Henderson Libraries
280 S. Green Valley Pkwy.
Henderson, NV 89012
702-492-7252
31431011061488

W9-AUZ-322

SIEGE
THOR

WRITER: **KIERON GILLEN**

THOR #607-609
ART: **BILLY TAN** & **BATT;** AND **RICH ELSON**
COLORISTS: **CHRISTINA STRAIN, PAUL MOUNTS, MATT HOLLINGSWORTH**
& **JUNE CHUNG**
LETTERER: **VIRTUAL CALLIGRAPHY'S JOE SABINO**
COVER ART: **MICO SUAYAN** & **LAURA MARTIN**

THOR #610
ART: **DOUG BRAITHWAITE**
COLORISTS: **ANDY TROY, DOUG BRAITHWAITE** & **PAUL MOUNTS**
LETTERER: **VIRTUAL CALLIGRAPHY'S JOE SABINO**
COVER ART: **MICO SUAYAN** & **LAURA MARTIN**

SIEGE: LOKI
ART: **JAMIE MCKELVIE**
COLORIST: **NATHAN FAIRBAIRN**
LETTERER: **VIRTUAL CALLIGRAPHY'S JOE CARAMAGNA**
COVER ART: **MARKO DJURDJEVIC**

ASSISTANT EDITOR: **ALEJANDRO ARBONA**
EDITOR: **RALPH MACCHIO**

NEW MUTANTS #11
ART: **NIKO HENRICHON**
LETTERER: **VIRTUAL CALLIGRAPHY'S JOE CARAMAGNA**
COVER ART: **TERRY DODSON** & **RACHEL DODSON**
ASSOCIATE EDITOR: **DANIEL KETCHUM**
EDITOR: **NICK LOWE**

COLLECTION EDITOR: **JENNIFER GRÜNWALD**
EDITORIAL ASSISTANTS: **JAMES EMMETT** & **JOE HOCHSTIEN** • ASSISTANT EDITOR: **ALEX STARBUCK**
EDITOR, SPECIAL PROJECTS: **MARK D. BEAZLEY** • SENIOR EDITOR, SPECIAL PROJECTS: **JEFF YOUNGQUIST**
SENIOR VICE PRESIDENT OF SALES: **DAVID GABRIEL** • BOOK DESIGNER: **RODOLFO MURAGUCHI**

EDITOR IN CHIEF: **JOE QUESADA** • PUBLISHER: **DAN BUCKLEY** • EXECUTIVE PRODUCER: **ALAN FINE**

SIEGE: THOR. Contains material originally published in magazine form as THOR #607-610, NEW MUTANTS #11 and SIEGE: LOKI. First printing 2010. ISBN# 978-0-7851-4813-5. Published by MARVEL WORLDWIDE, INC., a subsidiary of MARVEL ENTERTAINMENT, LLC. OFFICE OF PUBLICATION: 417 5th Avenue, New York, NY 10016. Copyright © 2010 Marvel Characters, Inc. All rights reserved. $19.99 per copy in the U.S. and $22.50 in Canada (GST #R127032852); Canadian Agreement #40668537. All characters featured in this issue and the distinctive names and likenesses thereof, and all related indicia are trademarks of Marvel Characters, Inc. No similarity between any of the names, characters, persons, and/or institutions in this magazine with those of any living or dead person or institution is intended, and any such similarity which may exist is purely coincidental. **Printed in the U.S.A.** ALAN FINE, EVP - Office of the President, Marvel Worldwide, Inc. and EVP & CMO Marvel Characters B.V.; DAN BUCKLEY, Chief Executive Officer and Publisher - Print, Animation & Digital Media; JIM SOKOLOWSKI, Chief Operating Officer; DAVID GABRIEL, SVP of Publishing Sales & Circulation; DAVID BOGART, SVP of Business Affairs & Talent Management; MICHAEL PASCIULLO, VP Merchandising & Communications; JIM O'KEEFE, VP of Operations & Logistics; DAN CARR, Executive Director of Publishing Technology; JUSTIN F. GABRIE, Director of Publishing & Editorial Operations; SUSAN CRESPI, Editorial Operations Manager; ALEX MORALES, Publishing Operations Manager; STAN LEE, Chairman Emeritus. For information regarding advertising in Marvel Comics or on Marvel.com, please contact Ron Stern, VP of Business Development, at rstern@marvel.com. For Marvel subscription inquiries, please call 800-217-9158. **Manufactured between 7/5/10 and 8/4/10 by R.R. DONNELLEY, INC., SALEM, VA, USA.**
10 9 8 7 6 5 4 3 2 1

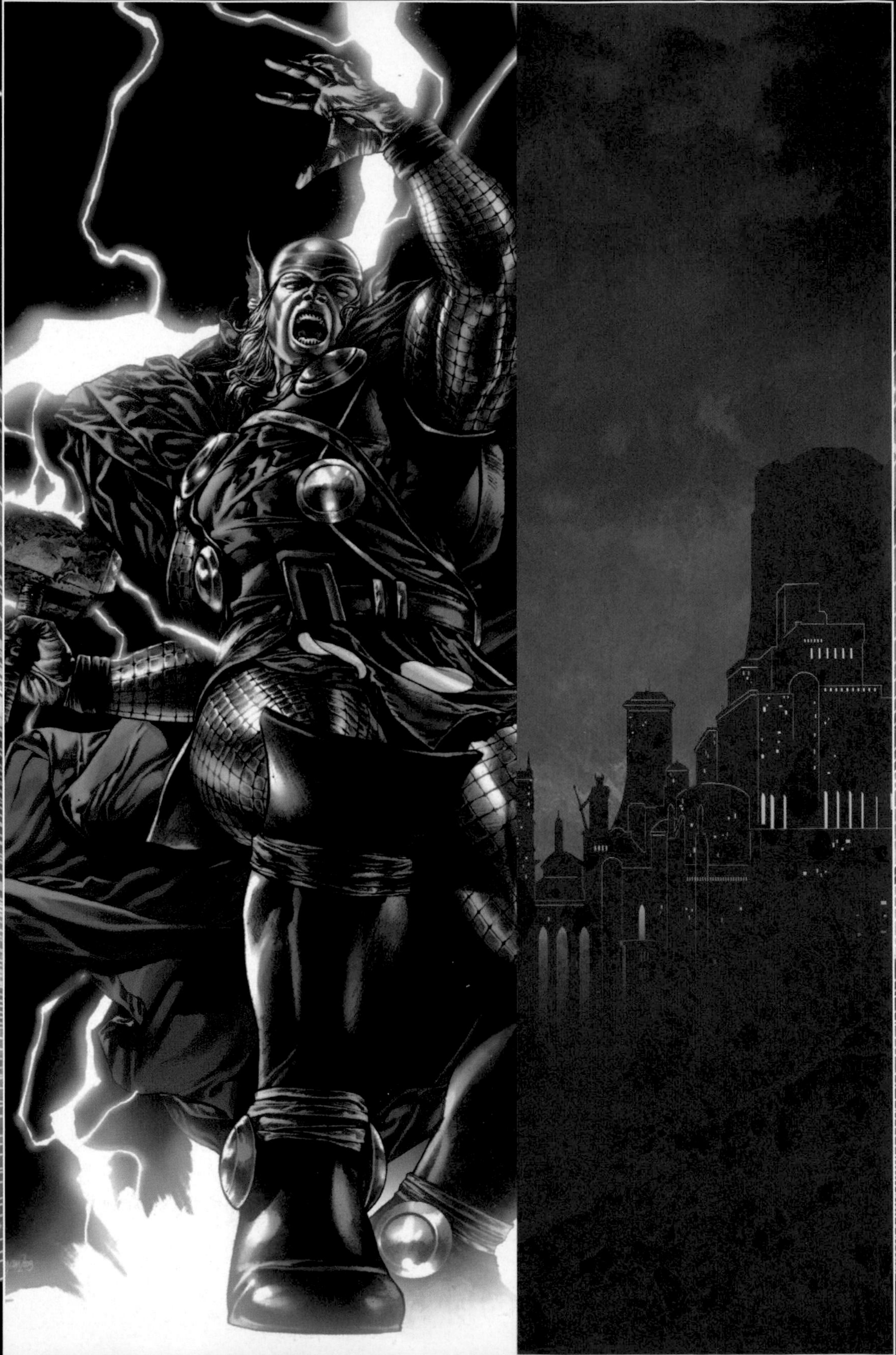

THOR #607

THOR #607 DEADPOOL VARIANT

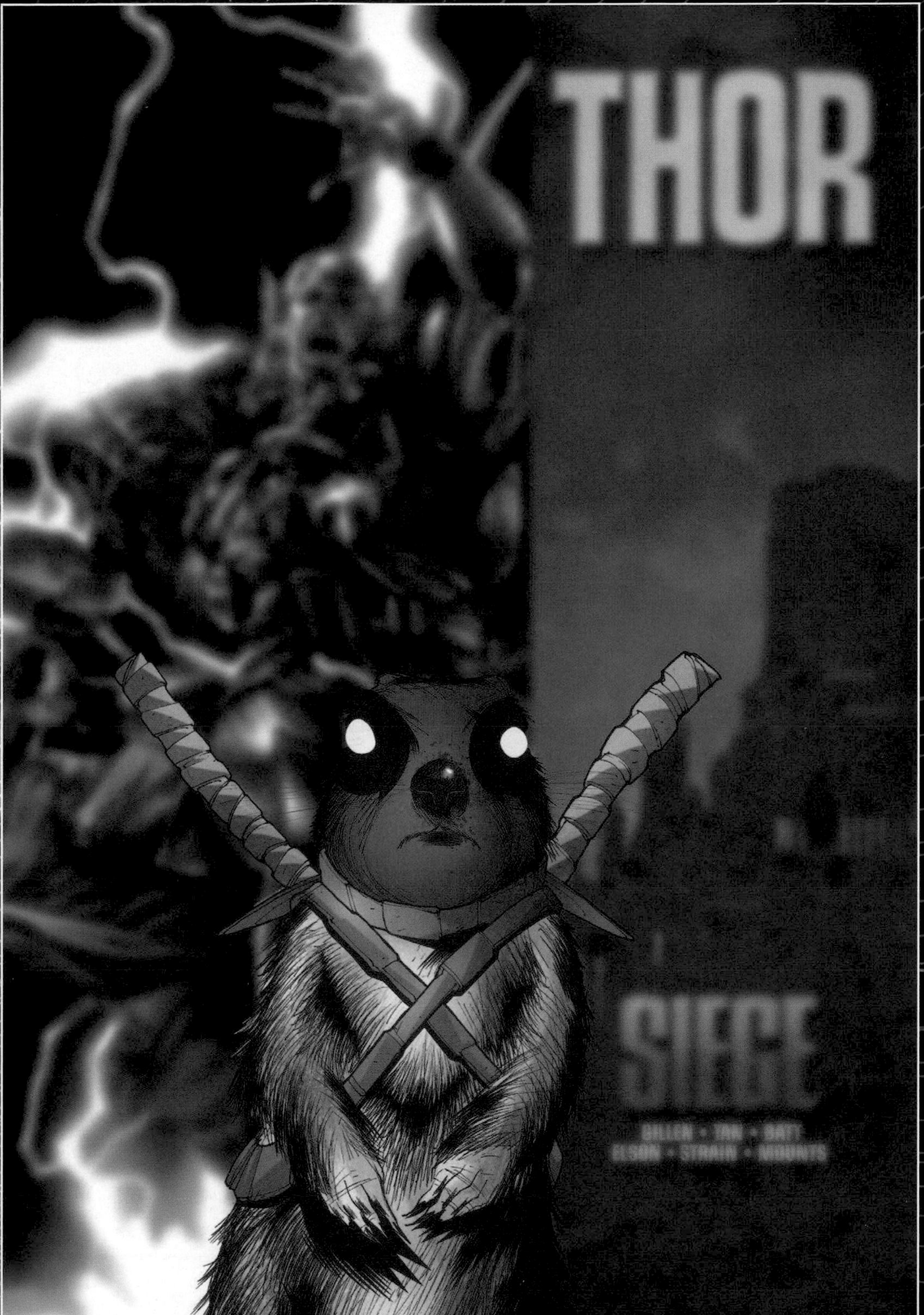
THOR
SIEGE

BY **JUAN DOE**

THOR

PREVIOUSLY...

DARK TIMES HAVE COME FOR THE GOD OF THUNDER.

THROUGH THE MANIPULATIONS OF HIS WICKED BROTHER, LOKI, THOR WAS CAST INTO EXILE. IN HIS ABSENCE, THEIR BROTHER BALDER WAS PLACED ON THE THRONE OF ASGARD...WITH LOKI AS ADVISER, WHISPERING POISON IN THE KING'S EAR.

BUT IT ISN'T MERELY BALDER WHO'S FALLEN UNDER LOKI'S INFLUENCE. AS A MEMBER OF NORMAN OSBORN'S CABAL OF SUPER VILLAINS, LOKI HAS MANAGED TO CONVINCE THE POWER-MAD OSBORN THAT ASGARD HAS NO PLACE BEING ON EARTH, IN ITS NEW HOME OUTSIDE THE SMALL TOWN OF BROXTON, OKLAHOMA...THAT ASGARD MUST BE REMOVED...

FABRICATING AN INCIDENT, OSBORN CAUSED A CATASTROPHE IN CHICAGO, KILLING HUNDREDS – AND MADE IT APPEAR AS THOUGH THE ASGARDIAN WARRIOR VOLSTAGG WAS RESPONSIBLE. AND AS DIRECTOR OF THE LAW ENFORCEMENT AGENCY H.A.M.M.E.R. AND LEADER OF A VILLAINOUS TEAM OF AVENGERS, IT'S OSBORN'S JOB TO LAY SIEGE TO ASGARD...

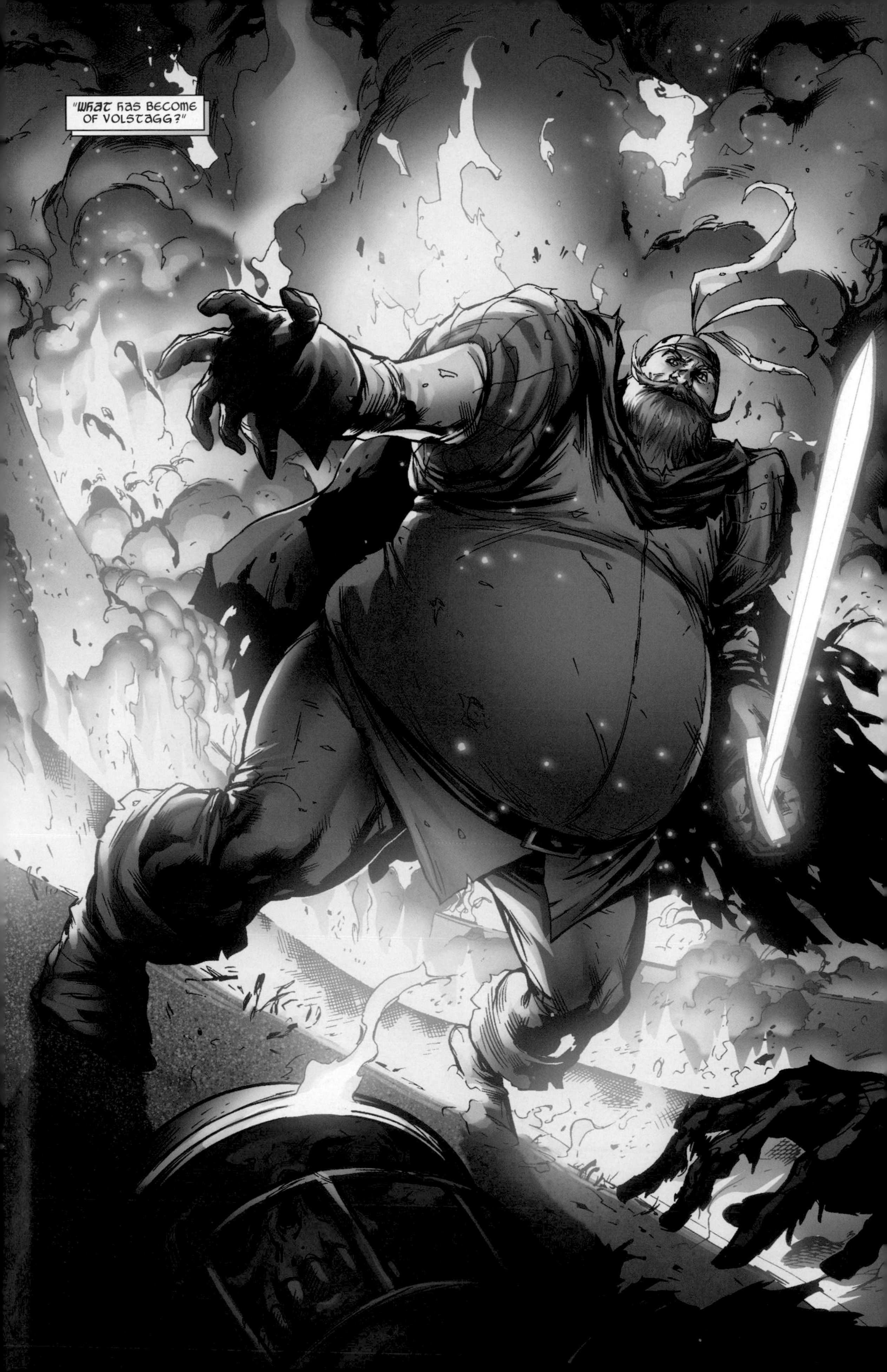
"WHAT HAS BECOME
OF VOLSTAGG?"

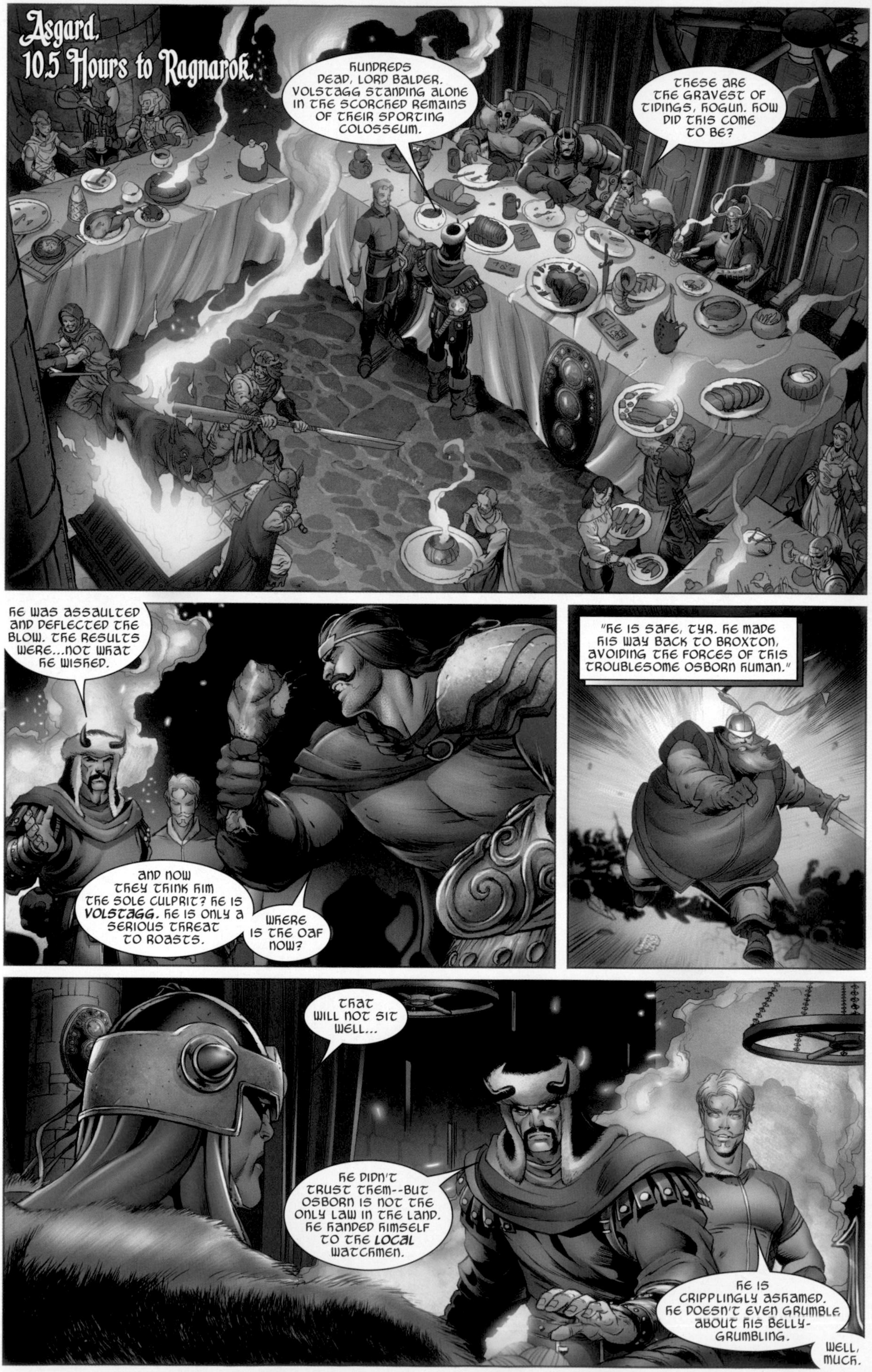
Asgard, 10.5 Hours to Ragnarok.
HUNDREDS DEAD, LORD BALDER. VOLSTAGG STANDING ALONE IN THE SCORCHED REMAINS OF THEIR SPORTING COLOSSEUM.
THESE ARE THE GRAVEST OF TIDINGS, HOGUN. HOW DID THIS COME TO BE?
HE WAS ASSAULTED AND DEFLECTED THE BLOW. THE RESULTS WERE...NOT WHAT HE WISHED.
AND NOW THEY THINK HIM THE SOLE CULPRIT? HE IS VOLSTAGG. HE IS ONLY A SERIOUS THREAT TO ROASTS.
WHERE IS THE OAF NOW?
"HE IS SAFE, TYR. HE MADE HIS WAY BACK TO BROXTON, AVOIDING THE FORCES OF THIS TROUBLESOME OSBORN HUMAN."
THAT WILL NOT SIT WELL...
HE DIDN'T TRUST THEM--BUT OSBORN IS NOT THE ONLY LAW IN THE LAND. HE HANDED HIMSELF TO THE LOCAL WATCHMEN.
HE IS CRIPPLINGLY ASHAMED. HE DOESN'T EVEN GRUMBLE ABOUT HIS BELLY-GRUMBLING.
WELL, MUCH.

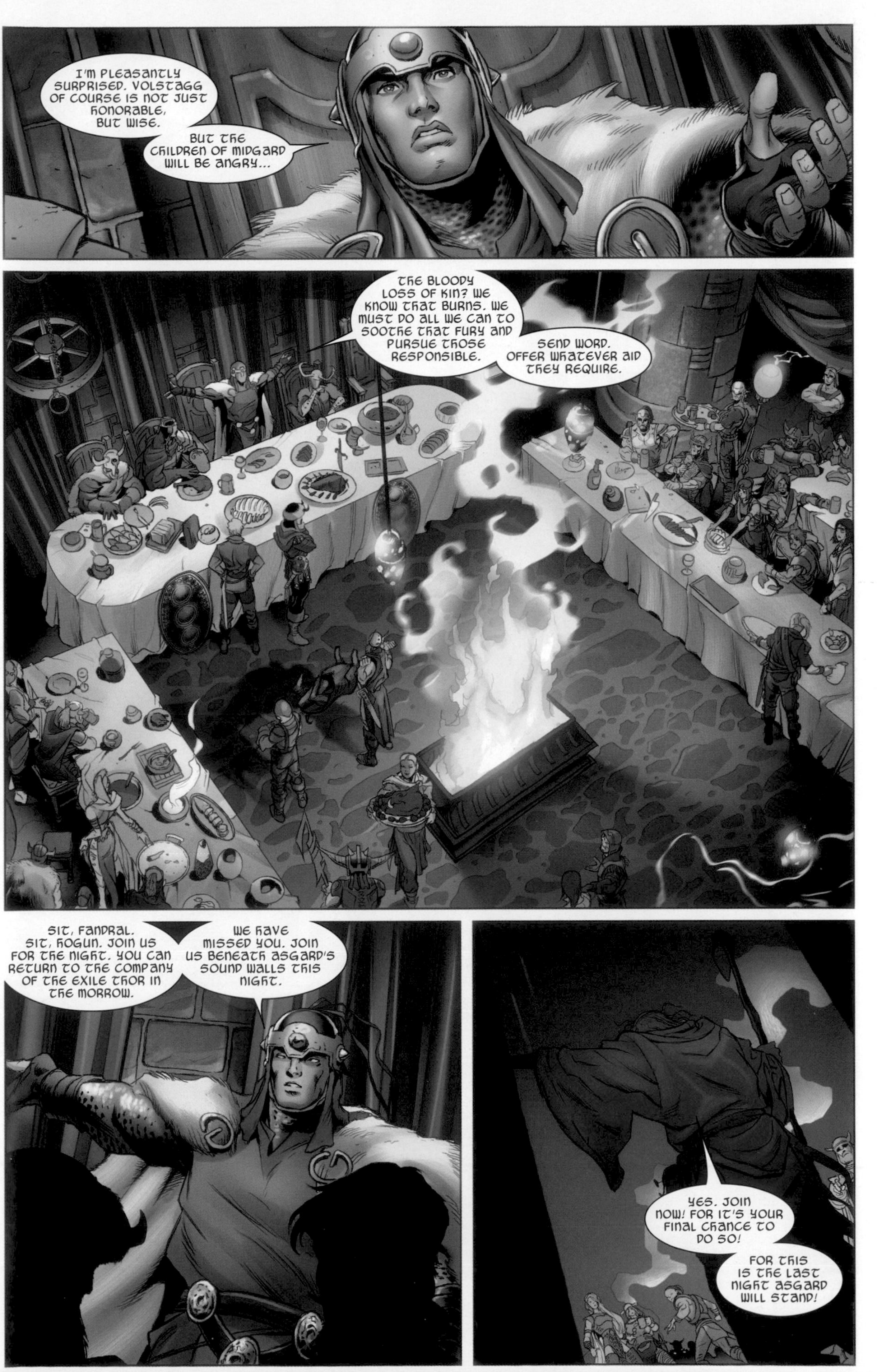
I'M PLEASANTLY SURPRISED. VOLSTAGG OF COURSE IS NOT JUST HONORABLE, BUT WISE.
BUT THE CHILDREN OF MIDGARD WILL BE ANGRY...
THE BLOODY LOSS OF KIN? WE KNOW THAT BURNS. WE MUST DO ALL WE CAN TO SOOTHE THAT FURY AND PURSUE THOSE RESPONSIBLE.
SEND WORD. OFFER WHATEVER AID THEY REQUIRE.
SIT, FANDRAL. SIT, HOGUN. JOIN US FOR THE NIGHT. YOU CAN RETURN TO THE COMPANY OF THE EXILE THOR IN THE MORROW.
WE HAVE MISSED YOU. JOIN US BENEATH ASGARD'S SOUND WALLS THIS NIGHT.
YES. JOIN NOW! FOR IT'S YOUR FINAL CHANCE TO DO SO!
FOR THIS IS THE LAST NIGHT ASGARD WILL STAND!

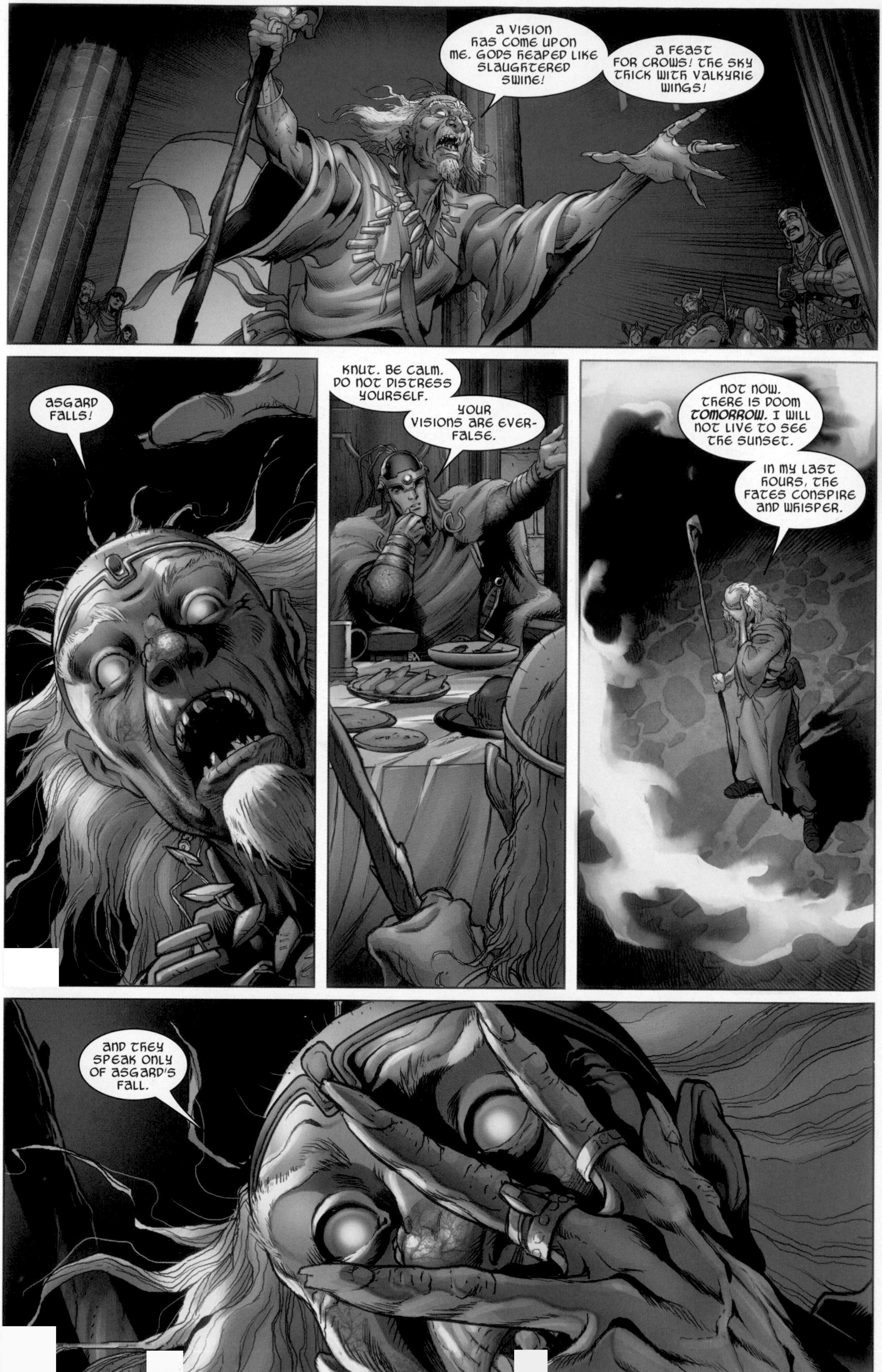
A VISION HAS COME UPON ME. GODS HEAPED LIKE SLAUGHTERED SWINE!
A FEAST FOR CROWS! THE SKY THICK WITH VALKYRIE WINGS!
ASGARD FALLS!
KNUT. BE CALM. DO NOT DISTRESS YOURSELF.
YOUR VISIONS ARE EVER-FALSE.
NOT NOW. THERE IS DOOM TOMORROW. I WILL NOT LIVE TO SEE THE SUNSET.
IN MY LAST HOURS, THE FATES CONSPIRE AND WHISPER.
AND THEY SPEAK ONLY OF ASGARD'S FALL.

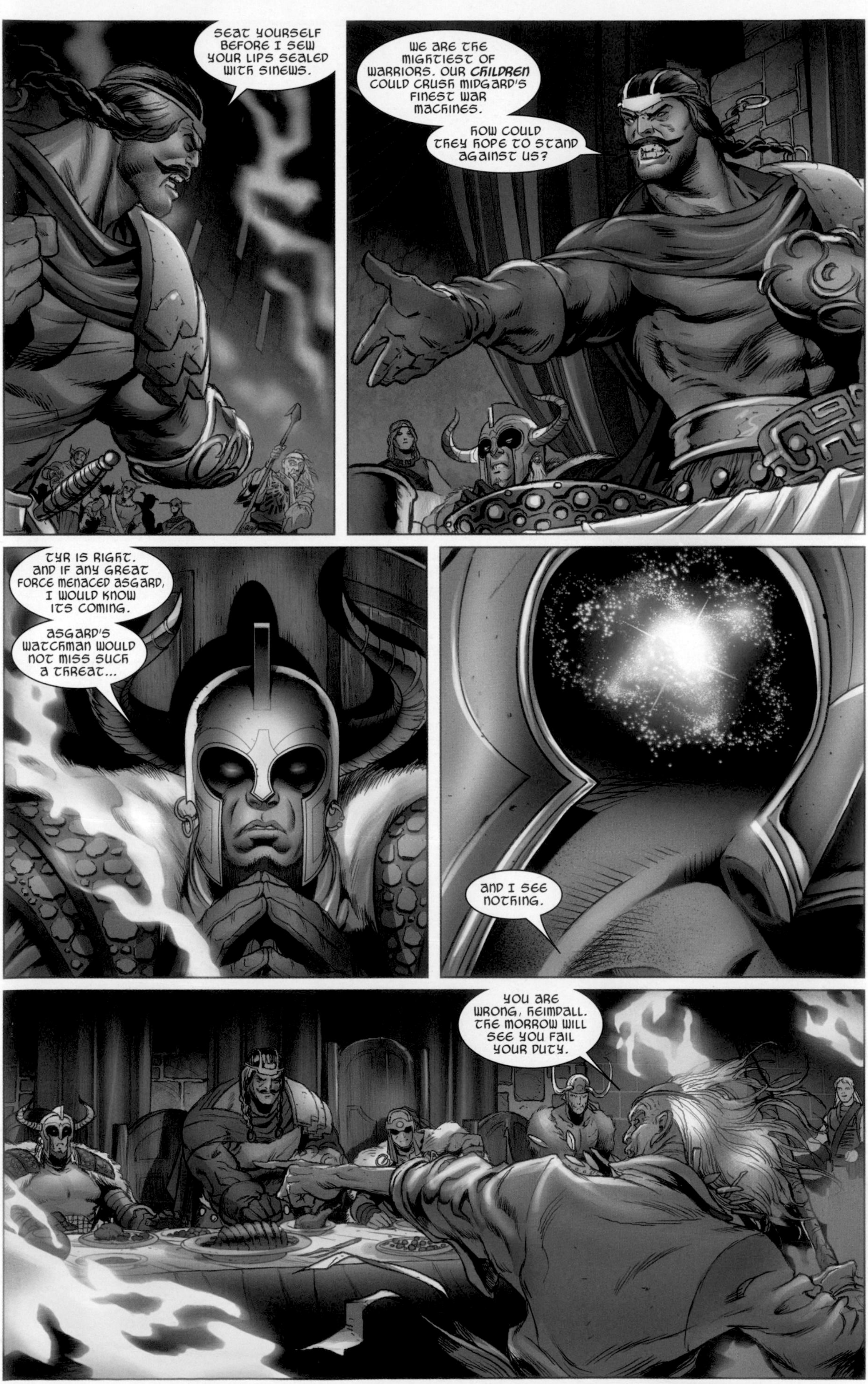
SEAT YOURSELF BEFORE I SEW YOUR LIPS SEALED WITH SINEWS.
WE ARE THE MIGHTIEST OF WARRIORS. OUR *CHILDREN* COULD CRUSH MIDGARD'S FINEST WAR MACHINES.
HOW COULD THEY HOPE TO STAND AGAINST US?
TYR IS RIGHT. AND IF ANY GREAT FORCE MENACED ASGARD, I WOULD KNOW ITS COMING.
ASGARD'S WATCHMAN WOULD NOT MISS SUCH A THREAT...
AND I SEE NOTHING.
YOU ARE WRONG, HEIMDALL. THE MORROW WILL SEE YOU FAIL YOUR DUTY.

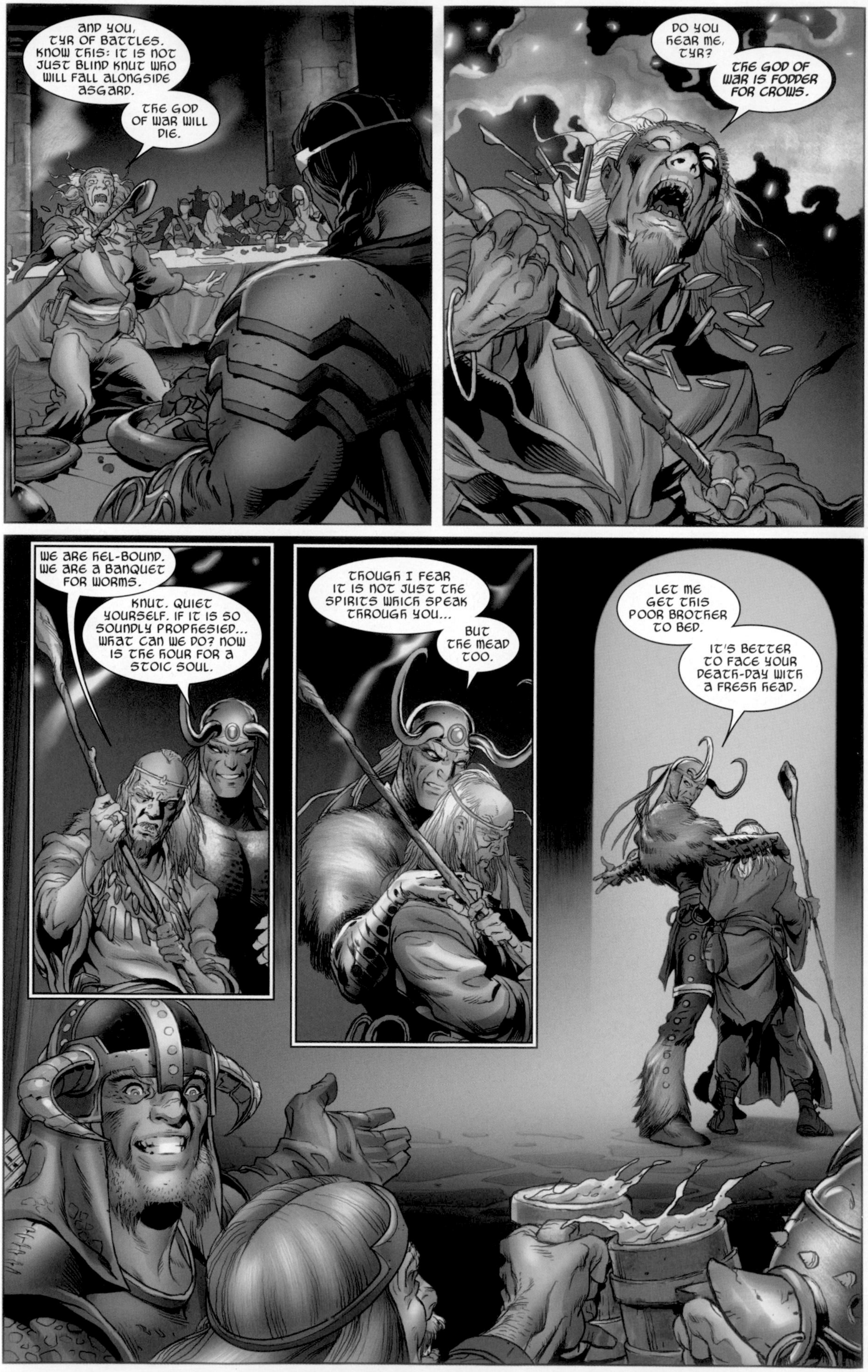
AND YOU, TYR OF BATTLES. KNOW THIS: IT IS NOT JUST BLIND KNUT WHO WILL FALL ALONGSIDE ASGARD.
THE GOD OF WAR WILL DIE.
DO YOU HEAR ME, TYR?
THE GOD OF WAR IS FODDER FOR CROWS.
WE ARE HEL-BOUND. WE ARE A BANQUET FOR WORMS.
KNUT. QUIET YOURSELF. IF IT IS SO SOUNDLY PROPHESIED... WHAT CAN WE DO? NOW IS THE HOUR FOR A STOIC SOUL.
THOUGH I FEAR IT IS NOT JUST THE SPIRITS WHICH SPEAK THROUGH YOU...
BUT THE MEAD TOO.
LET ME GET THIS POOR BROTHER TO BED.
IT'S BETTER TO FACE YOUR DEATH-DAY WITH A FRESH HEAD.

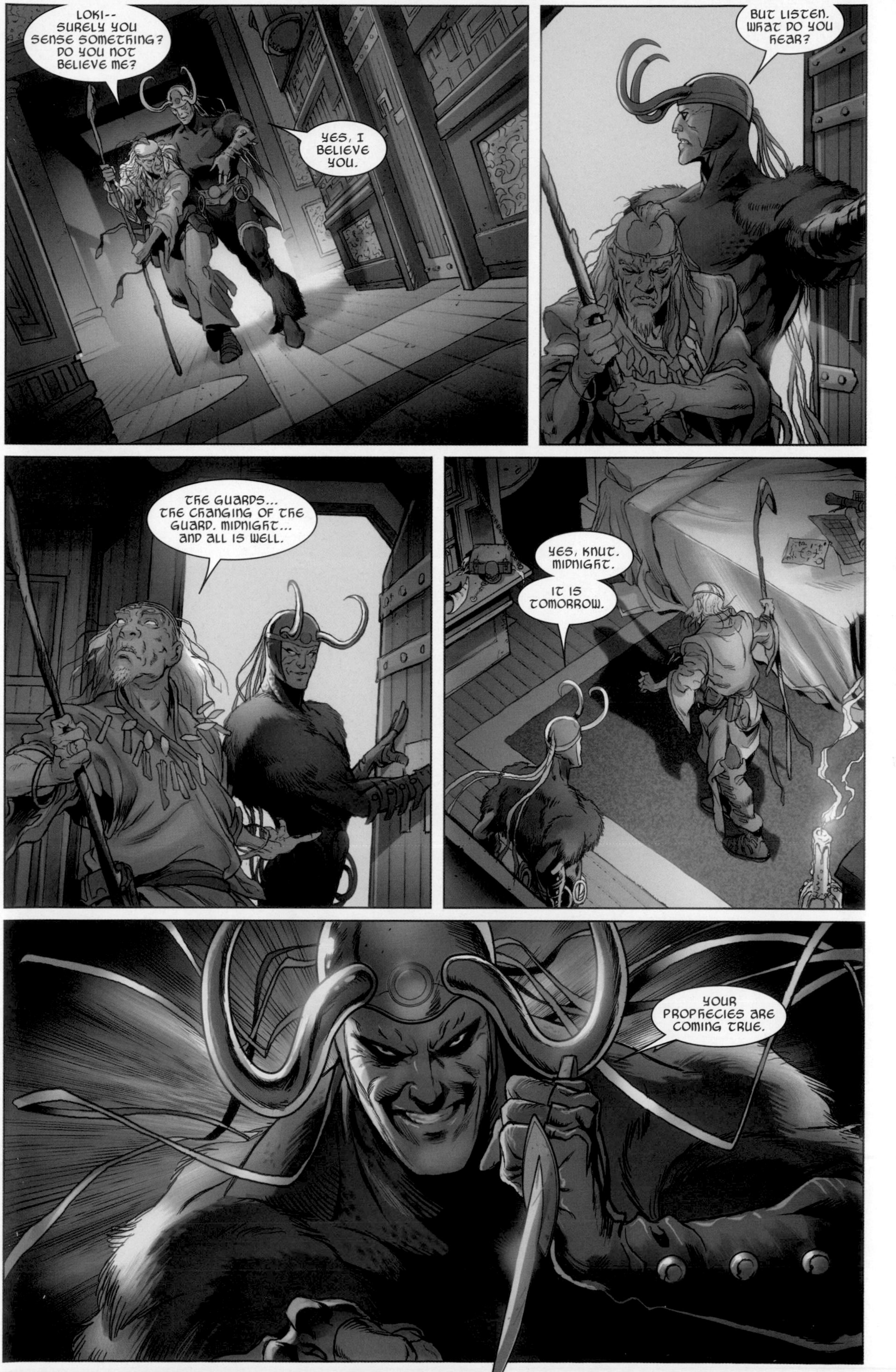
LOKI-- SURELY YOU SENSE SOMETHING? DO YOU NOT BELIEVE ME?
YES, I BELIEVE YOU.
BUT LISTEN. WHAT DO YOU HEAR?
THE GUARDS... THE CHANGING OF THE GUARD. MIDNIGHT... AND ALL IS WELL.
YES, KNUT. MIDNIGHT.
IT IS TOMORROW.
YOUR PROPHECIES ARE COMING TRUE.

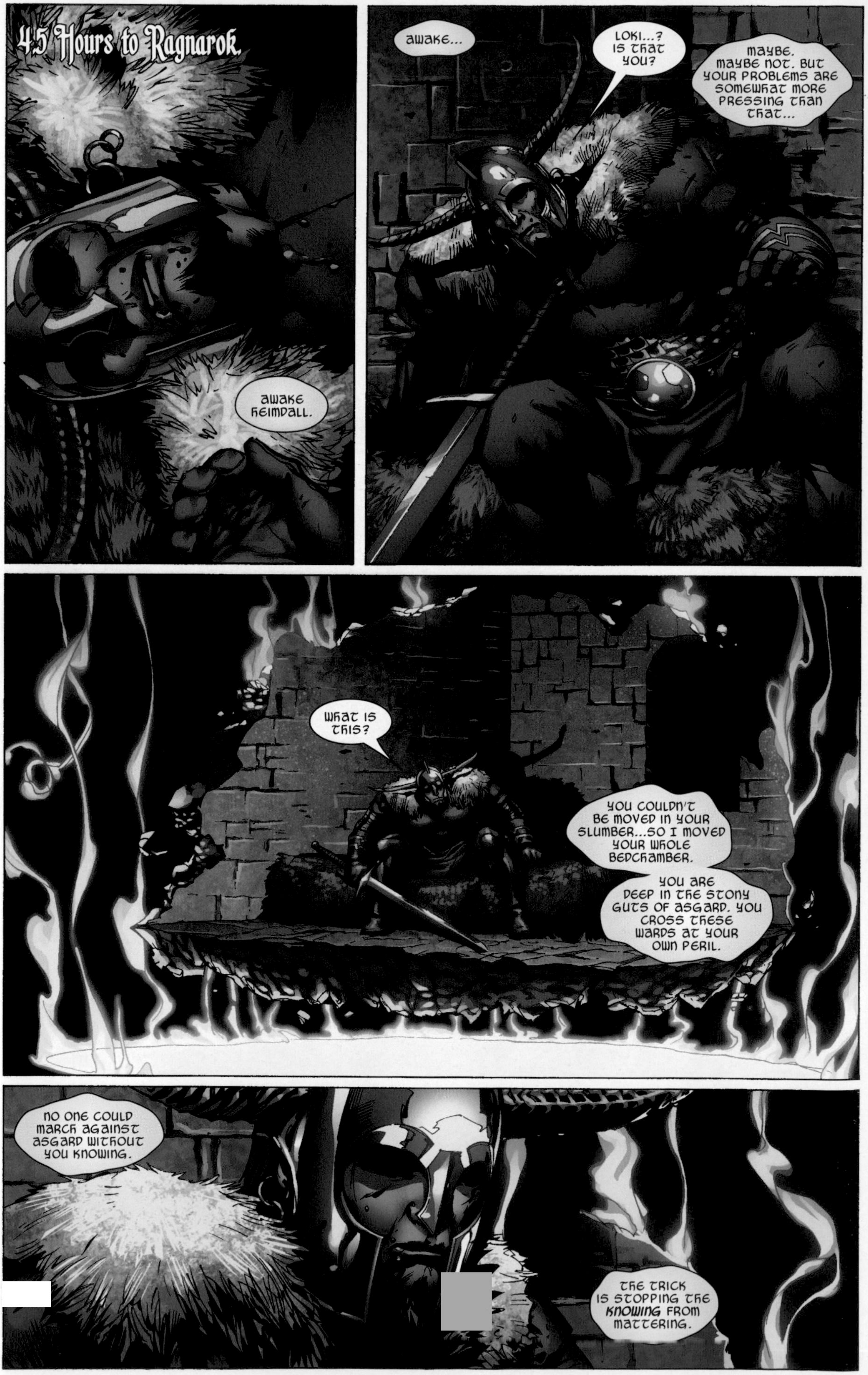
4.5 Hours to Ragnarok.
AWAKE HEIMDALL.
AWAKE...
LOKI...? IS THAT YOU?
MAYBE. MAYBE NOT. BUT YOUR PROBLEMS ARE SOMEWHAT MORE PRESSING THAN THAT...
WHAT IS THIS?
YOU COULDN'T BE MOVED IN YOUR SLUMBER...SO I MOVED YOUR WHOLE BEDCHAMBER.
YOU ARE DEEP IN THE STONY GUTS OF ASGARD. YOU CROSS THESE WARDS AT YOUR OWN PERIL.
NO ONE COULD MARCH AGAINST ASGARD WITHOUT YOU KNOWING.
THE TRICK IS STOPPING THE *KNOWING* FROM MATTERING.

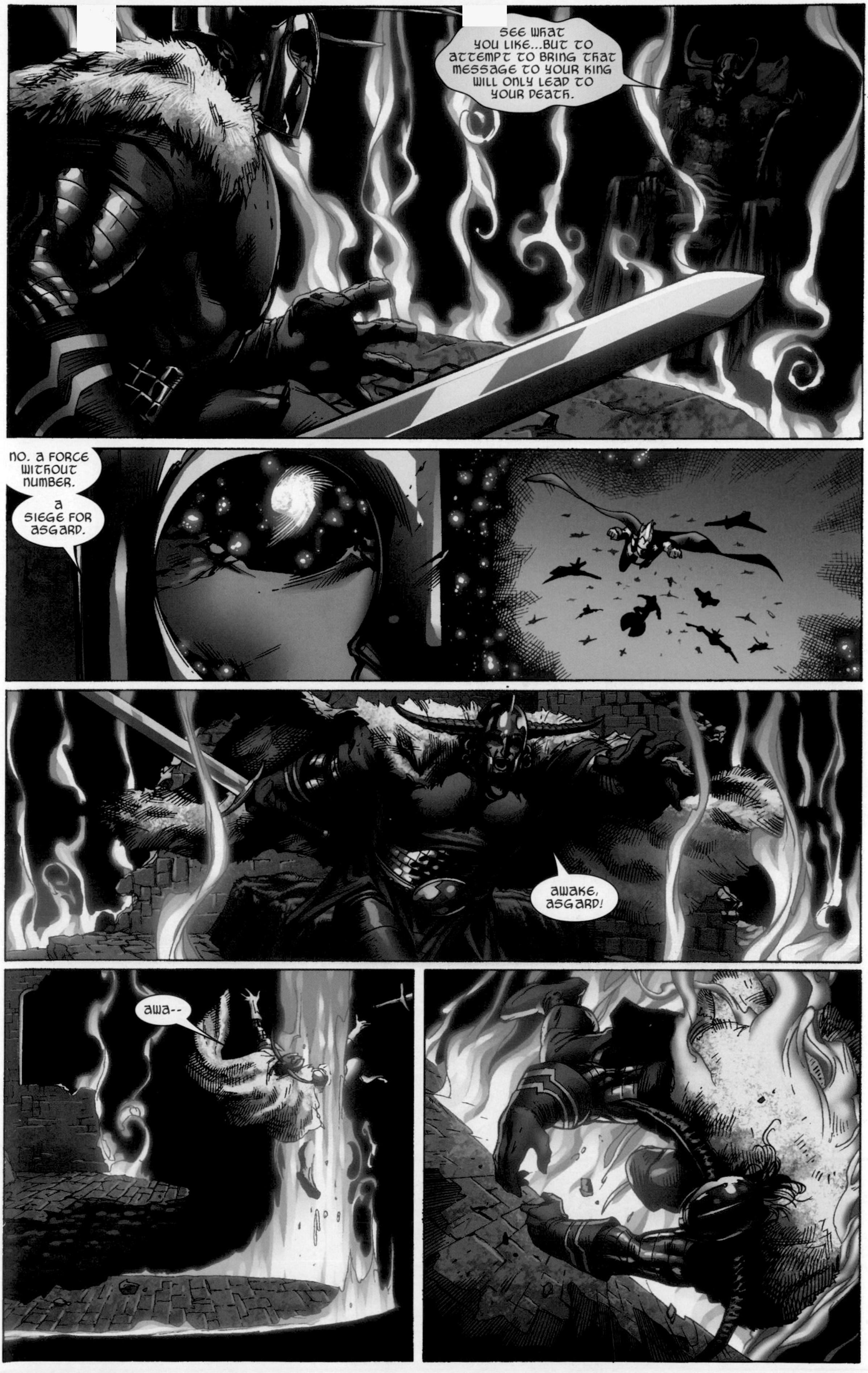
SEE WHAT YOU LIKE...BUT TO ATTEMPT TO BRING THAT MESSAGE TO YOUR KING WILL ONLY LEAD TO YOUR DEATH.
NO. A FORCE WITHOUT NUMBER.
A SIEGE FOR ASGARD.
AWAKE, ASGARD!
AWA--

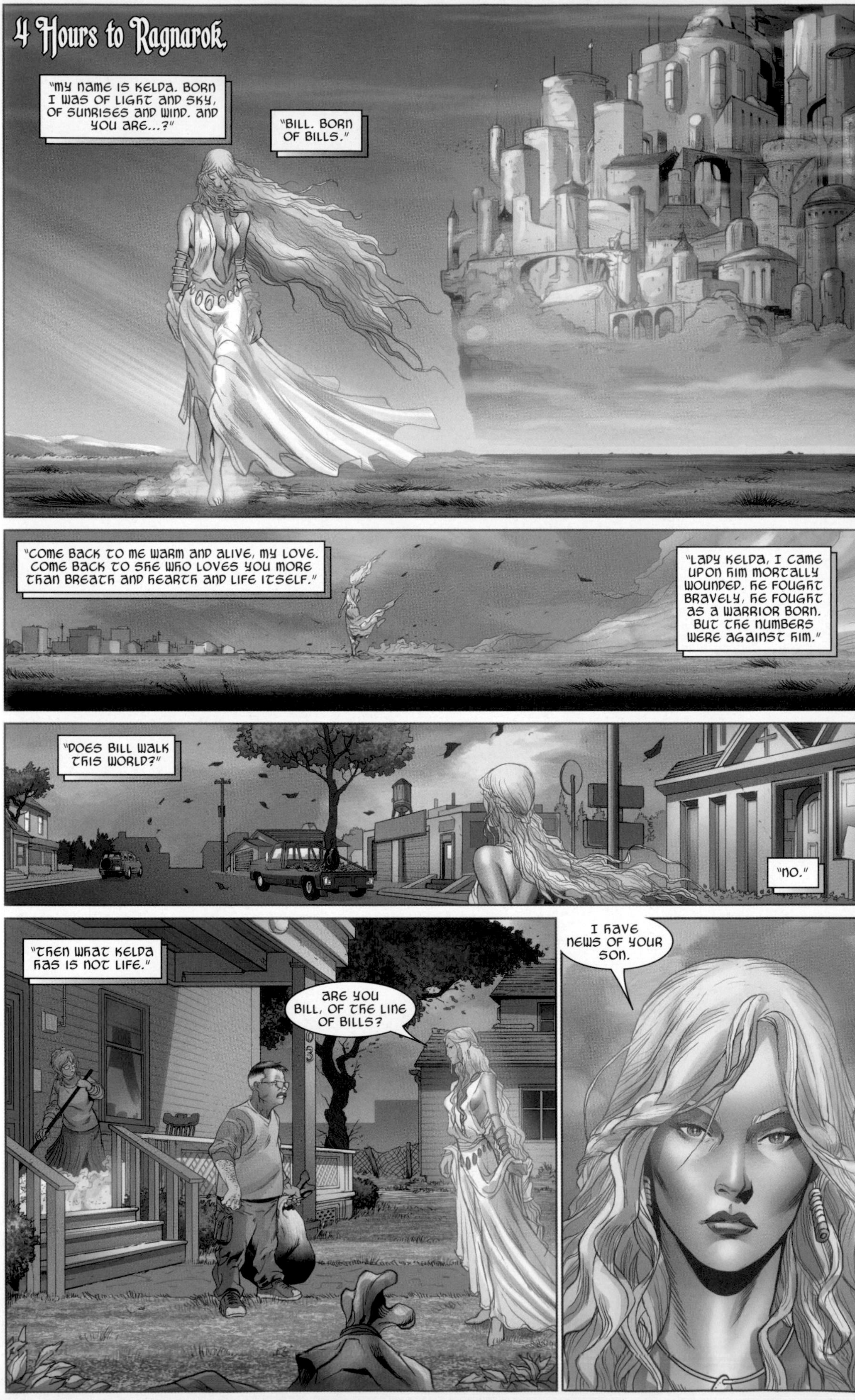
4 Hours to Ragnarok.
"MY NAME IS KELDA. BORN I WAS OF LIGHT AND SKY, OF SUNRISES AND WIND. AND YOU ARE...?"
"BILL. BORN OF BILLS."
"COME BACK TO ME WARM AND ALIVE, MY LOVE. COME BACK TO SHE WHO LOVES YOU MORE THAN BREATH AND HEARTH AND LIFE ITSELF."
"LADY KELDA, I CAME UPON HIM MORTALLY WOUNDED. HE FOUGHT BRAVELY, HE FOUGHT AS A WARRIOR BORN. BUT THE NUMBERS WERE AGAINST HIM."
"DOES BILL WALK THIS WORLD?"
"NO."
"THEN WHAT KELDA HAS IS NOT LIFE."
ARE YOU BILL, OF THE LINE OF BILLS?
I HAVE NEWS OF YOUR SON.

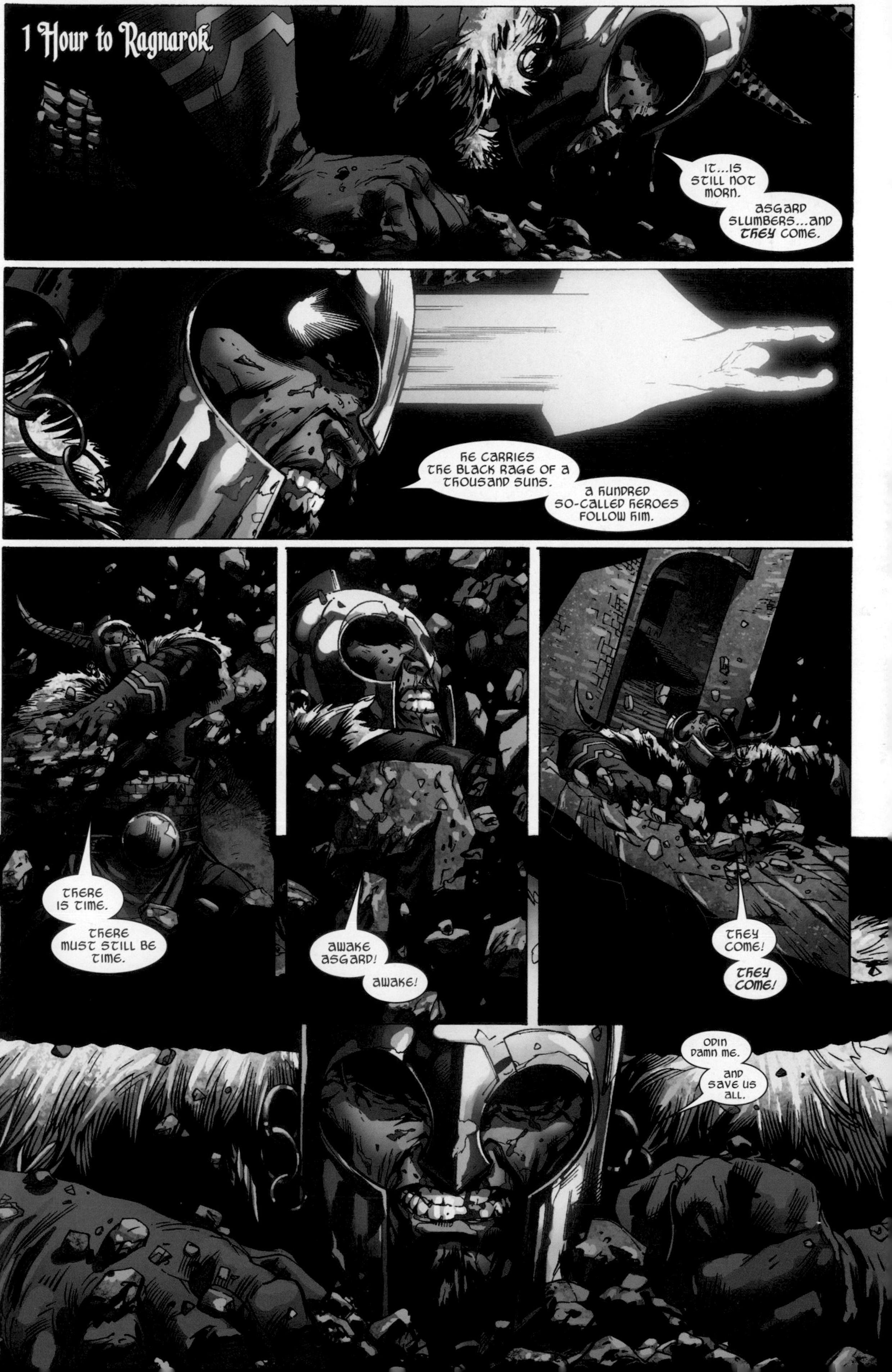
1 Hour to Ragnarok.
IT...IS STILL NOT MORN.
ASGARD SLUMBERS...AND THEY COME.
HE CARRIES THE BLACK RAGE OF A THOUSAND SUNS.
A HUNDRED SO-CALLED HEROES FOLLOW HIM.
THERE IS TIME.
THERE MUST STILL BE TIME.
AWAKE ASGARD!
AWAKE!
THEY COME!
THEY COME!
ODIN DAMN ME.
AND SAVE US ALL.

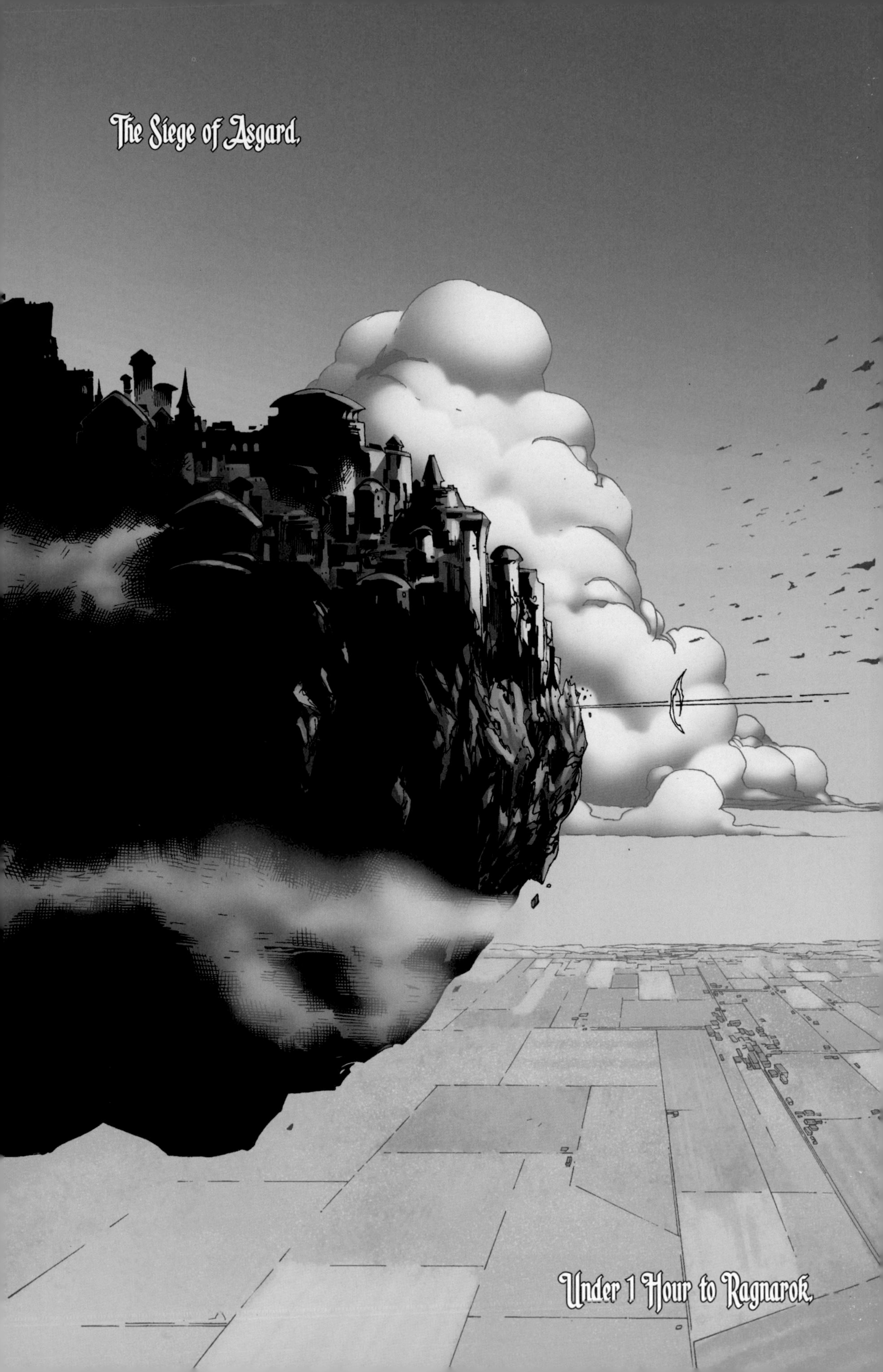
The Siege of Asgard.
Under 1 Hour to Ragnarok.

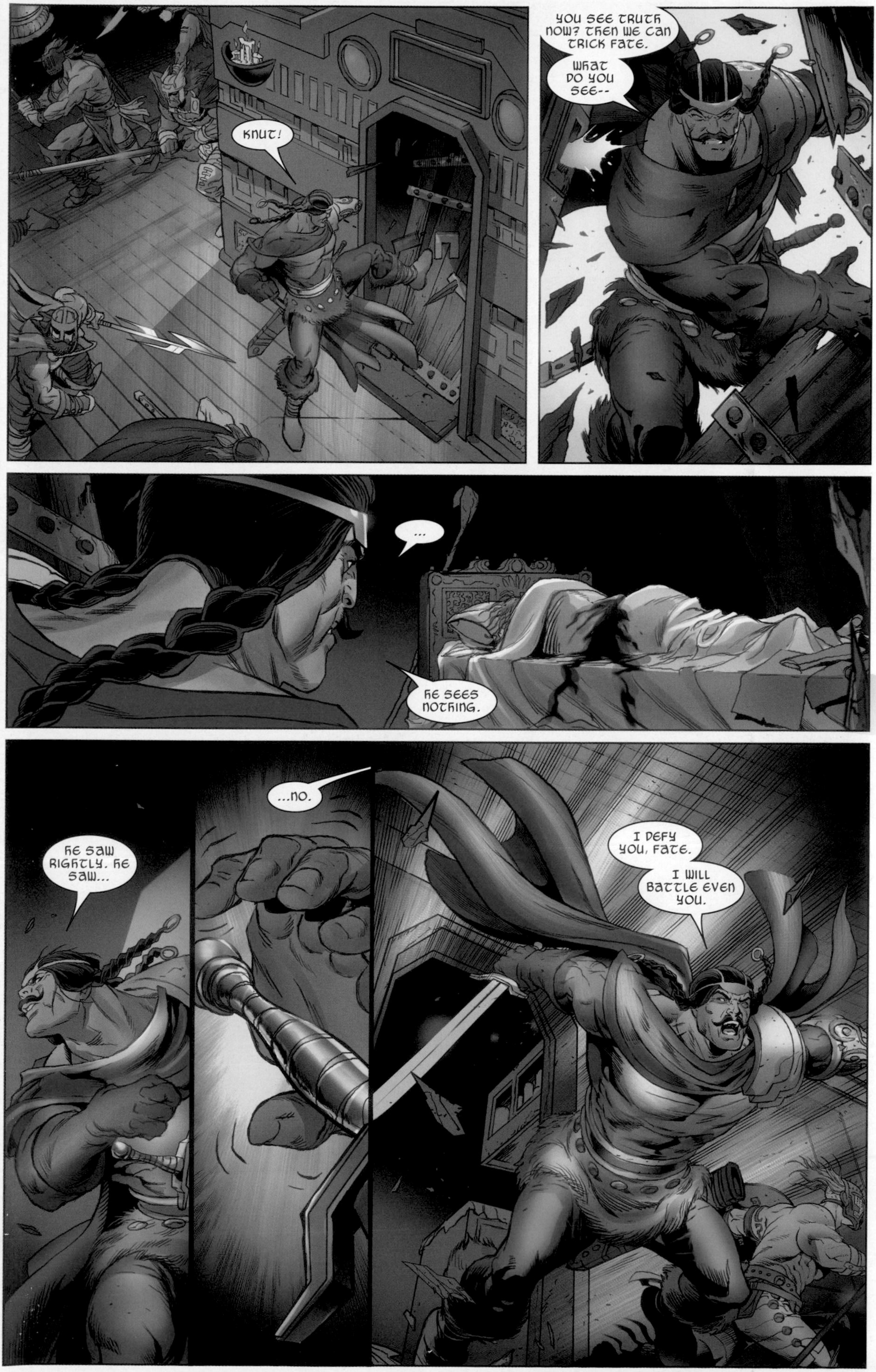
KNUT!
YOU SEE TRUTH NOW? THEN WE CAN TRICK FATE.
WHAT DO YOU SEE--
...
HE SEES NOTHING.
HE SAW RIGHTLY. HE SAW...
...NO.
I DEFY YOU, FATE.
I WILL BATTLE EVEN YOU.

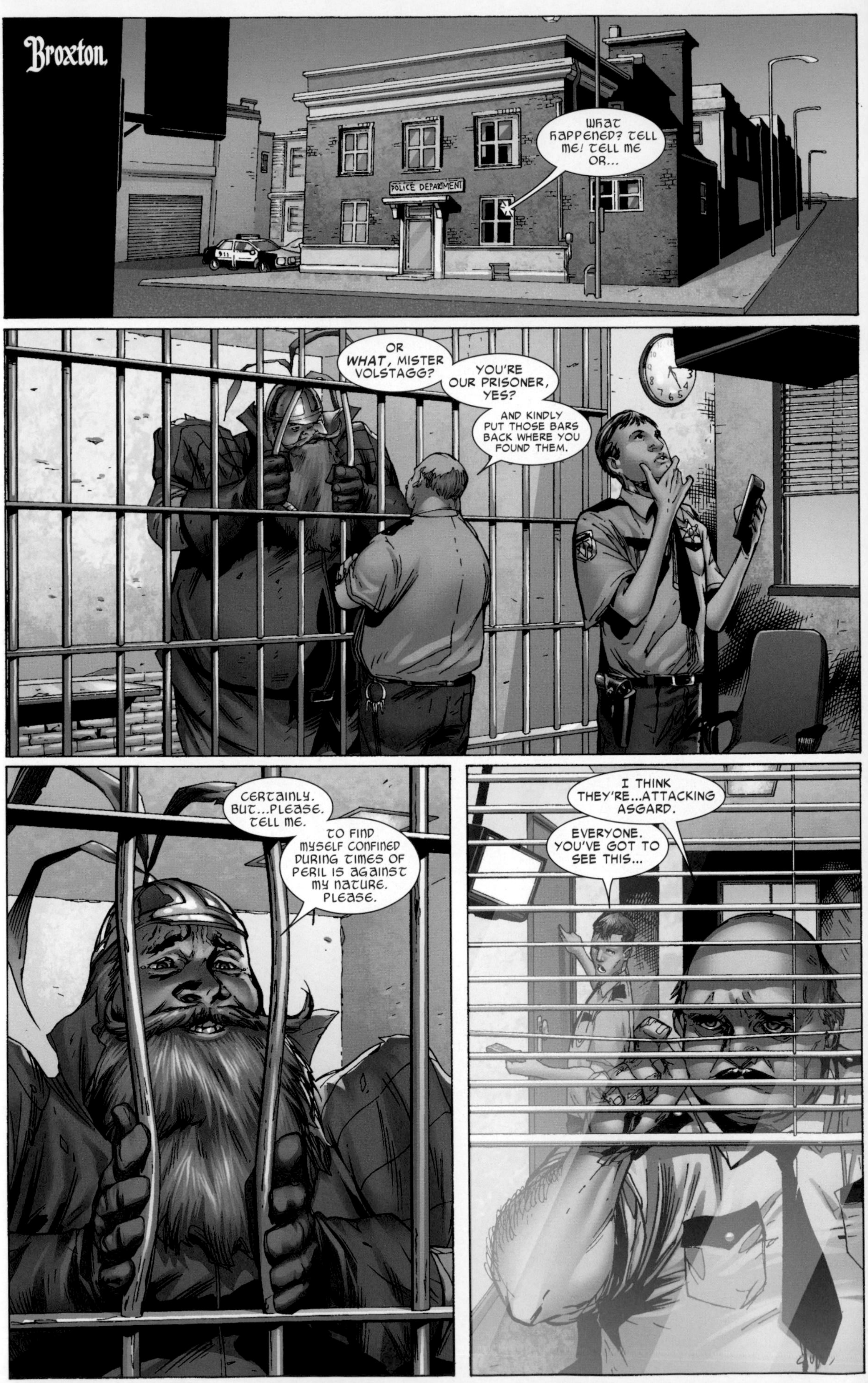
Broxton.
POLICE DEPARTMENT
WHAT HAPPENED? TELL ME! TELL ME OR...
OR WHAT, MISTER VOLSTAGG?
YOU'RE OUR PRISONER, YES?
AND KINDLY PUT THOSE BARS BACK WHERE YOU FOUND THEM.
CERTAINLY. BUT...PLEASE. TELL ME.
TO FIND MYSELF CONFINED DURING TIMES OF PERIL IS AGAINST MY NATURE. PLEASE.
I THINK THEY'RE...ATTACKING ASGARD.
EVERYONE. YOU'VE GOT TO SEE THIS...

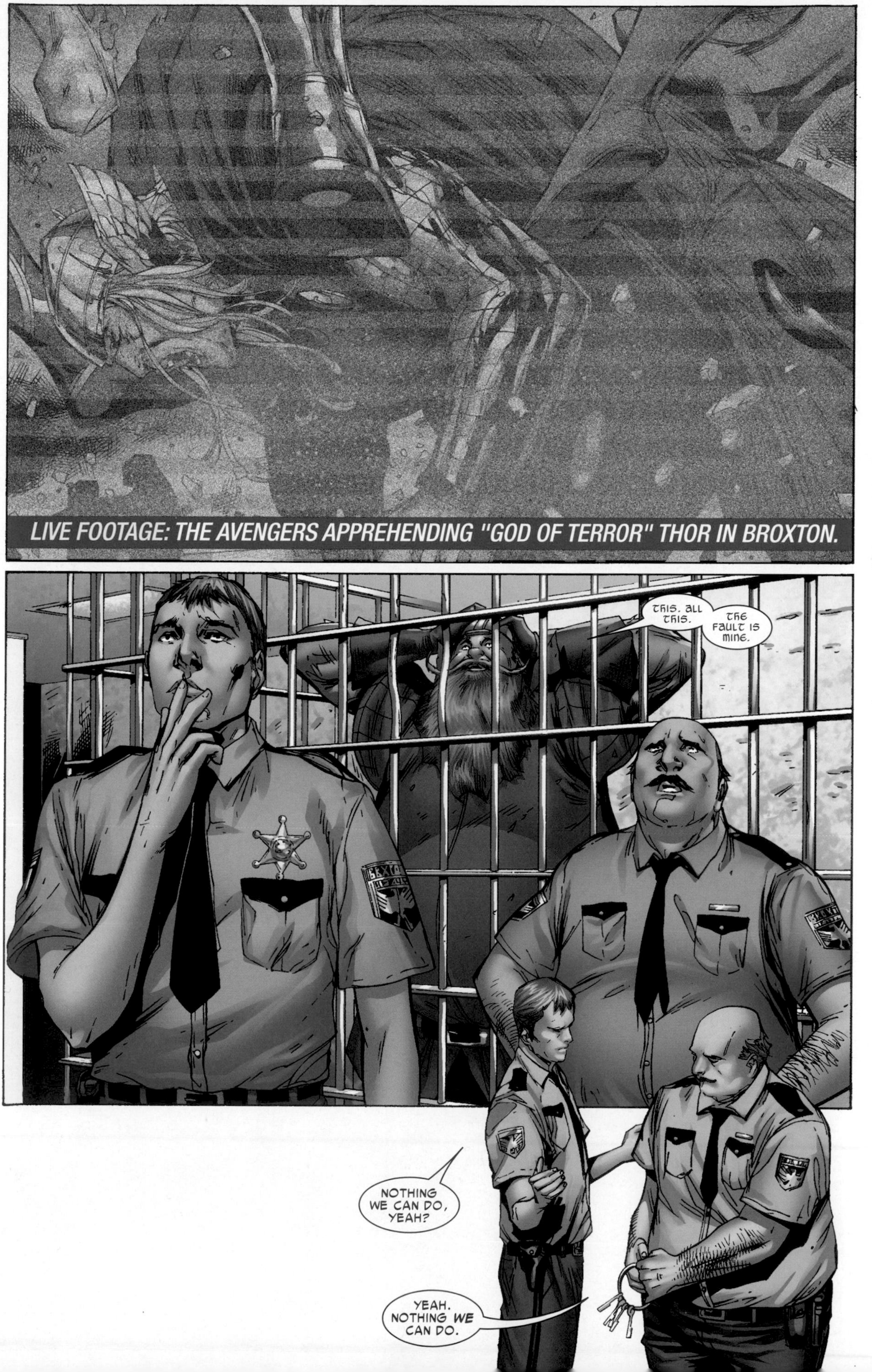
LIVE FOOTAGE: THE AVENGERS APPREHENDING "GOD OF TERROR" THOR IN BROXTON.
THIS. ALL THIS.
THE FAULT IS MINE.
NOTHING WE CAN DO, YEAH?
YEAH. NOTHING WE CAN DO.

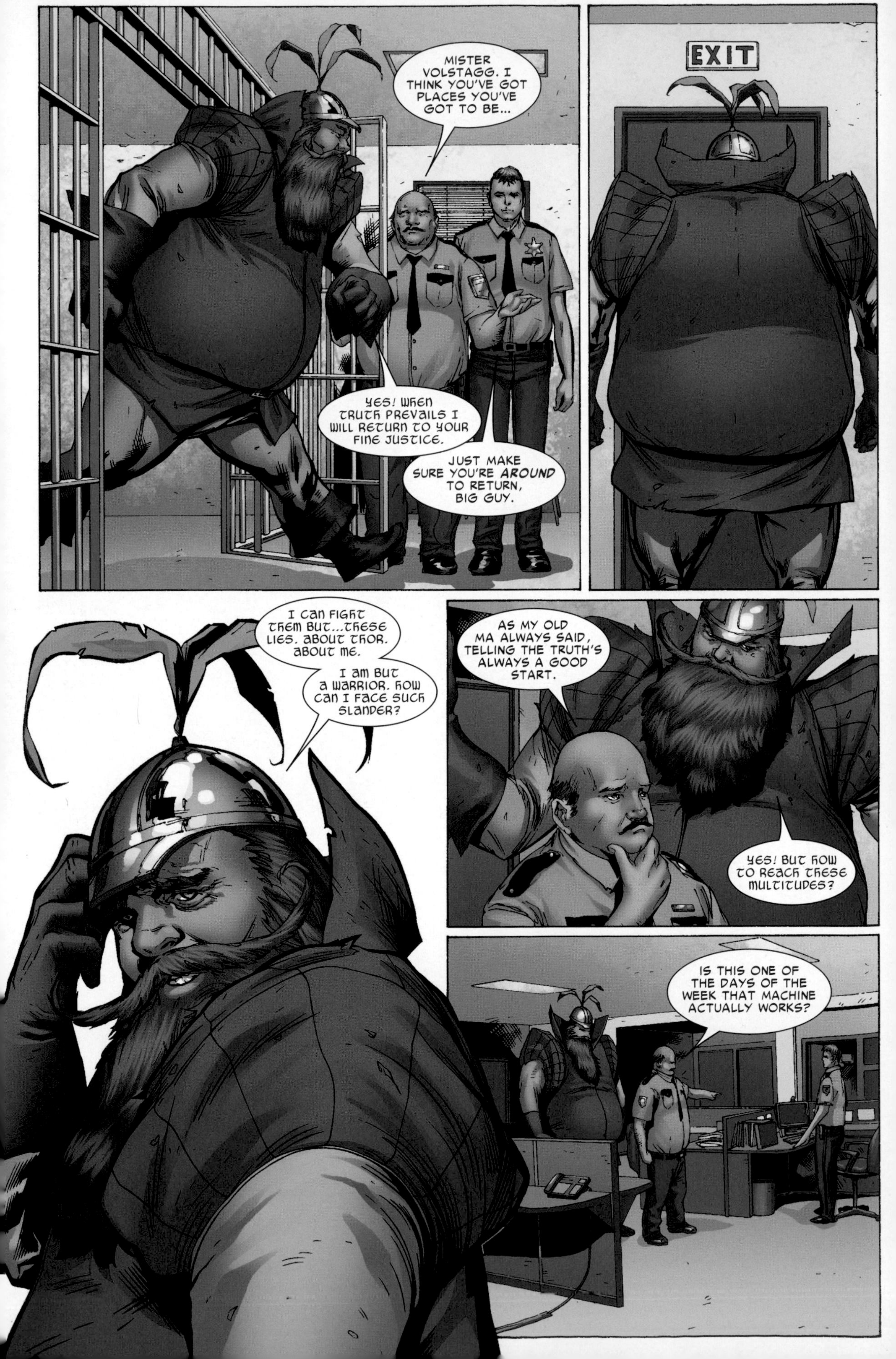
MISTER VOLSTAGG. I THINK YOU'VE GOT PLACES YOU'VE GOT TO BE...
YES! WHEN TRUTH PREVAILS I WILL RETURN TO YOUR FINE JUSTICE.
JUST MAKE SURE YOU'RE AROUND TO RETURN, BIG GUY.
EXIT
I CAN FIGHT THEM BUT...THESE LIES. ABOUT THOR. ABOUT ME.
I AM BUT A WARRIOR. HOW CAN I FACE SUCH SLANDER?
AS MY OLD MA ALWAYS SAID, TELLING THE TRUTH'S ALWAYS A GOOD START.
YES! BUT HOW TO REACH THESE MULTITUDES?
IS THIS ONE OF THE DAYS OF THE WEEK THAT MACHINE ACTUALLY WORKS?

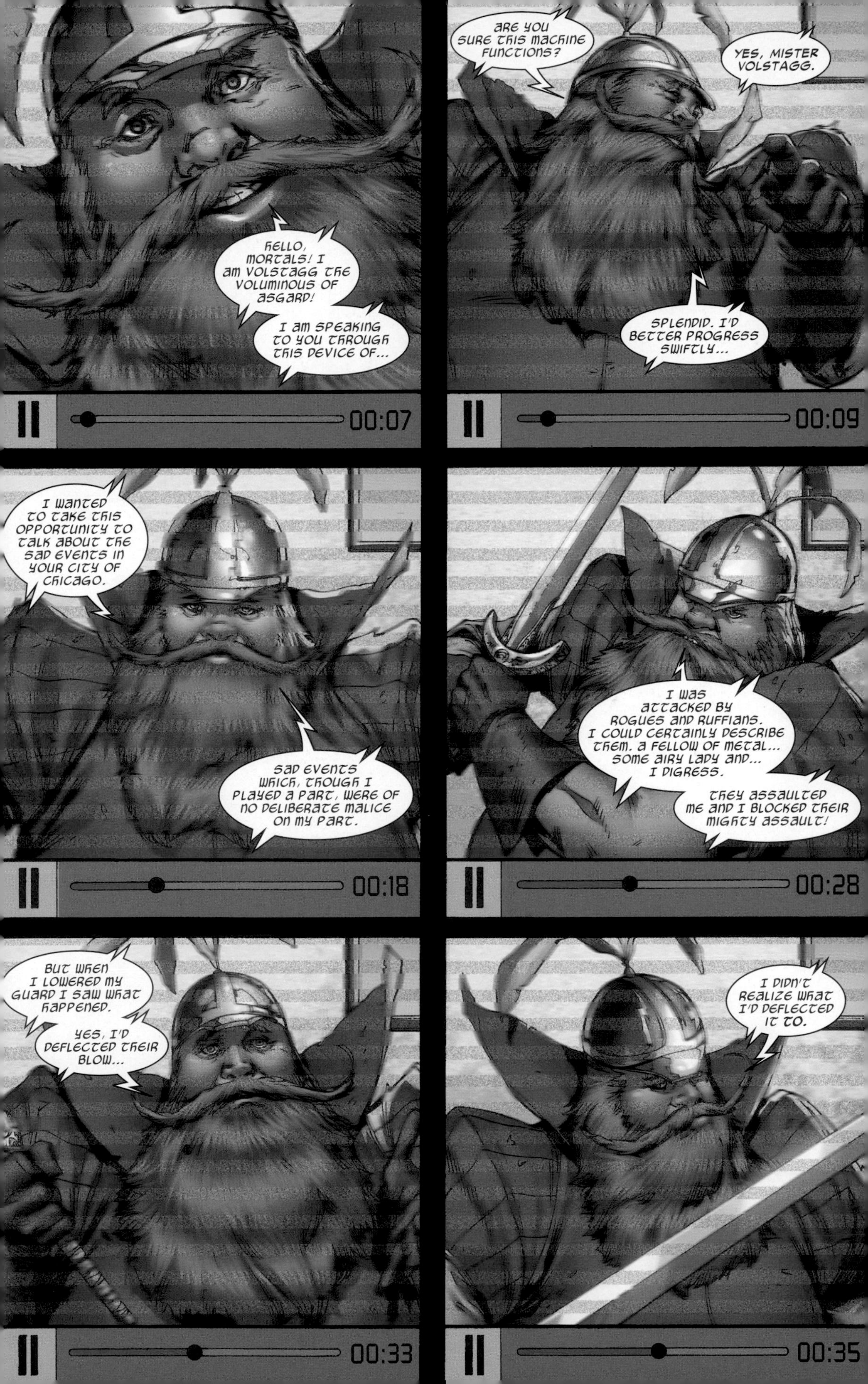
HELLO, MORTALS! I AM VOLSTAGG THE VOLUMINOUS OF ASGARD!
I AM SPEAKING TO YOU THROUGH THIS DEVICE OF...
00:07
ARE YOU SURE THIS MACHINE FUNCTIONS?
YES, MISTER VOLSTAGG.
SPLENDID. I'D BETTER PROGRESS SWIFTLY...
00:09
I WANTED TO TAKE THIS OPPORTUNITY TO TALK ABOUT THE SAD EVENTS IN YOUR CITY OF CHICAGO.
SAD EVENTS WHICH, THOUGH I PLAYED A PART, WERE OF NO DELIBERATE MALICE ON MY PART.
00:18
I WAS ATTACKED BY ROGUES AND RUFFIANS. I COULD CERTAINLY DESCRIBE THEM. A FELLOW OF METAL... SOME AIRY LADY AND... I DIGRESS.
THEY ASSAULTED ME AND I BLOCKED THEIR MIGHTY ASSAULT!
00:28
BUT WHEN I LOWERED MY GUARD I SAW WHAT HAPPENED.
YES, I'D DEFLECTED THEIR BLOW...
00:33
I DIDN'T REALIZE WHAT I'D DEFLECTED IT TO.
00:35

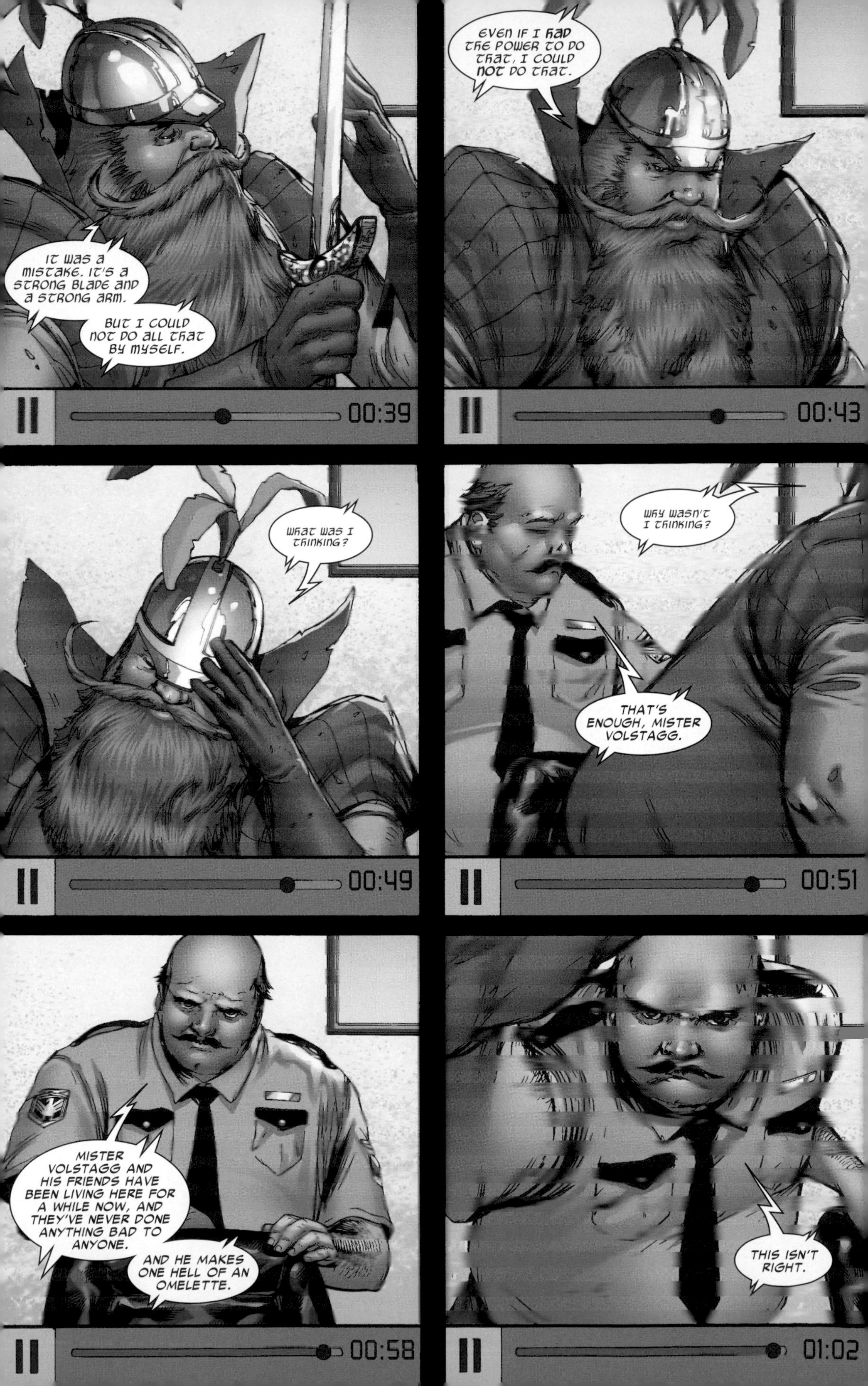
IT WAS A MISTAKE. IT'S A STRONG BLADE AND A STRONG ARM.
BUT I COULD NOT DO ALL THAT BY MYSELF.
00:39
EVEN IF I HAD THE POWER TO DO THAT, I COULD NOT DO THAT.
00:43
WHAT WAS I THINKING?
00:49
WHY WASN'T I THINKING?
THAT'S ENOUGH, MISTER VOLSTAGG.
00:51
MISTER VOLSTAGG AND HIS FRIENDS HAVE BEEN LIVING HERE FOR A WHILE NOW, AND THEY'VE NEVER DONE ANYTHING BAD TO ANYONE.
AND HE MAKES ONE HELL OF AN OMELETTE.
00:58
THIS ISN'T RIGHT.
01:02

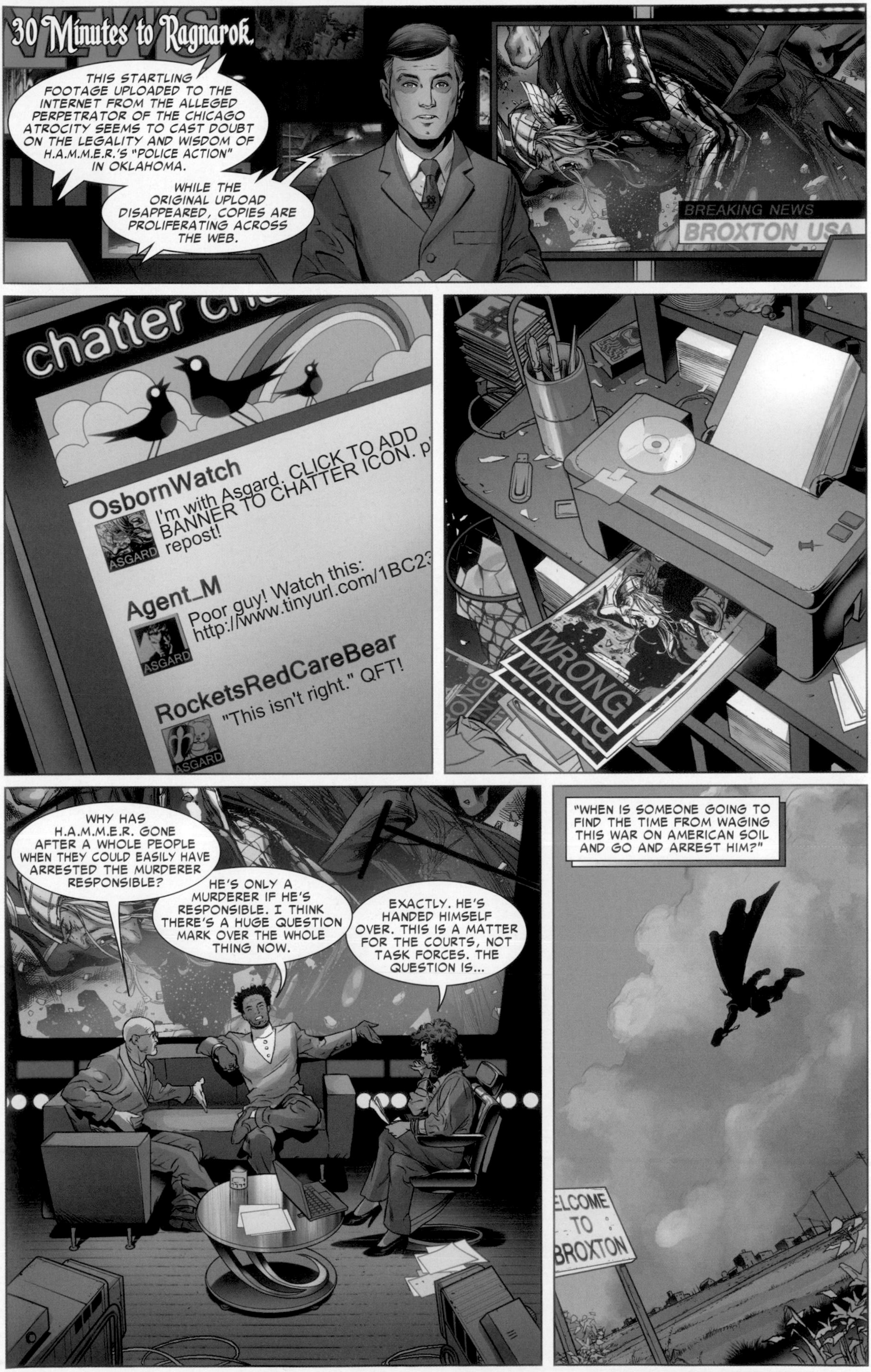
30 Minutes to Ragnarok.
THIS STARTLING FOOTAGE UPLOADED TO THE INTERNET FROM THE ALLEGED PERPETRATOR OF THE CHICAGO ATROCITY SEEMS TO CAST DOUBT ON THE LEGALITY AND WISDOM OF H.A.M.M.E.R.'S "POLICE ACTION" IN OKLAHOMA.
WHILE THE ORIGINAL UPLOAD DISAPPEARED, COPIES ARE PROLIFERATING ACROSS THE WEB.
BREAKING NEWS
BROXTON USA
chatter
OsbornWatch
I'm with Asgard. CLICK TO ADD BANNER TO CHATTER ICON. repost!
ASGARD
Agent_M
Poor guy! Watch this: http://www.tinyurl.com/1BC23
ASGARD
RocketsRedCareBear
"This isn't right." QFT!
ASGARD
WRONG
WRONG
WHY HAS H.A.M.M.E.R. GONE AFTER A WHOLE PEOPLE WHEN THEY COULD EASILY HAVE ARRESTED THE MURDERER RESPONSIBLE?
HE'S ONLY A MURDERER IF HE'S RESPONSIBLE. I THINK THERE'S A HUGE QUESTION MARK OVER THE WHOLE THING NOW.
EXACTLY. HE'S HANDED HIMSELF OVER. THIS IS A MATTER FOR THE COURTS, NOT TASK FORCES. THE QUESTION IS...
"WHEN IS SOMEONE GOING TO FIND THE TIME FROM WAGING THIS WAR ON AMERICAN SOIL AND GO AND ARREST HIM?"
ELCOME TO BROXTON

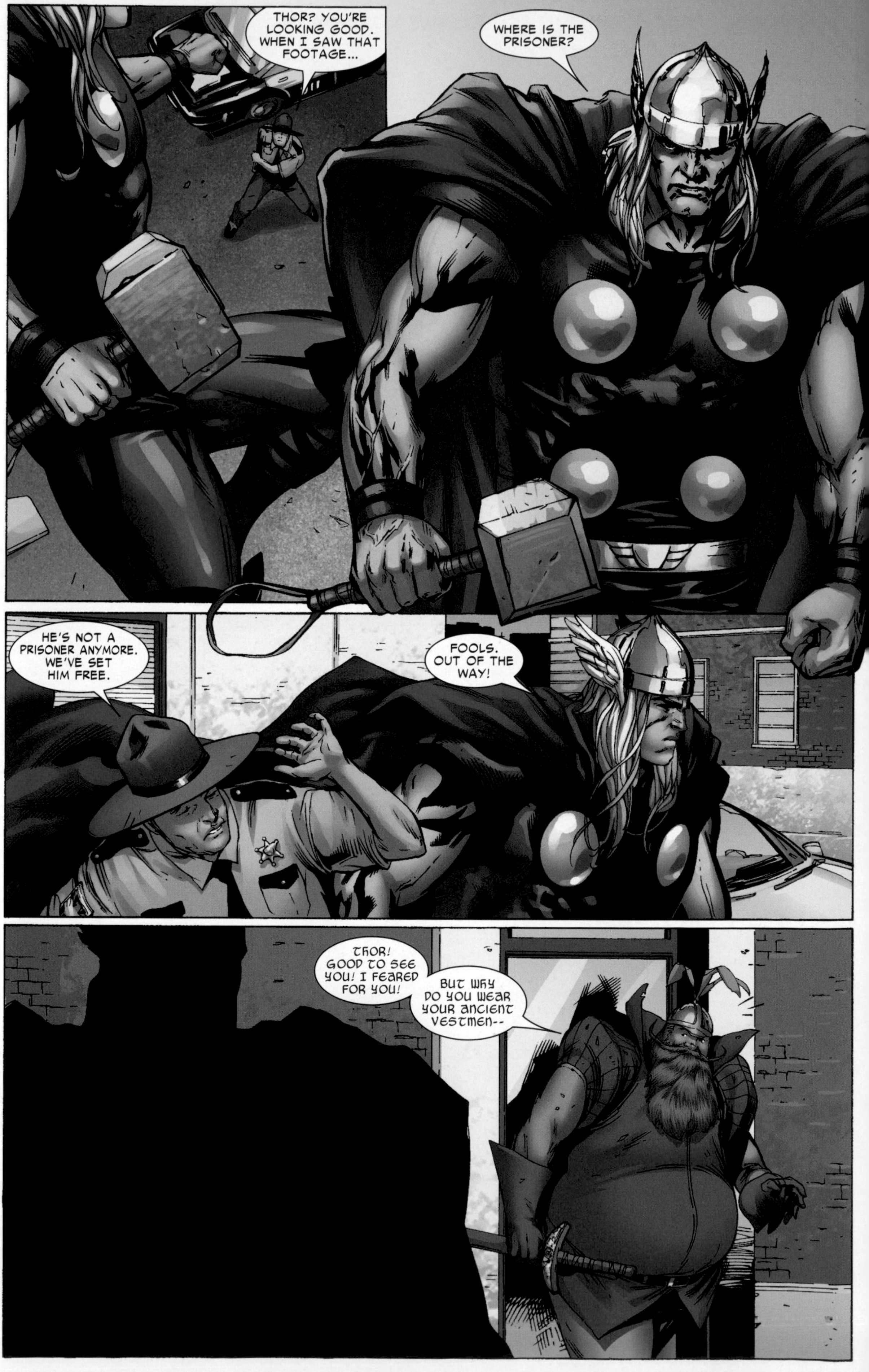
THOR? YOU'RE LOOKING GOOD. WHEN I SAW THAT FOOTAGE...
WHERE IS THE PRISONER?
HE'S NOT A PRISONER ANYMORE. WE'VE SET HIM FREE.
FOOLS. OUT OF THE WAY!
THOR! GOOD TO SEE YOU! I FEARED FOR YOU!
BUT WHY DO YOU WEAR YOUR ANCIENT VESTMEN--

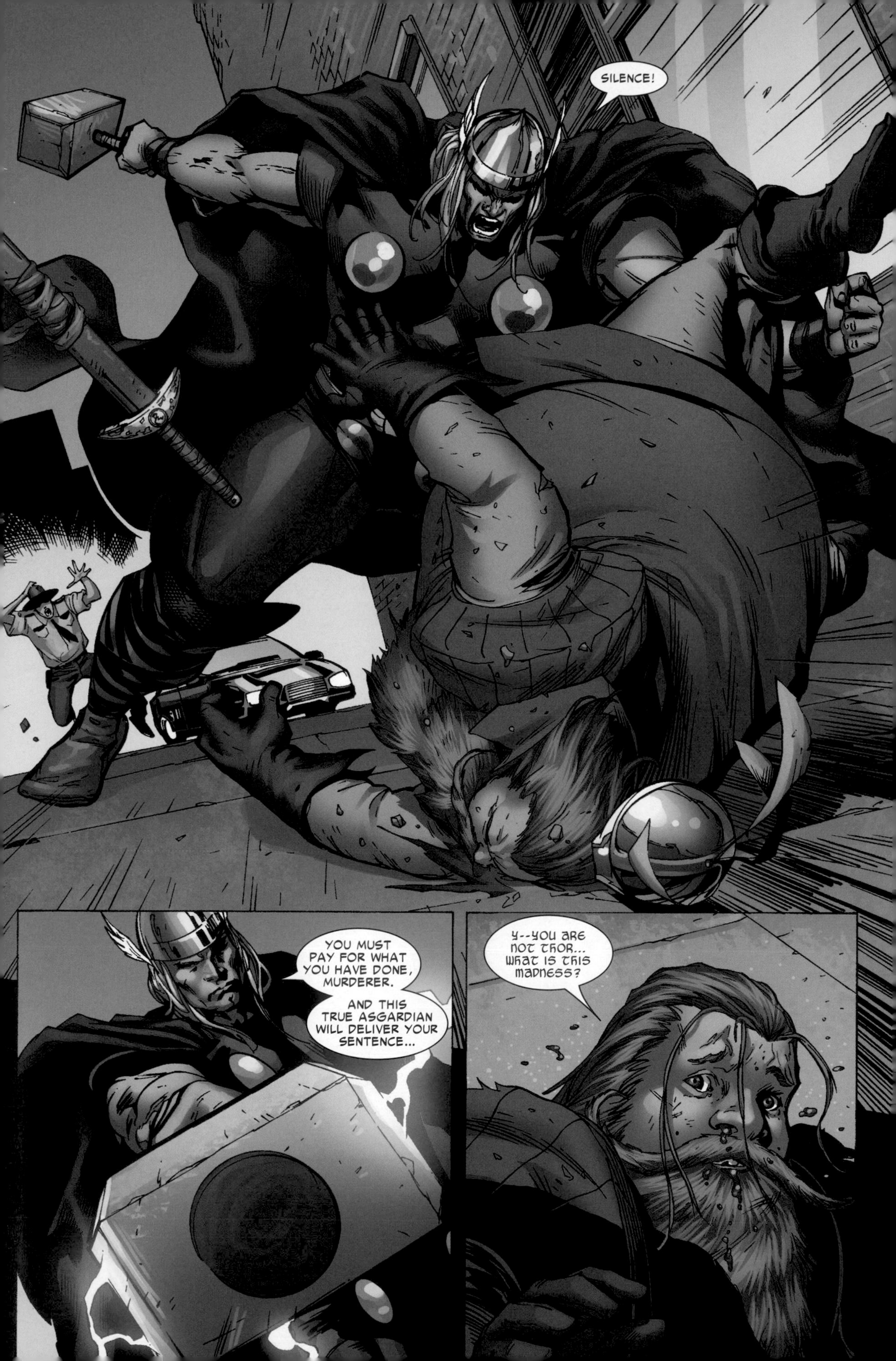
SILENCE!
YOU MUST PAY FOR WHAT YOU HAVE DONE, MURDERER.
AND THIS TRUE ASGARDIAN WILL DELIVER YOUR SENTENCE...
Y--YOU ARE NOT THOR... WHAT IS THIS MADNESS?

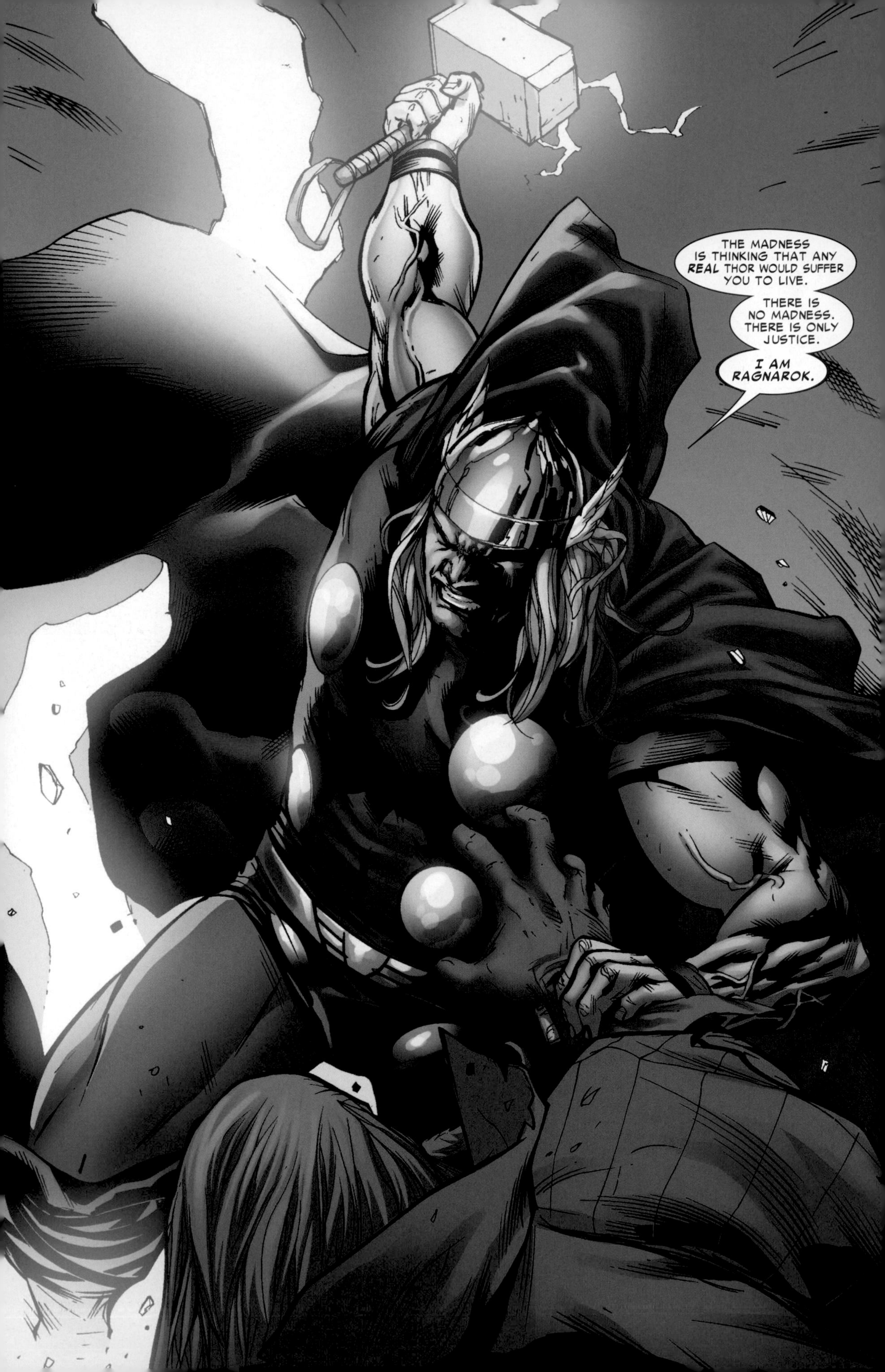
THE MADNESS IS THINKING THAT ANY *REAL* THOR WOULD SUFFER YOU TO LIVE.
THERE IS NO MADNESS. THERE IS ONLY JUSTICE.
I AM RAGNAROK.

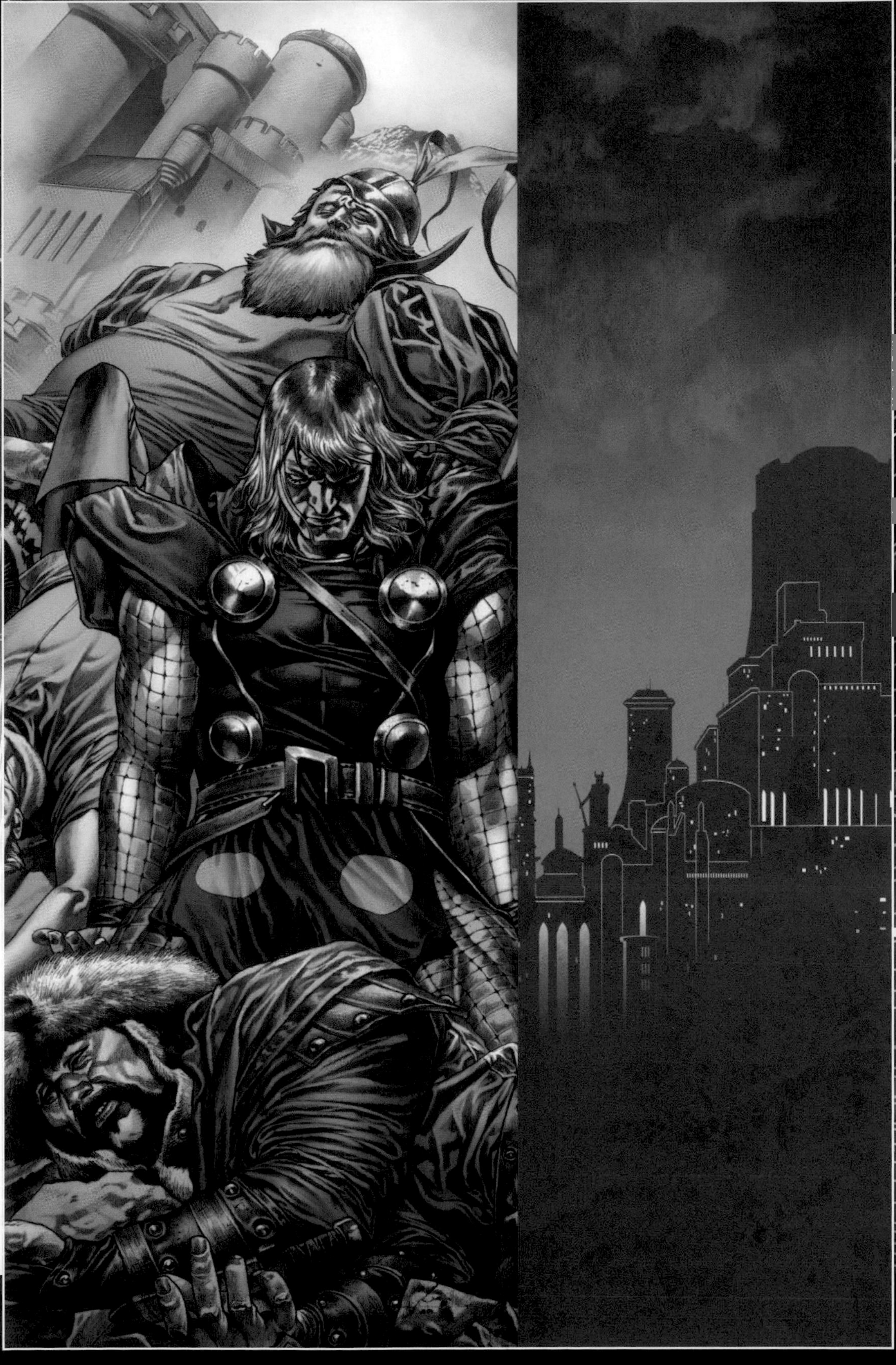

THOR #608

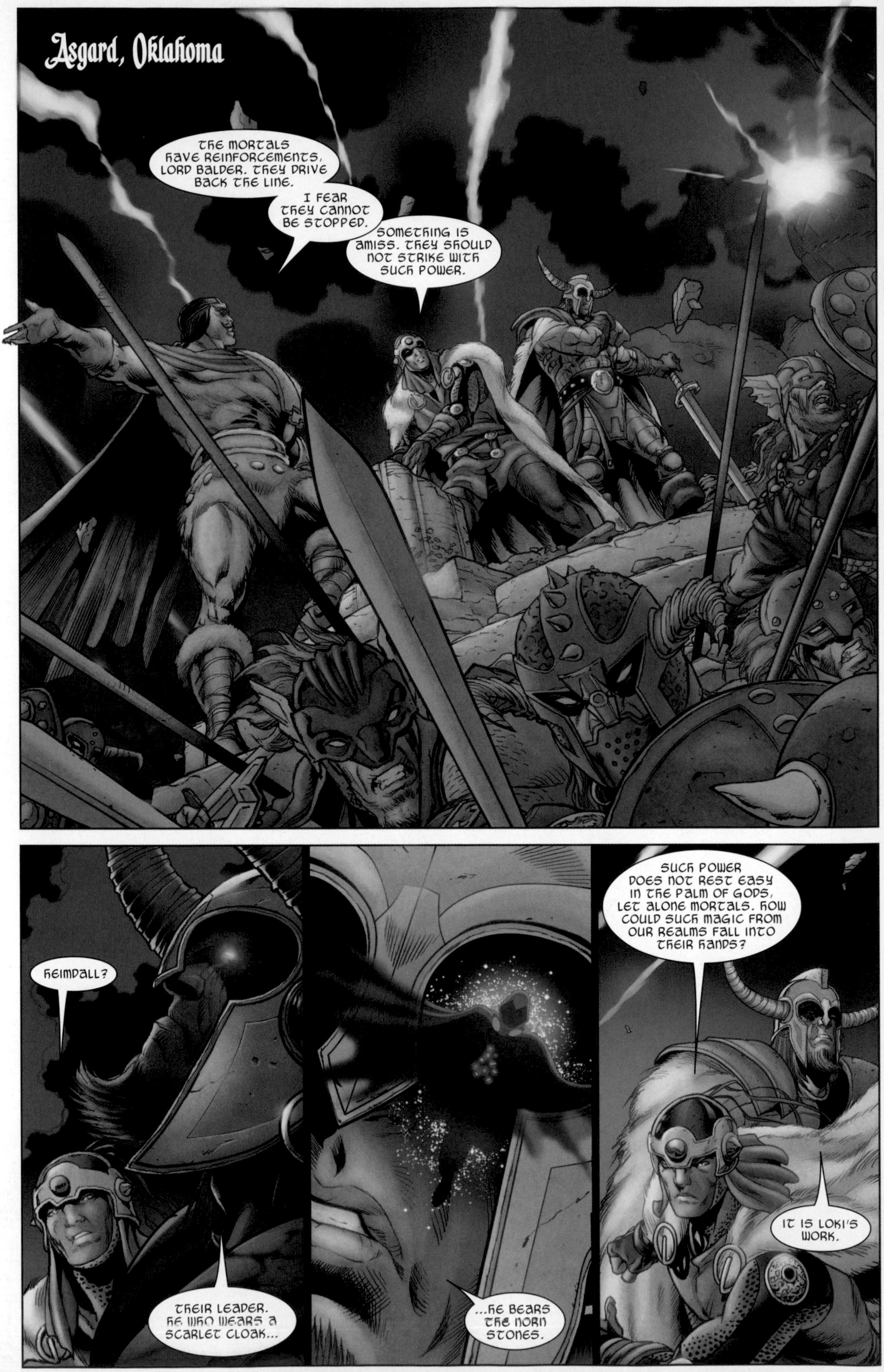
Asgard, Oklahoma
THE MORTALS HAVE REINFORCEMENTS, LORD BALDER. THEY DRIVE BACK THE LINE.
I FEAR THEY CANNOT BE STOPPED.
SOMETHING IS AMISS. THEY SHOULD NOT STRIKE WITH SUCH POWER.
HEIMDALL?
THEIR LEADER. HE WHO WEARS A SCARLET CLOAK...
...HE BEARS THE NORN STONES.
SUCH POWER DOES NOT REST EASY IN THE PALM OF GODS, LET ALONE MORTALS. HOW COULD SUCH MAGIC FROM OUR REALMS FALL INTO THEIR HANDS?
IT IS LOKI'S WORK.

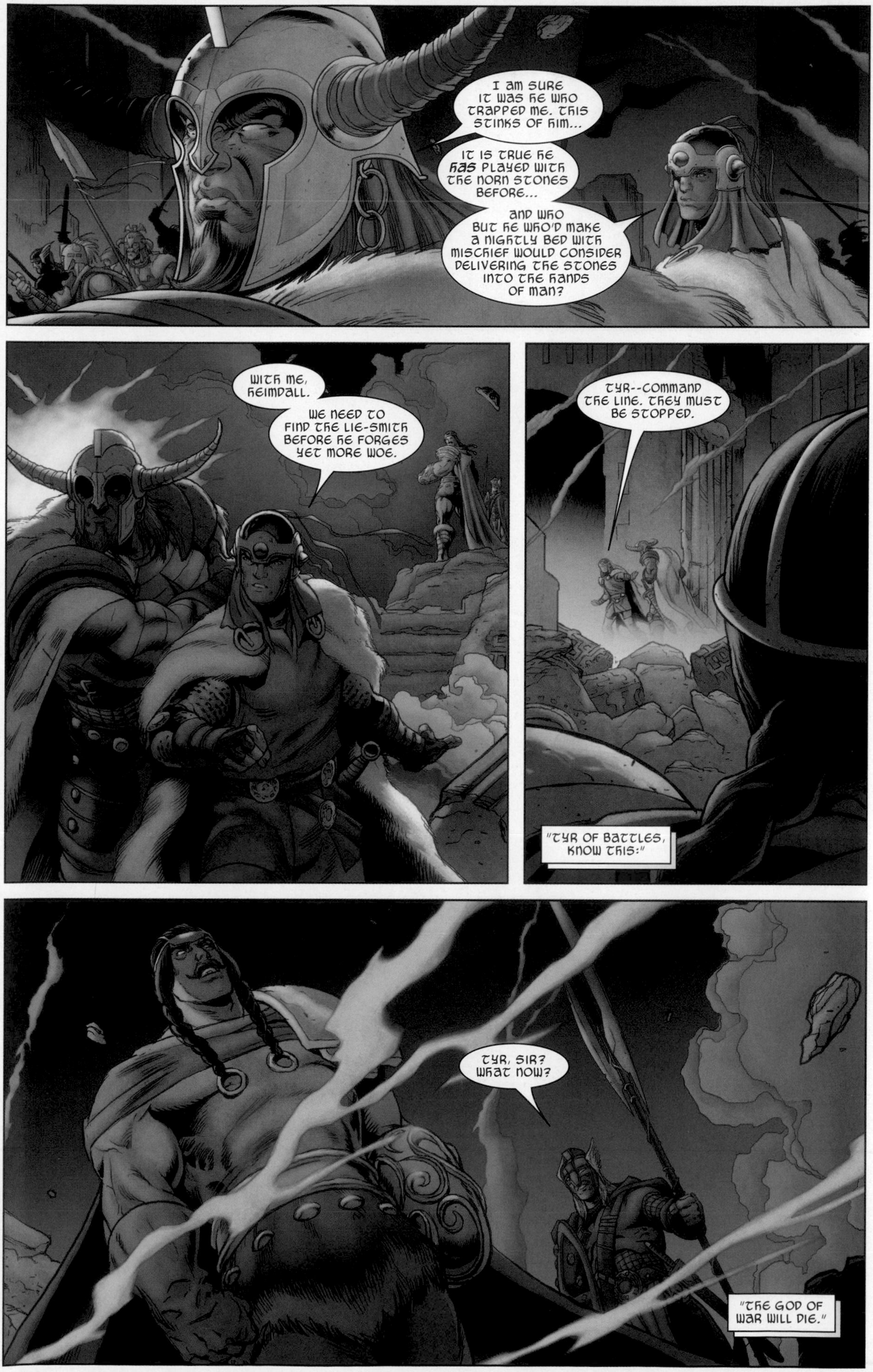
I AM SURE IT WAS HE WHO TRAPPED ME. THIS STINKS OF HIM...
IT IS TRUE HE HAS PLAYED WITH THE NORN STONES BEFORE...
AND WHO BUT HE WHO'D MAKE A NIGHTLY BED WITH MISCHIEF WOULD CONSIDER DELIVERING THE STONES INTO THE HANDS OF MAN?
WITH ME, HEIMDALL.
WE NEED TO FIND THE LIE-SMITH BEFORE HE FORGES YET MORE WOE.
TYR--COMMAND THE LINE. THEY MUST BE STOPPED.
"TYR OF BATTLES, KNOW THIS:"
TYR, SIR? WHAT NOW?
"THE GOD OF WAR WILL DIE."

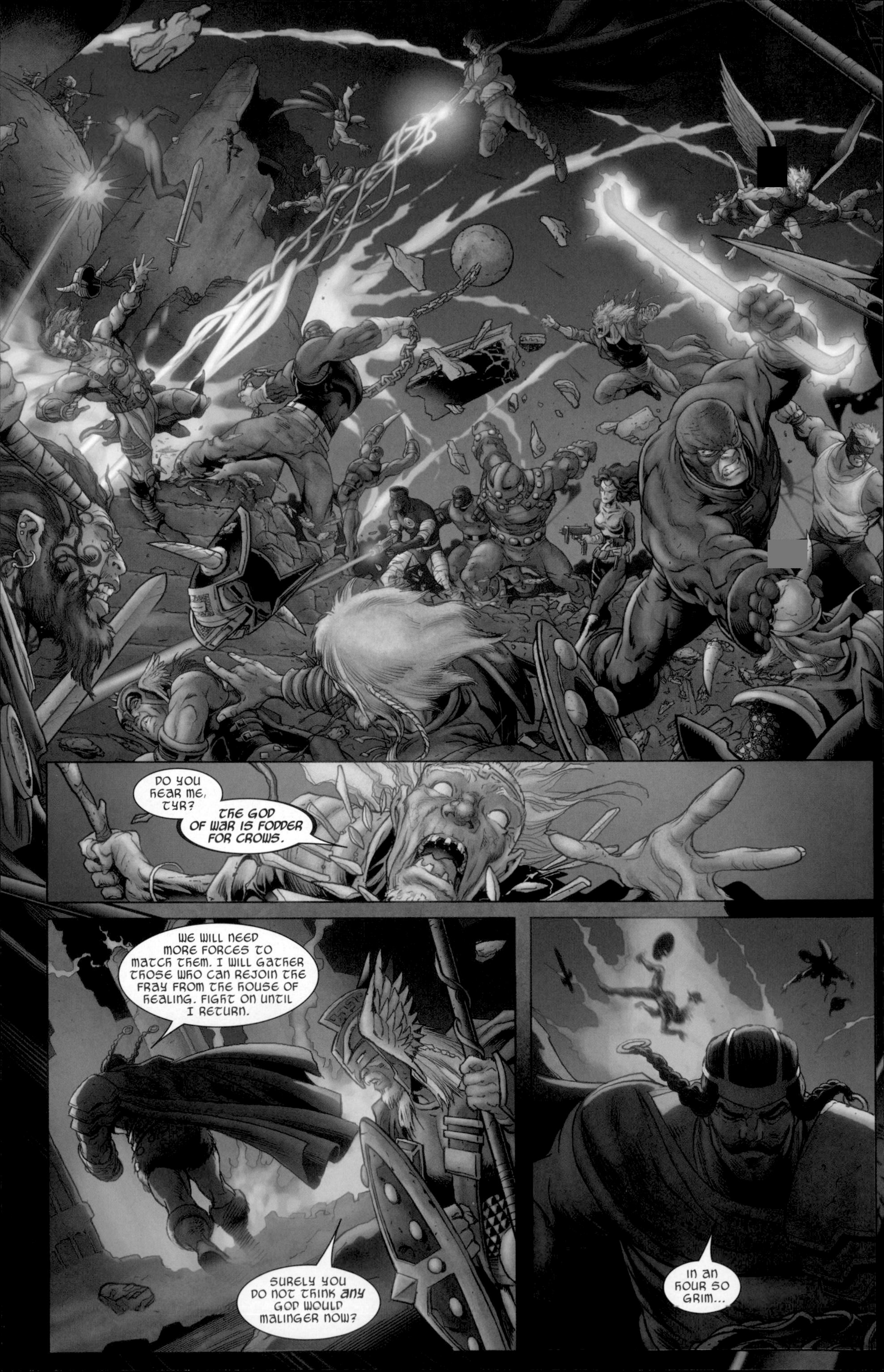

DO YOU HEAR ME, TYR?
THE GOD OF WAR IS FODDER FOR CROWS.
WE WILL NEED MORE FORCES TO MATCH THEM. I WILL GATHER THOSE WHO CAN REJOIN THE FRAY FROM THE HOUSE OF HEALING. FIGHT ON UNTIL I RETURN.
SURELY YOU DO NOT THINK ANY GOD WOULD MALINGER NOW?
IN AN HOUR SO GRIM...

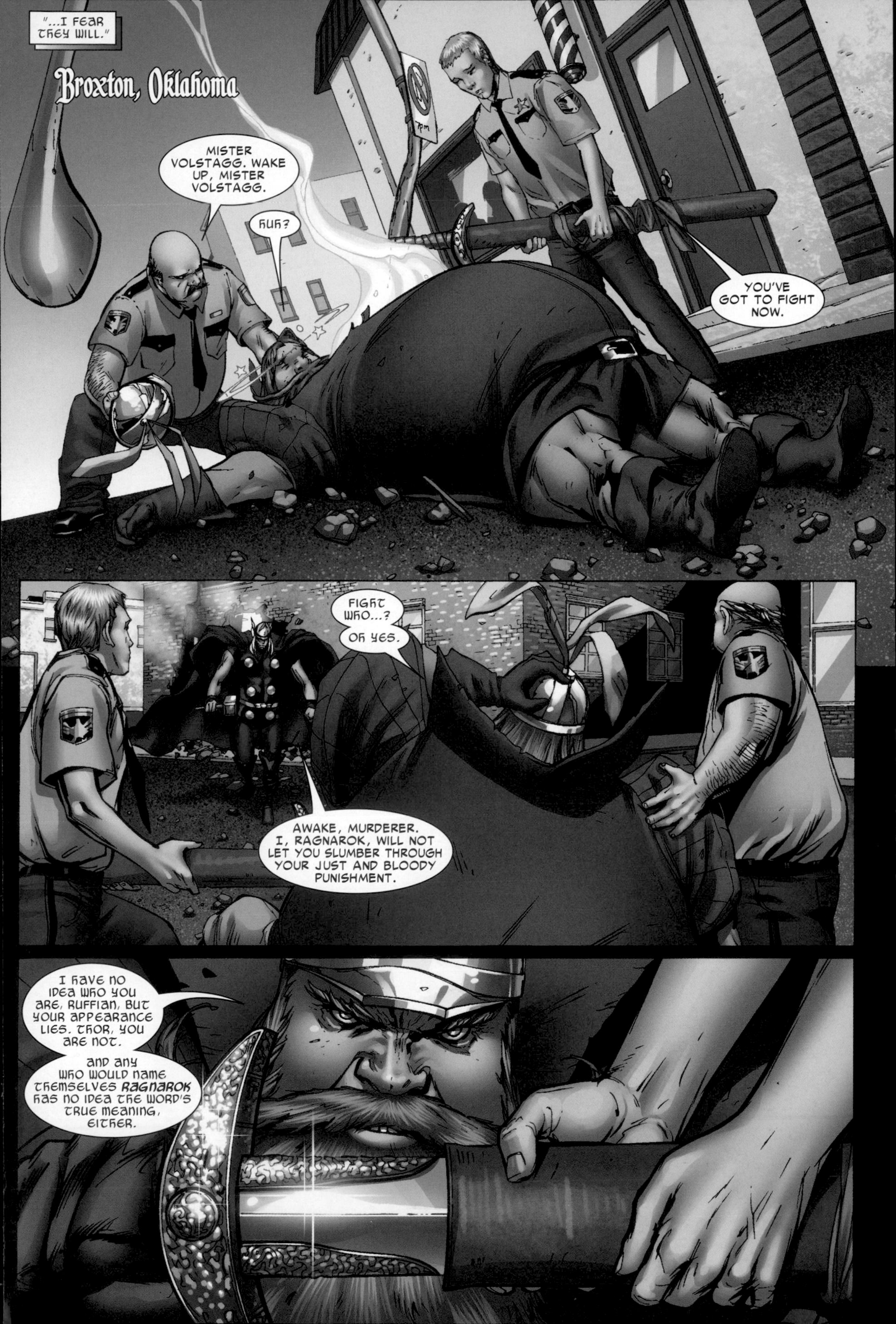

"...I FEAR THEY WILL."
Broxton, Oklahoma
MISTER VOLSTAGG. WAKE UP, MISTER VOLSTAGG.
HUH?
YOU'VE GOT TO FIGHT NOW.
FIGHT WHO...?
OH YES.
AWAKE, MURDERER. I, RAGNAROK, WILL NOT LET YOU SLUMBER THROUGH YOUR JUST AND BLOODY PUNISHMENT.
I HAVE NO IDEA WHO YOU ARE, RUFFIAN, BUT YOUR APPEARANCE LIES. THOR, YOU ARE NOT.
AND ANY WHO WOULD NAME THEMSELVES RAGNAROK HAS NO IDEA THE WORD'S TRUE MEANING, EITHER.

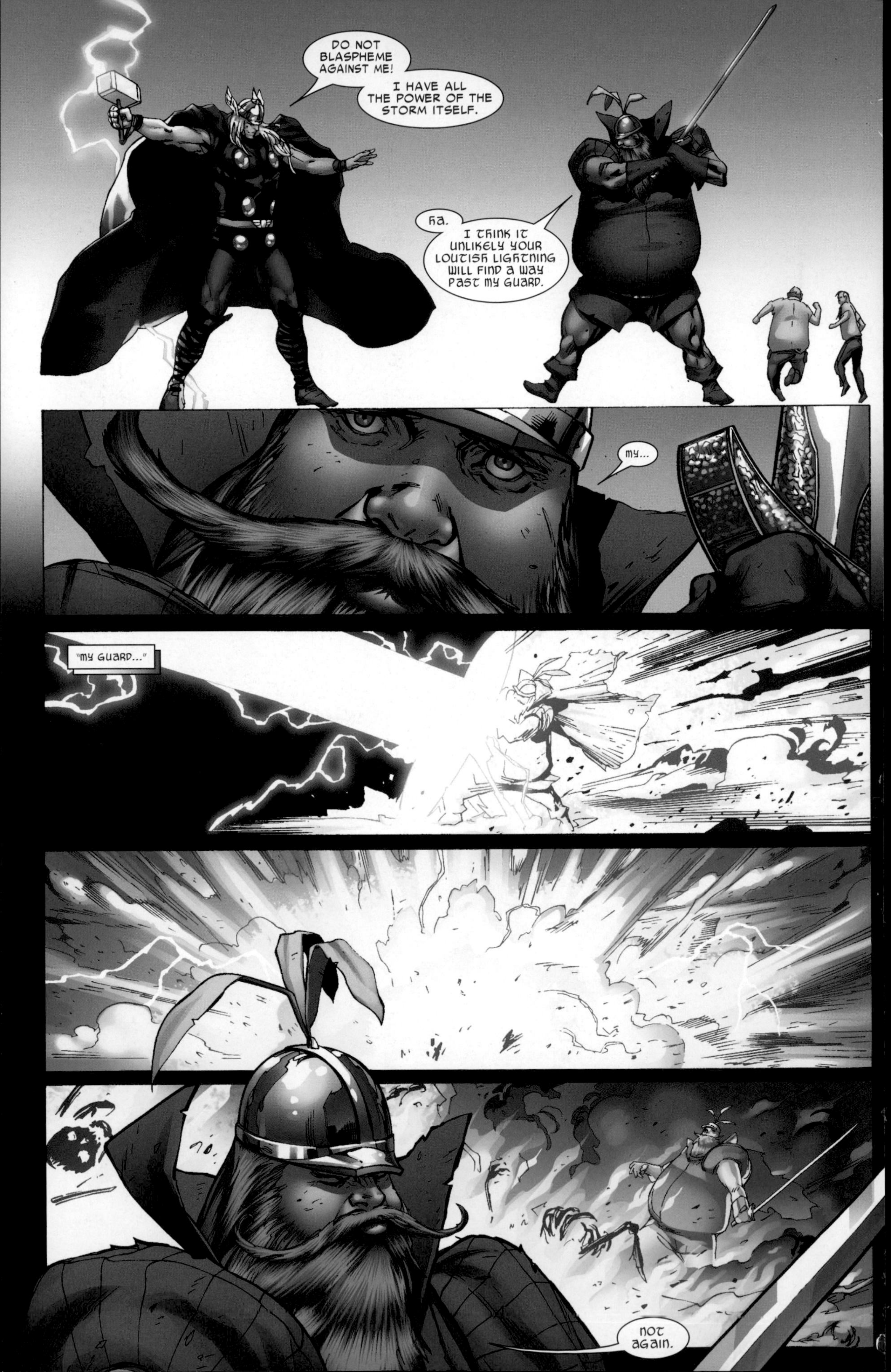
DO NOT BLASPHEME AGAINST ME!
I HAVE ALL THE POWER OF THE STORM ITSELF.
HA.
I THINK IT UNLIKELY YOUR LOUTISH LIGHTNING WILL FIND A WAY PAST MY GUARD.
MY...
"MY GUARD..."
NOT AGAIN.

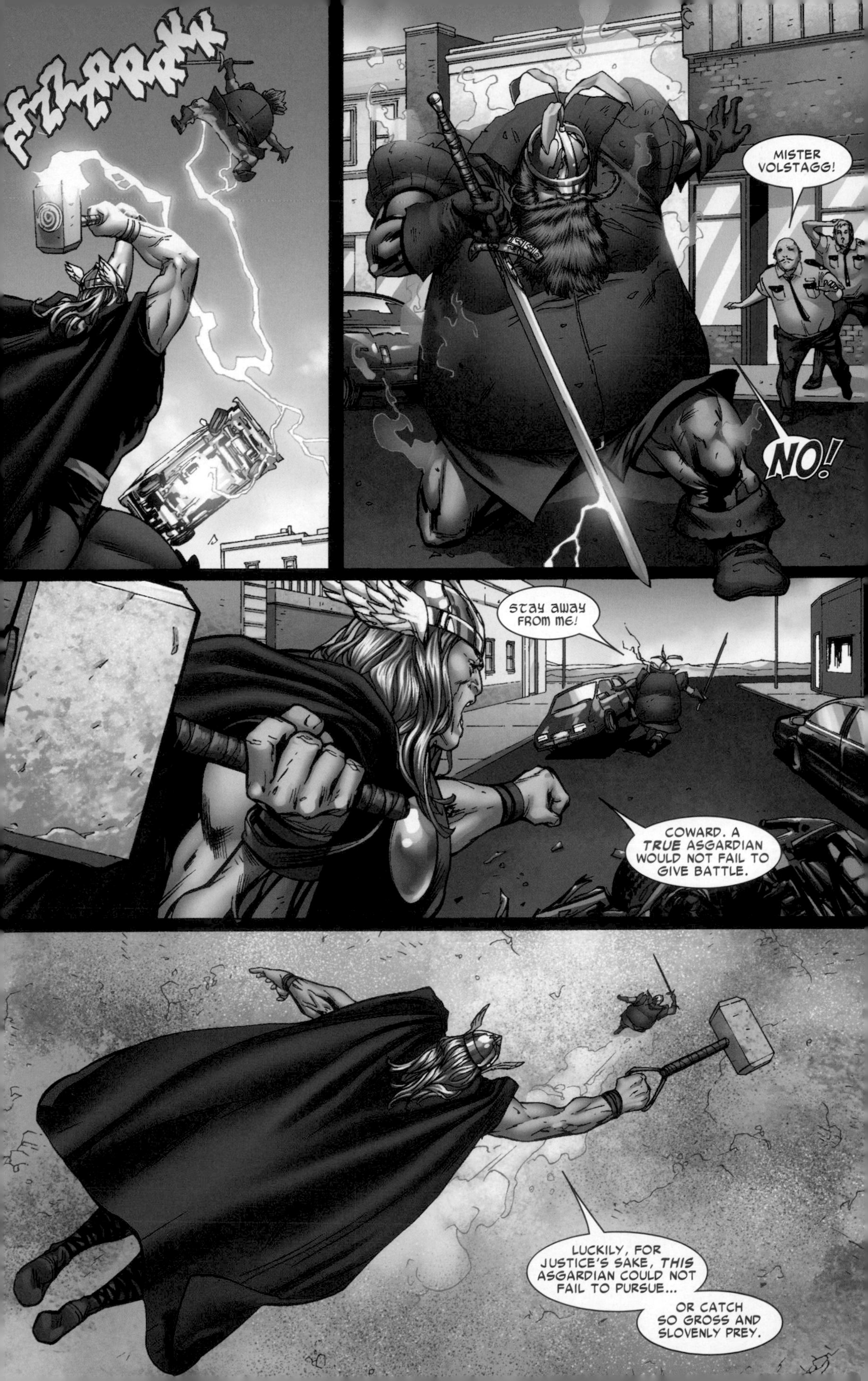
FZZRRAKK
MISTER VOLSTAGG!
NO!
STAY AWAY FROM ME!
COWARD. A *TRUE* ASGARDIAN WOULD NOT FAIL TO GIVE BATTLE.
LUCKILY, FOR JUSTICE'S SAKE, *THIS* ASGARDIAN COULD NOT FAIL TO PURSUE...
OR CATCH SO GROSS AND SLOVENLY PREY.

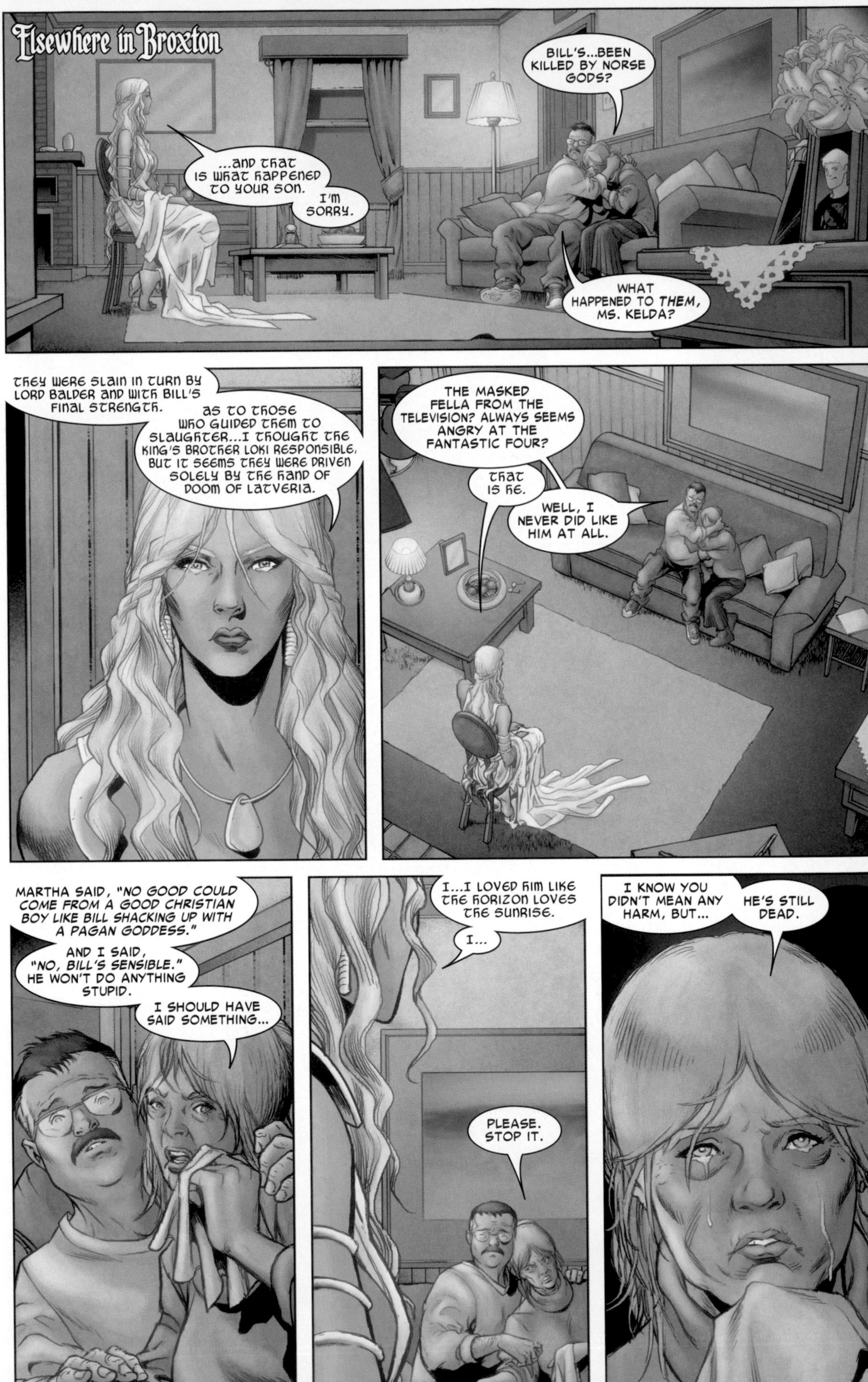
Elsewhere in Broxton
...AND THAT IS WHAT HAPPENED TO YOUR SON.
I'M SORRY.
BILL'S...BEEN KILLED BY NORSE GODS?
WHAT HAPPENED TO THEM, MS. KELDA?
THEY WERE SLAIN IN TURN BY LORD BALDER AND WITH BILL'S FINAL STRENGTH.
AS TO THOSE WHO GUIDED THEM TO SLAUGHTER...I THOUGHT THE KING'S BROTHER LOKI RESPONSIBLE, BUT IT SEEMS THEY WERE DRIVEN SOLELY BY THE HAND OF DOOM OF LATVERIA.
THE MASKED FELLA FROM THE TELEVISION? ALWAYS SEEMS ANGRY AT THE FANTASTIC FOUR?
THAT IS HE.
WELL, I NEVER DID LIKE HIM AT ALL.
MARTHA SAID, "NO GOOD COULD COME FROM A GOOD CHRISTIAN BOY LIKE BILL SHACKING UP WITH A PAGAN GODDESS."
AND I SAID, "NO, BILL'S SENSIBLE." HE WON'T DO ANYTHING STUPID.
I SHOULD HAVE SAID SOMETHING...
I...I LOVED HIM LIKE THE HORIZON LOVES THE SUNRISE.
I...
PLEASE. STOP IT.
I KNOW YOU DIDN'T MEAN ANY HARM, BUT...
HE'S STILL DEAD.

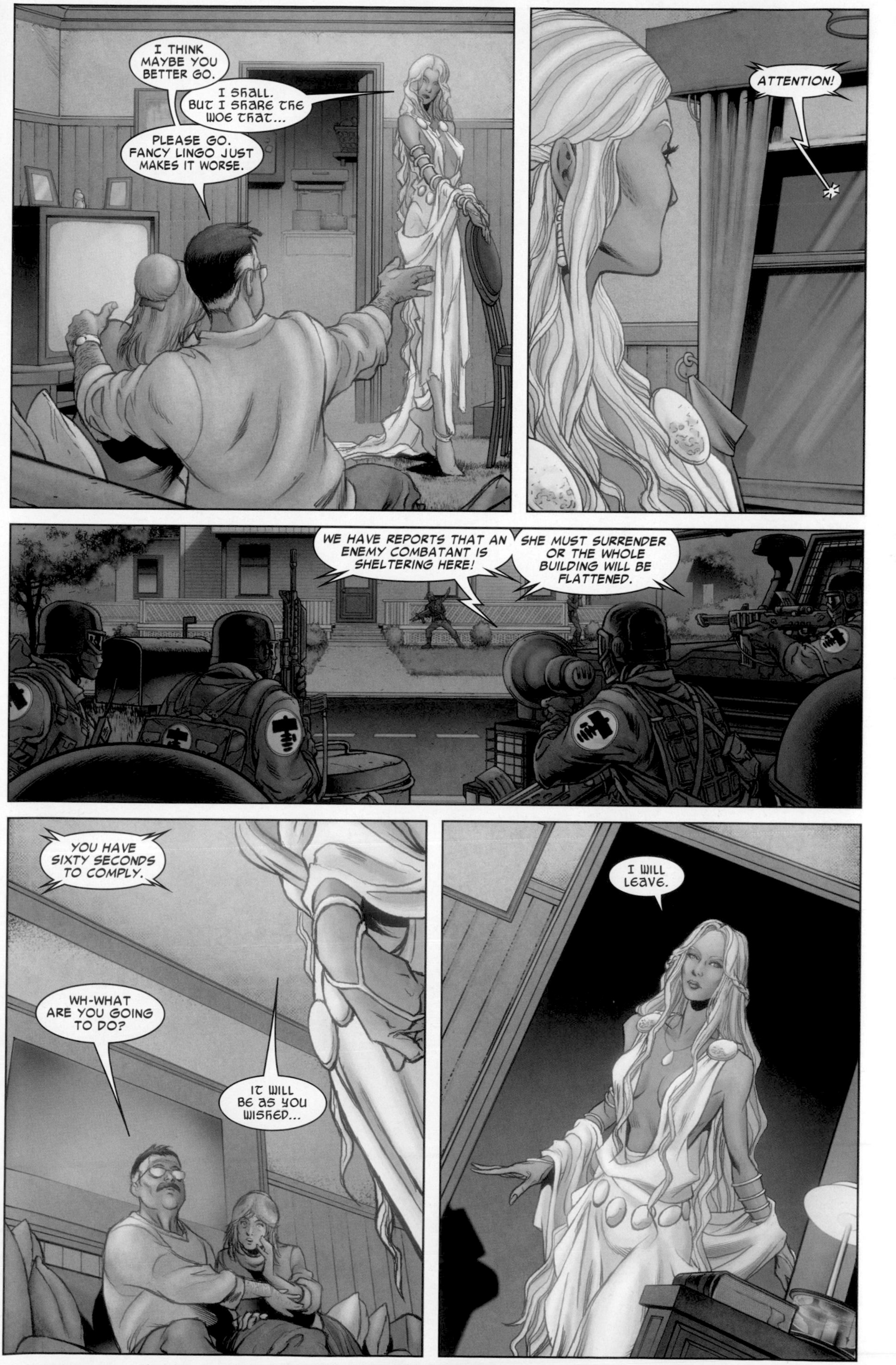
I THINK MAYBE YOU BETTER GO.
I SHALL. BUT I SHARE THE WOE THAT...
PLEASE GO. FANCY LINGO JUST MAKES IT WORSE.
ATTENTION!
WE HAVE REPORTS THAT AN ENEMY COMBATANT IS SHELTERING HERE!
SHE MUST SURRENDER OR THE WHOLE BUILDING WILL BE FLATTENED.
YOU HAVE SIXTY SECONDS TO COMPLY.
WH-WHAT ARE YOU GOING TO DO?
IT WILL BE AS YOU WISHED...
I WILL LEAVE.

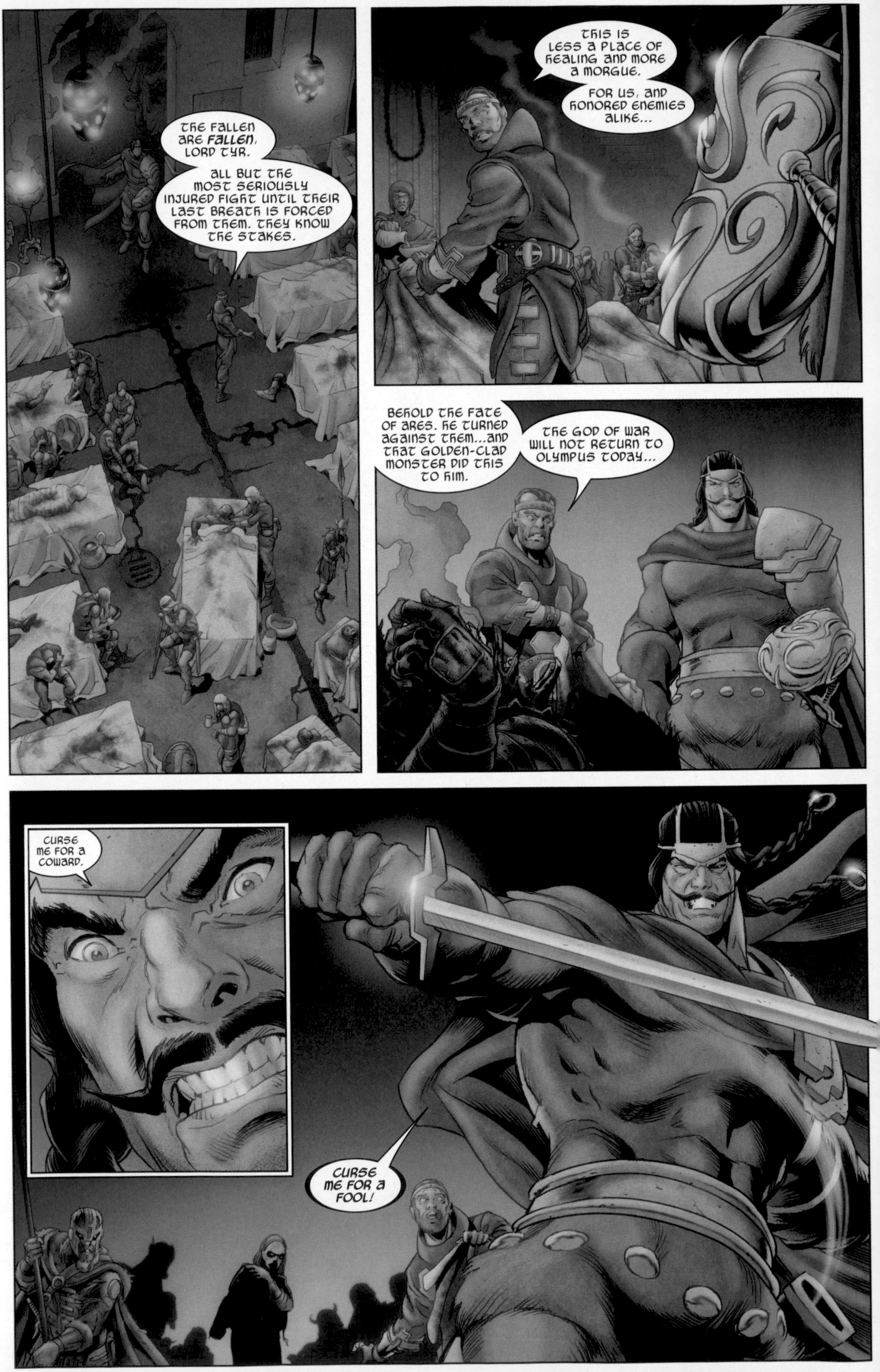
THE FALLEN ARE FALLEN, LORD TYR.
ALL BUT THE MOST SERIOUSLY INJURED FIGHT UNTIL THEIR LAST BREATH IS FORCED FROM THEM. THEY KNOW THE STAKES.
THIS IS LESS A PLACE OF HEALING AND MORE A MORGUE.
FOR US, AND HONORED ENEMIES ALIKE...
BEHOLD THE FATE OF ARES. HE TURNED AGAINST THEM...AND THAT GOLDEN-CLAD MONSTER DID THIS TO HIM.
THE GOD OF WAR WILL NOT RETURN TO OLYMPUS TODAY...
CURSE ME FOR A COWARD.
CURSE ME FOR A FOOL!

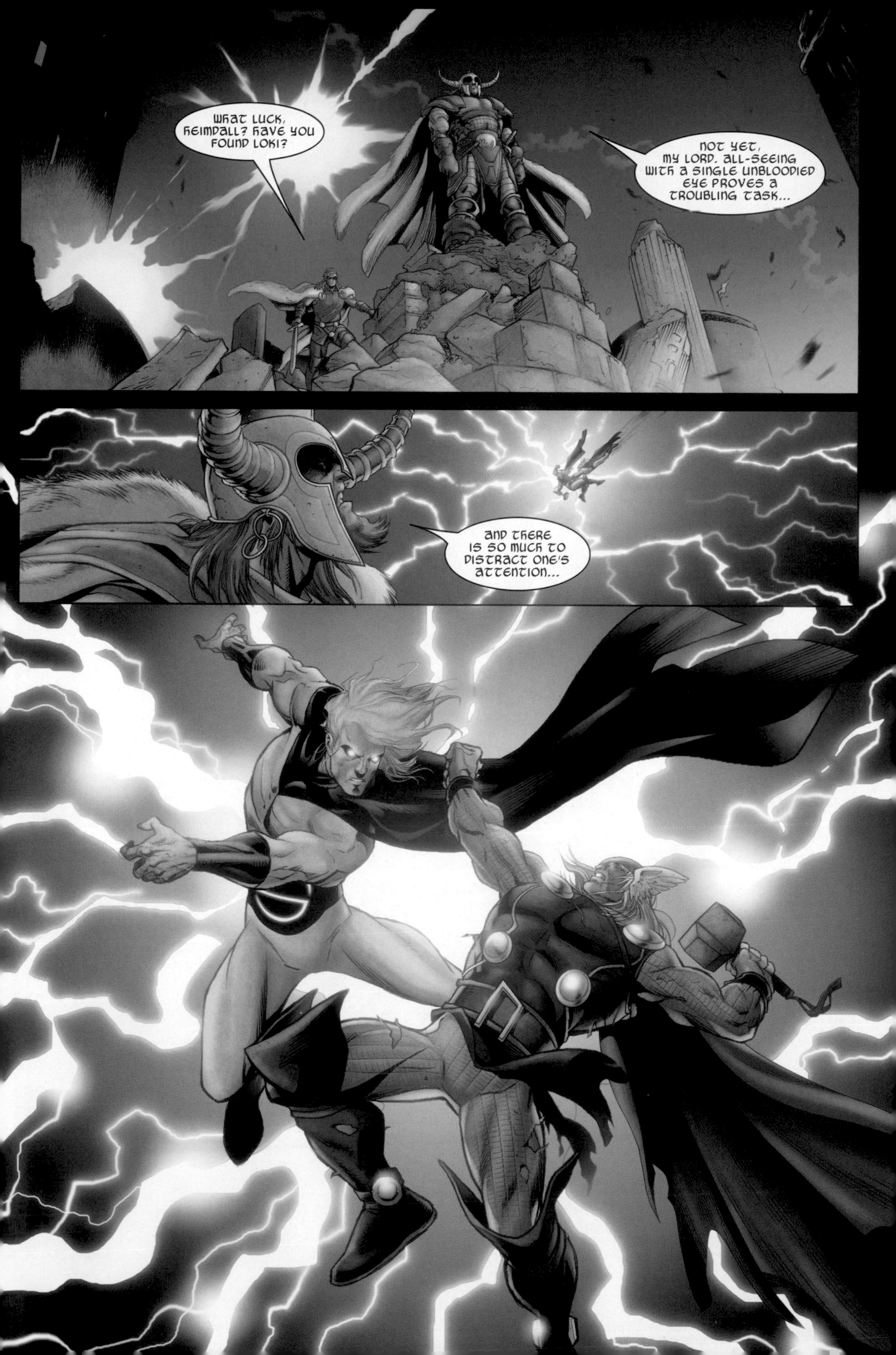
WHAT LUCK, HEIMDALL? HAVE YOU FOUND LOKI?
NOT YET, MY LORD. ALL-SEEING WITH A SINGLE UNBLOODIED EYE PROVES A TROUBLING TASK...
AND THERE IS SO MUCH TO DISTRACT ONE'S ATTENTION...

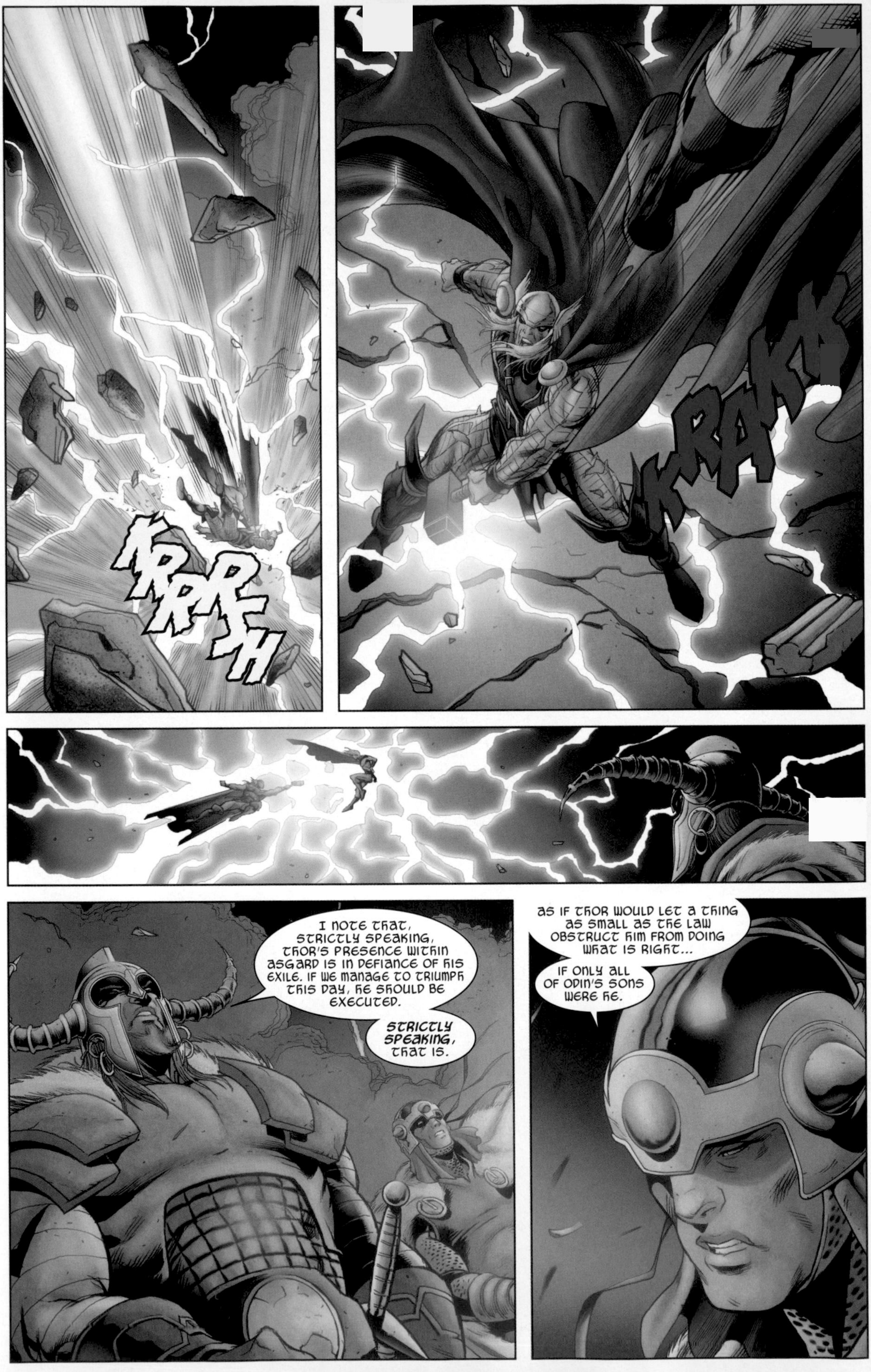
KRRASH
KRAKK
I NOTE THAT, STRICTLY SPEAKING, THOR'S PRESENCE WITHIN ASGARD IS IN DEFIANCE OF HIS EXILE. IF WE MANAGE TO TRIUMPH THIS DAY, HE SHOULD BE EXECUTED.
STRICTLY SPEAKING, THAT IS.
AS IF THOR WOULD LET A THING AS SMALL AS THE LAW OBSTRUCT HIM FROM DOING WHAT IS RIGHT...
IF ONLY ALL OF ODIN'S SONS WERE HE.

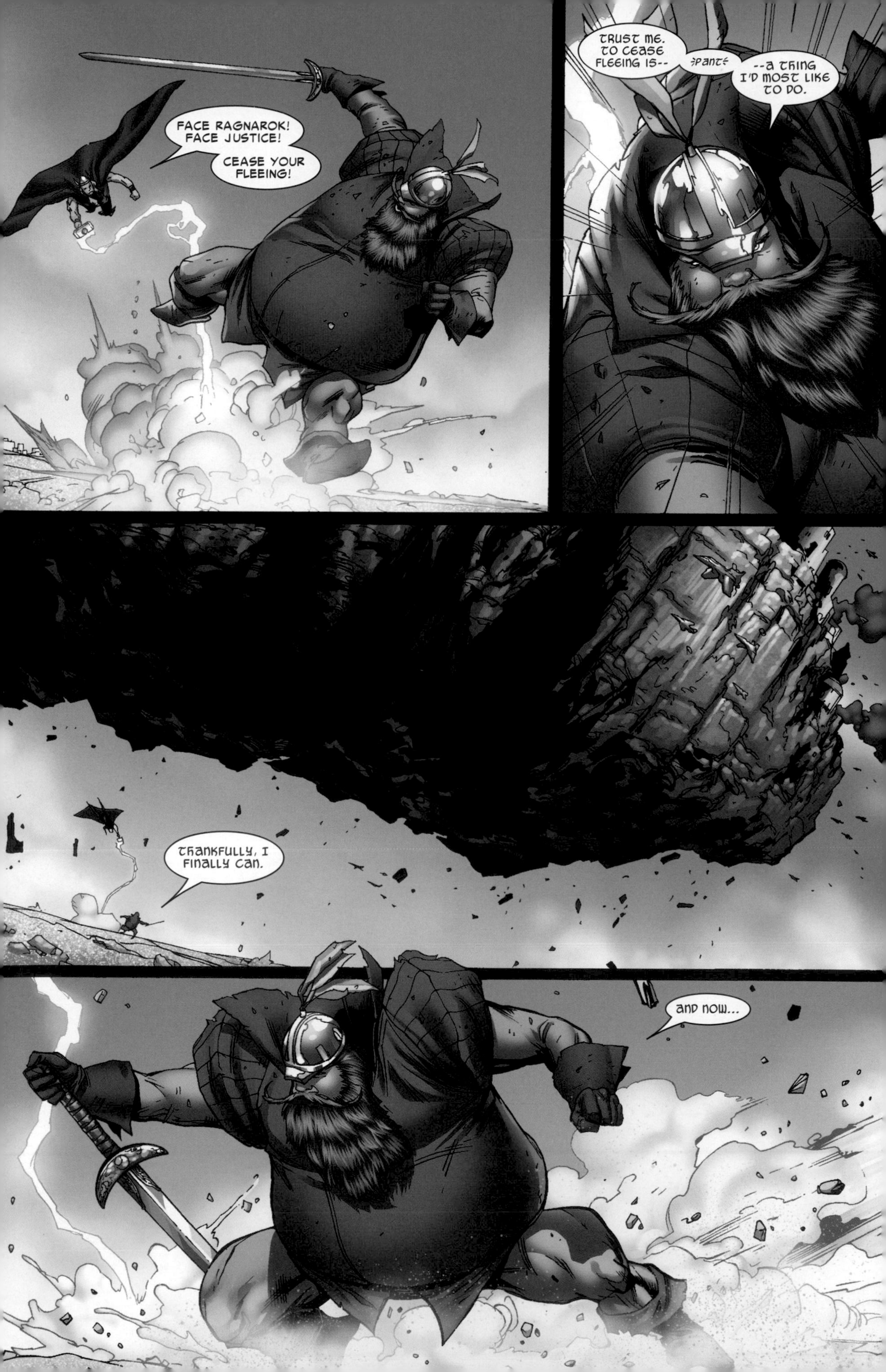
FACE RAGNAROK! FACE JUSTICE!
CEASE YOUR FLEEING!
TRUST ME. TO CEASE FLEEING IS--
PANT
--A THING I'D MOST LIKE TO DO.
THANKFULLY, I FINALLY CAN.
AND NOW...

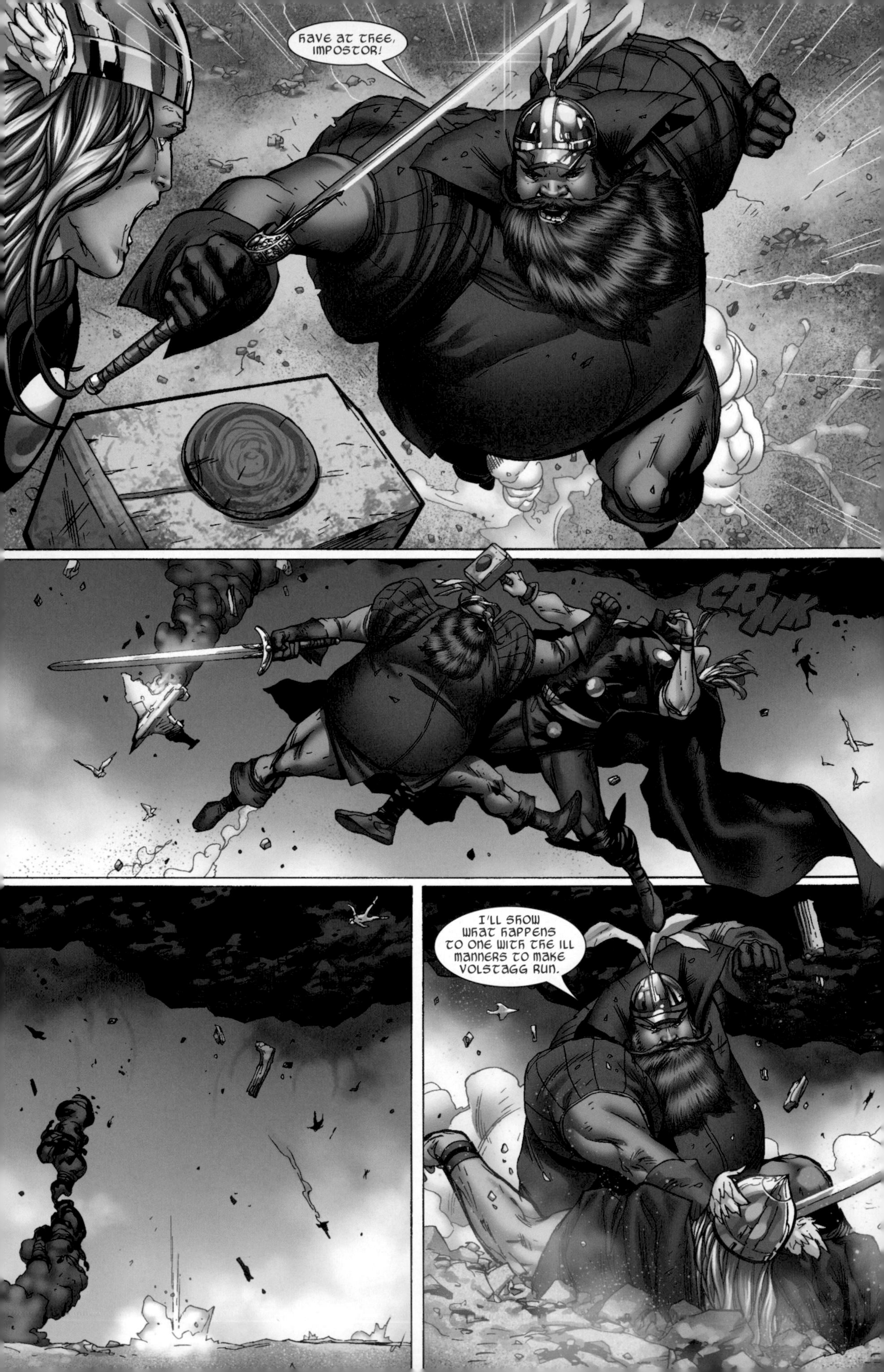
HAVE AT THEE, IMPOSTOR!
CRNK
I'LL SHOW WHAT HAPPENS TO ONE WITH THE ILL MANNERS TO MAKE VOLSTAGG RUN.

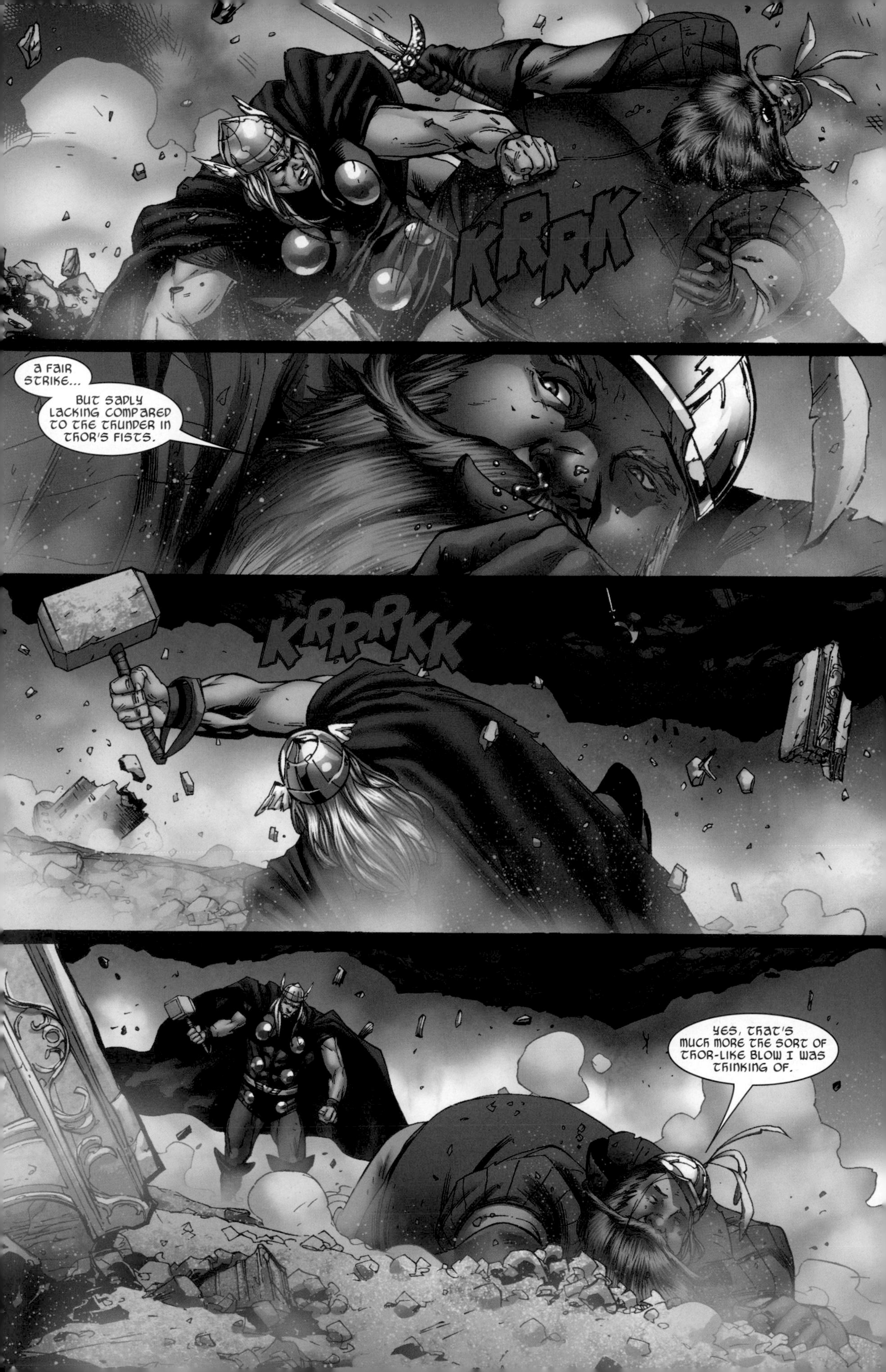
KRRK
A FAIR STRIKE...
BUT SADLY LACKING COMPARED TO THE THUNDER IN THOR'S FISTS.
KRRRKK
YES, THAT'S MUCH MORE THE SORT OF THOR-LIKE BLOW I WAS THINKING OF.

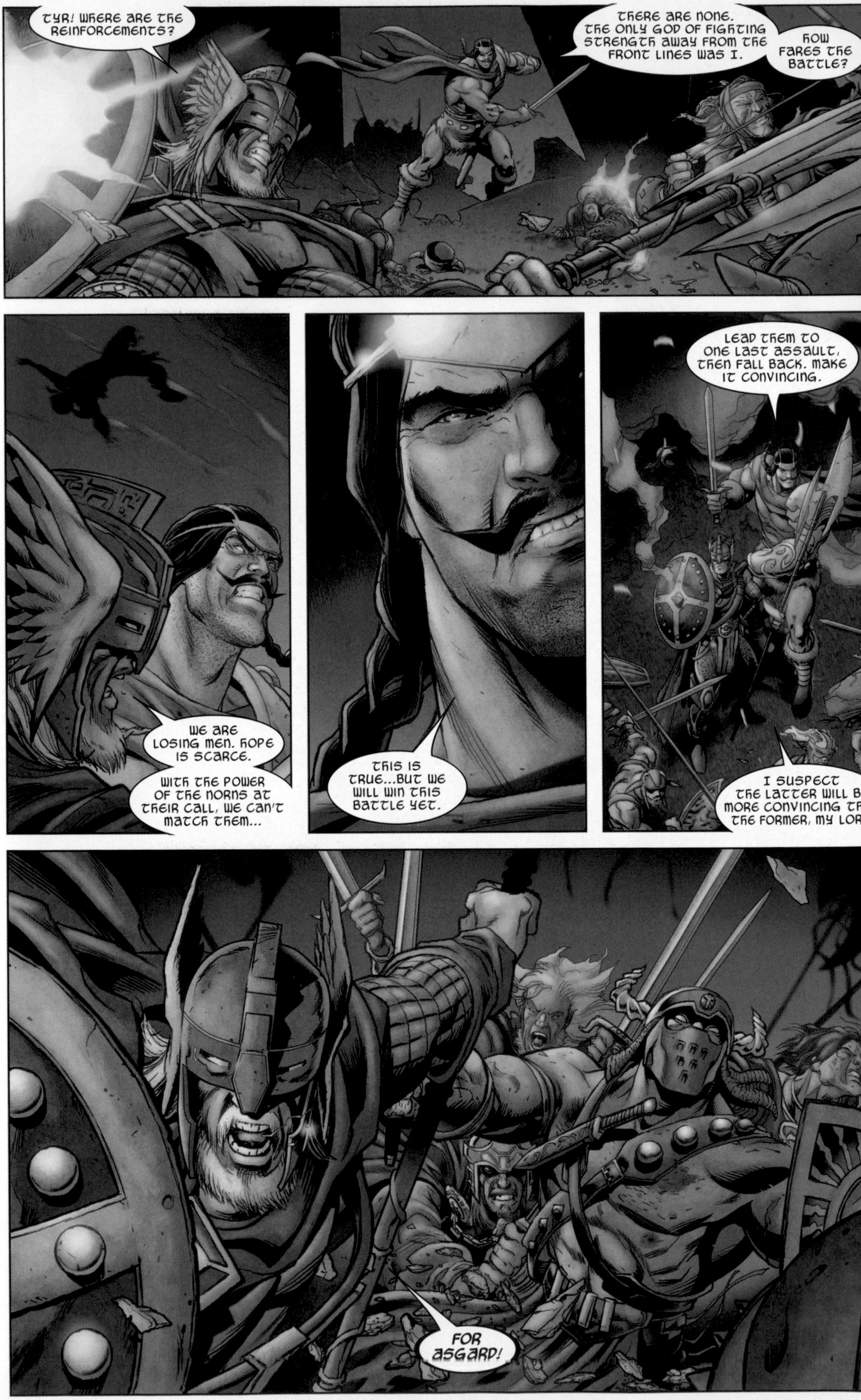
TYR! WHERE ARE THE REINFORCEMENTS?
THERE ARE NONE. THE ONLY GOD OF FIGHTING STRENGTH AWAY FROM THE FRONT LINES WAS I.
HOW FARES THE BATTLE?
WE ARE LOSING MEN. HOPE IS SCARCE.
WITH THE POWER OF THE NORNS AT THEIR CALL, WE CAN'T MATCH THEM...
THIS IS TRUE...BUT WE WILL WIN THIS BATTLE YET.
LEAD THEM TO ONE LAST ASSAULT, THEN FALL BACK. MAKE IT CONVINCING.
I SUSPECT THE LATTER WILL BE MORE CONVINCING THAN THE FORMER, MY LORD.
FOR ASGARD!

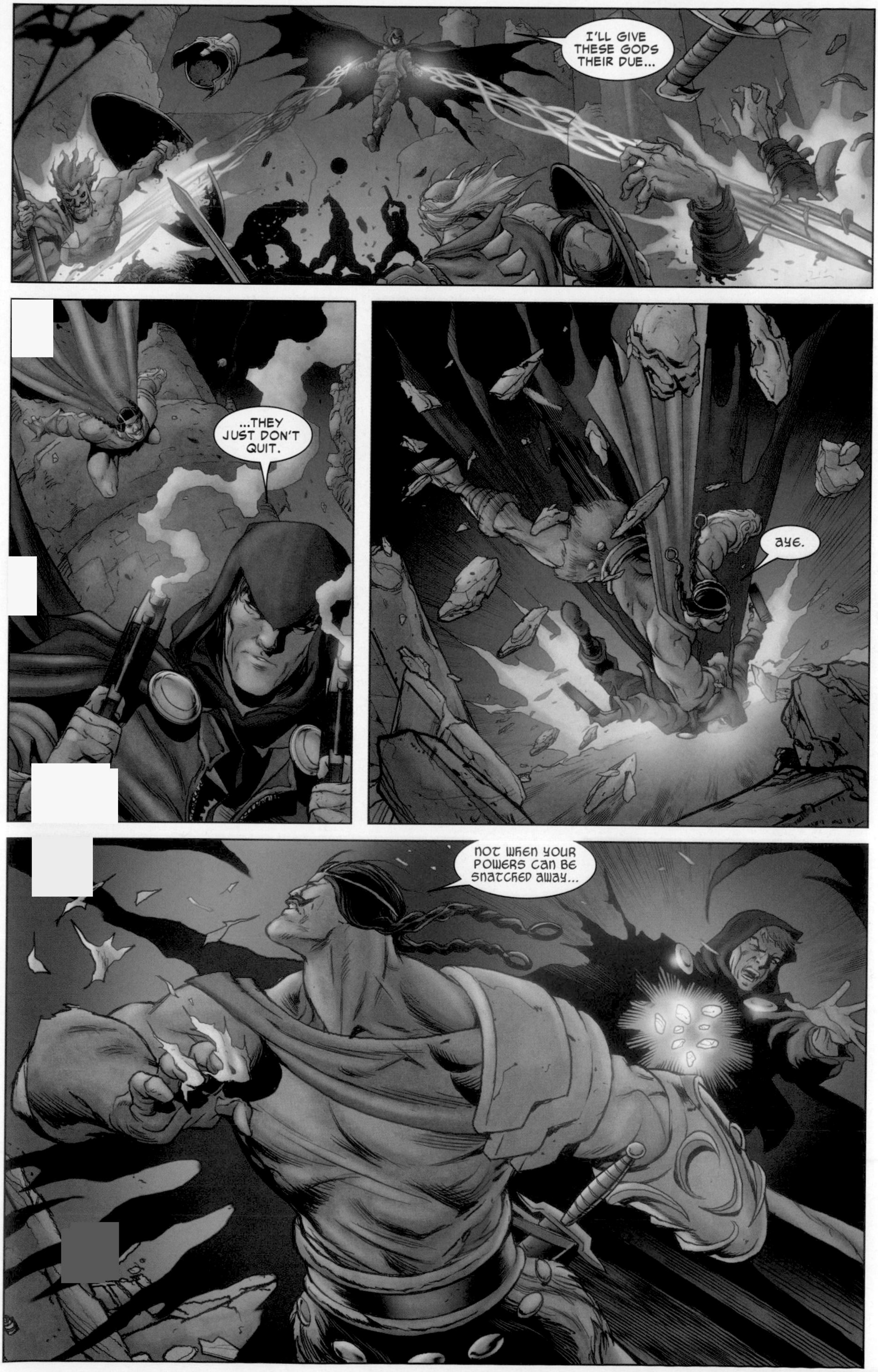
I'LL GIVE THESE GODS THEIR DUE...
...THEY JUST DON'T QUIT.
AYE.
NOT WHEN YOUR POWERS CAN BE SNATCHED AWAY...

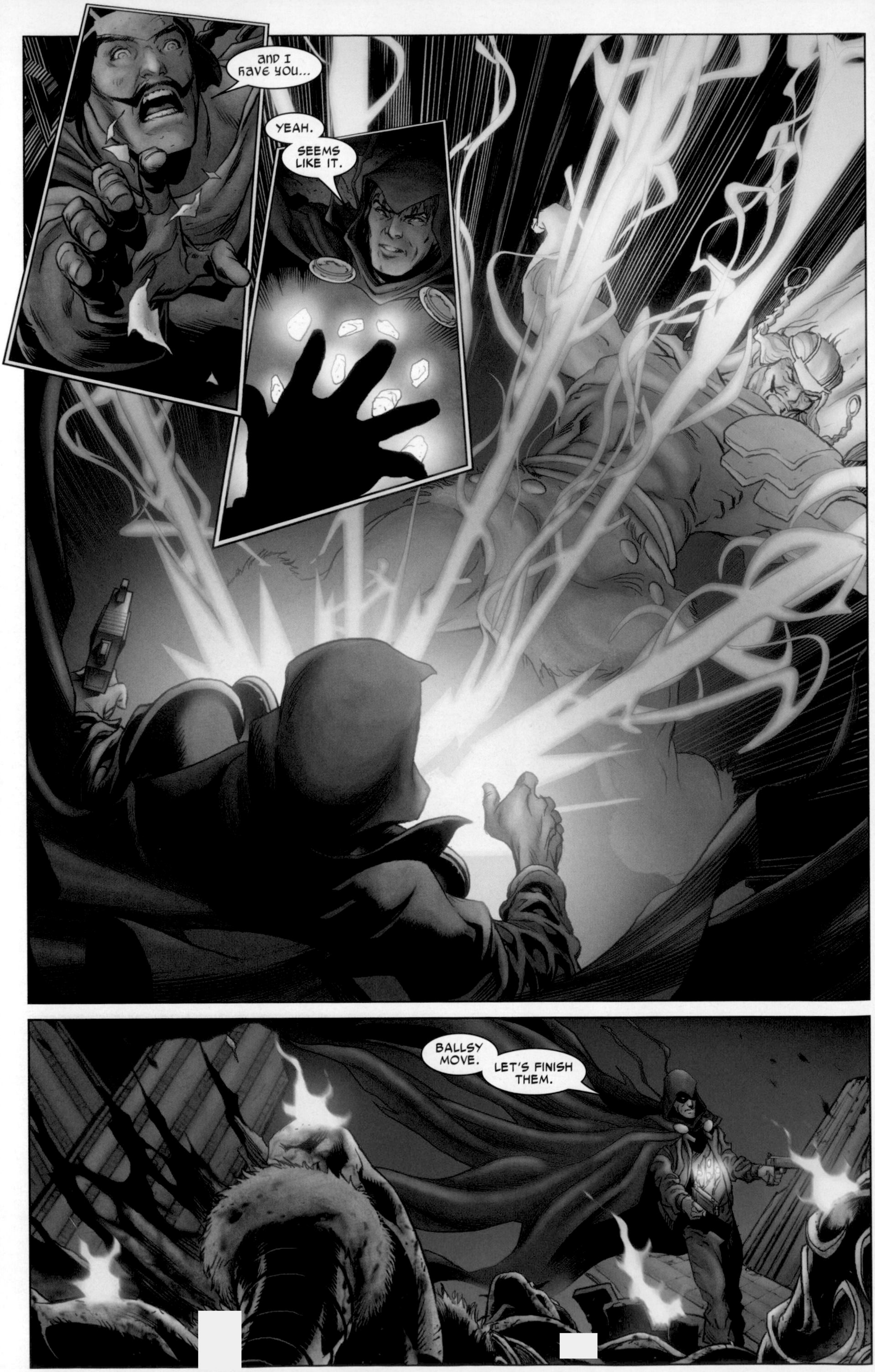
AND I HAVE YOU...
YEAH.
SEEMS LIKE IT.
BALLSY MOVE.
LET'S FINISH THEM.

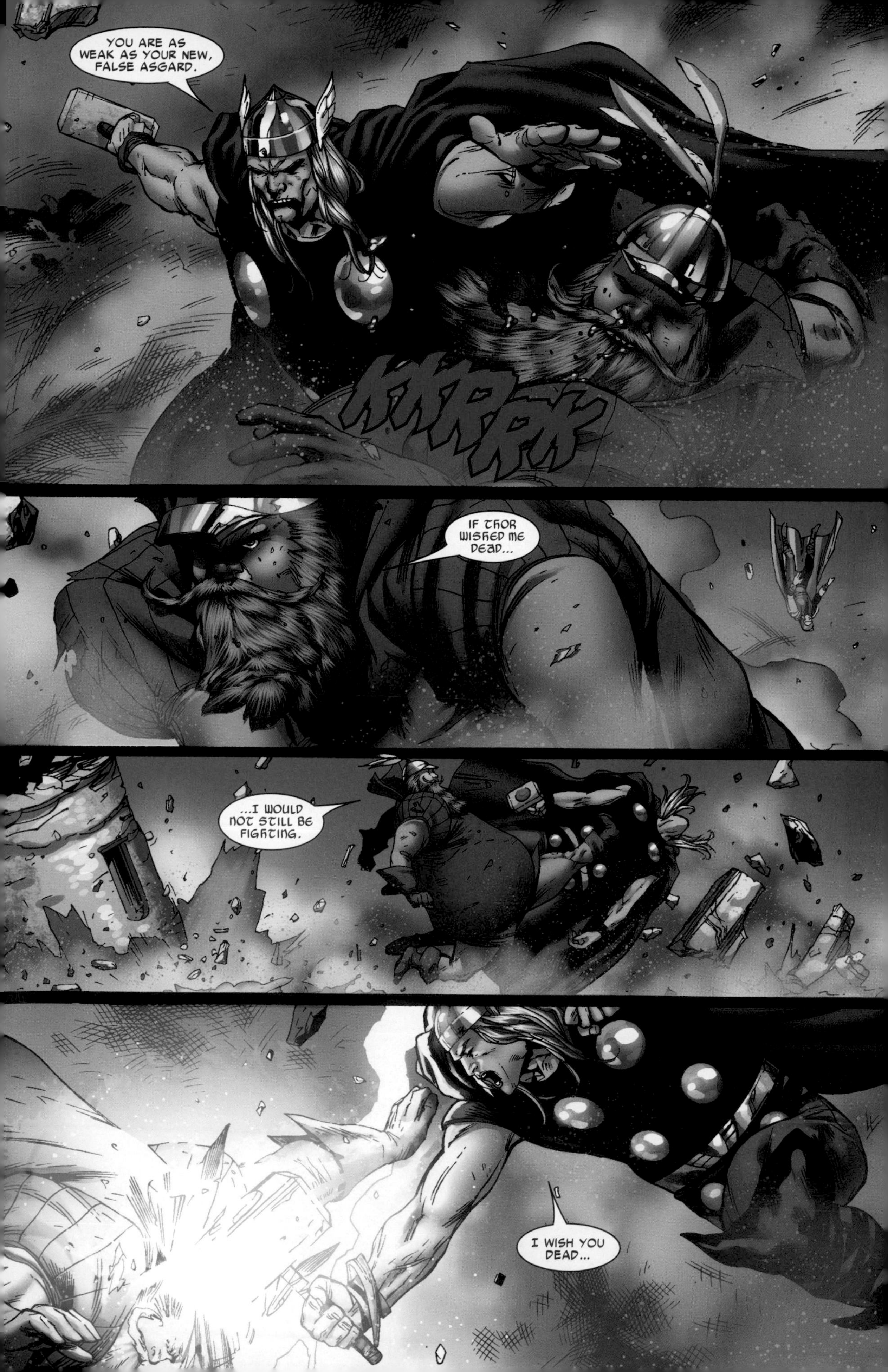
YOU ARE AS WEAK AS YOUR NEW, FALSE ASGARD.
KKRRK
IF THOR WISHED ME DEAD...
...I WOULD NOT STILL BE FIGHTING.
I WISH YOU DEAD...

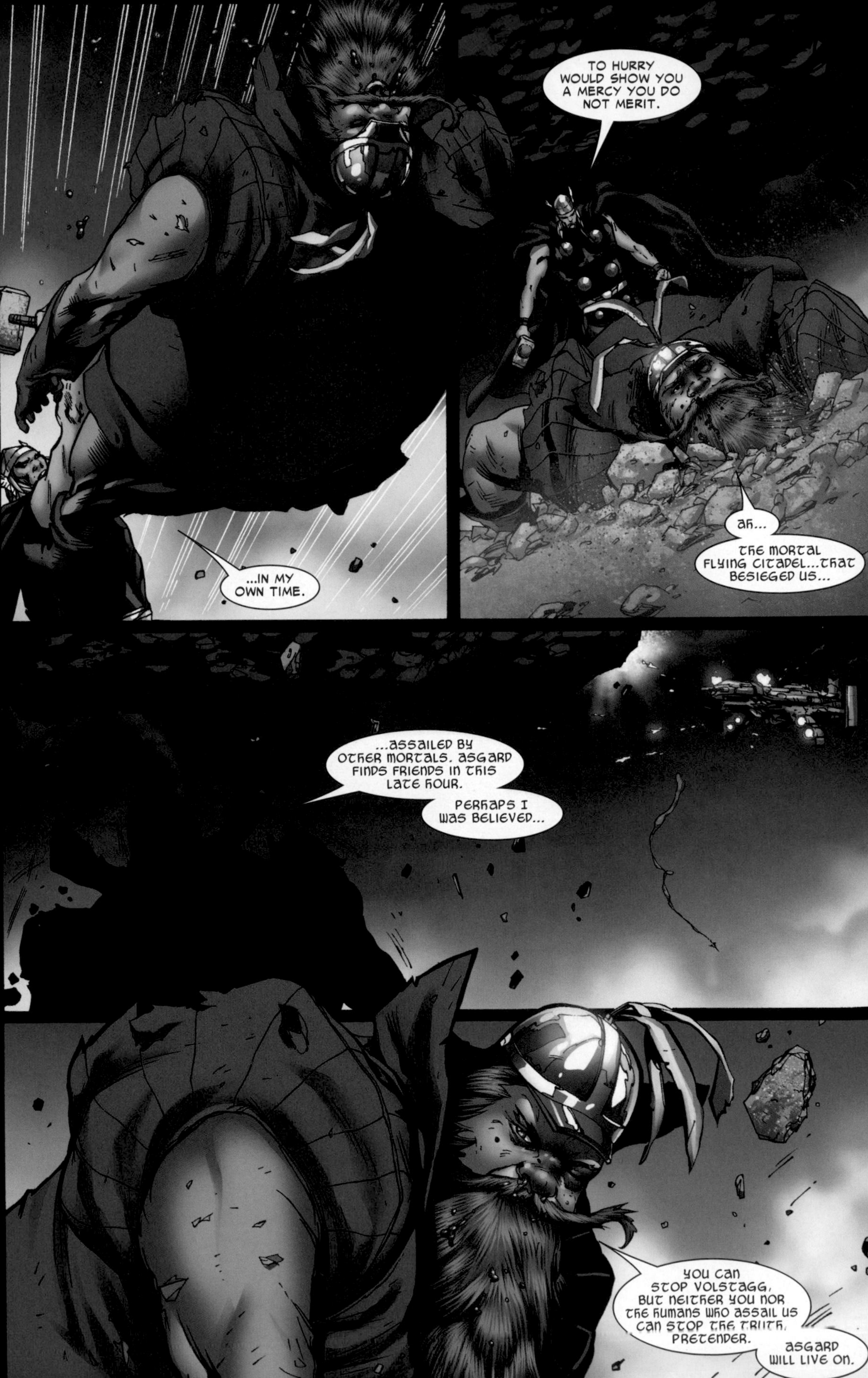
...IN MY OWN TIME.
TO HURRY WOULD SHOW YOU A MERCY YOU DO NOT MERIT.
AH...
THE MORTAL FLYING CITADEL...THAT BESIEGED US...
...ASSAILED BY OTHER MORTALS. ASGARD FINDS FRIENDS IN THIS LATE HOUR.
PERHAPS I WAS BELIEVED...
YOU CAN STOP VOLSTAGG, BUT NEITHER YOU NOR THE HUMANS WHO ASSAIL US CAN STOP THE TRUTH, PRETENDER.
ASGARD WILL LIVE ON.

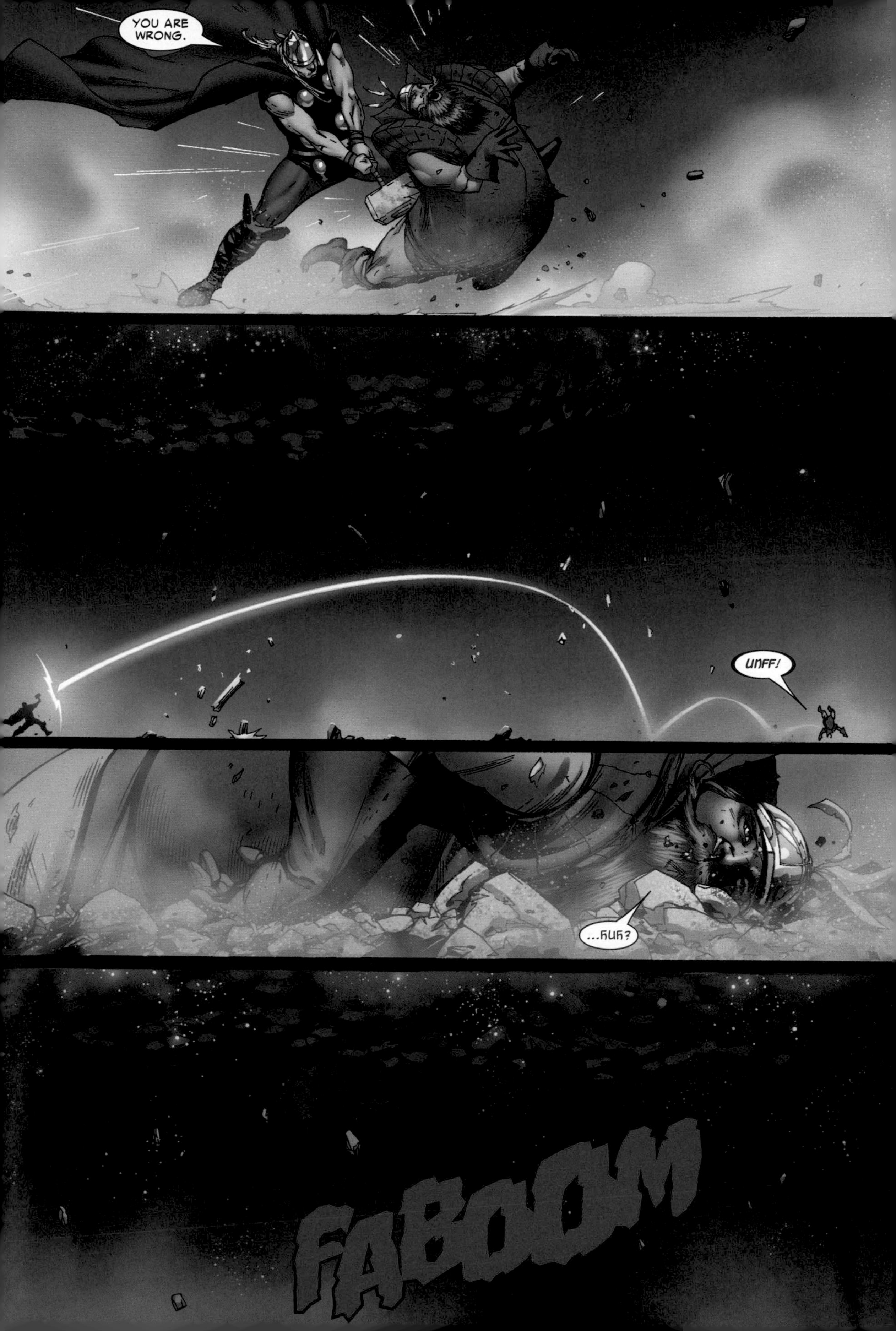
YOU ARE WRONG.
UNFF!
...HUH?
FABOOM

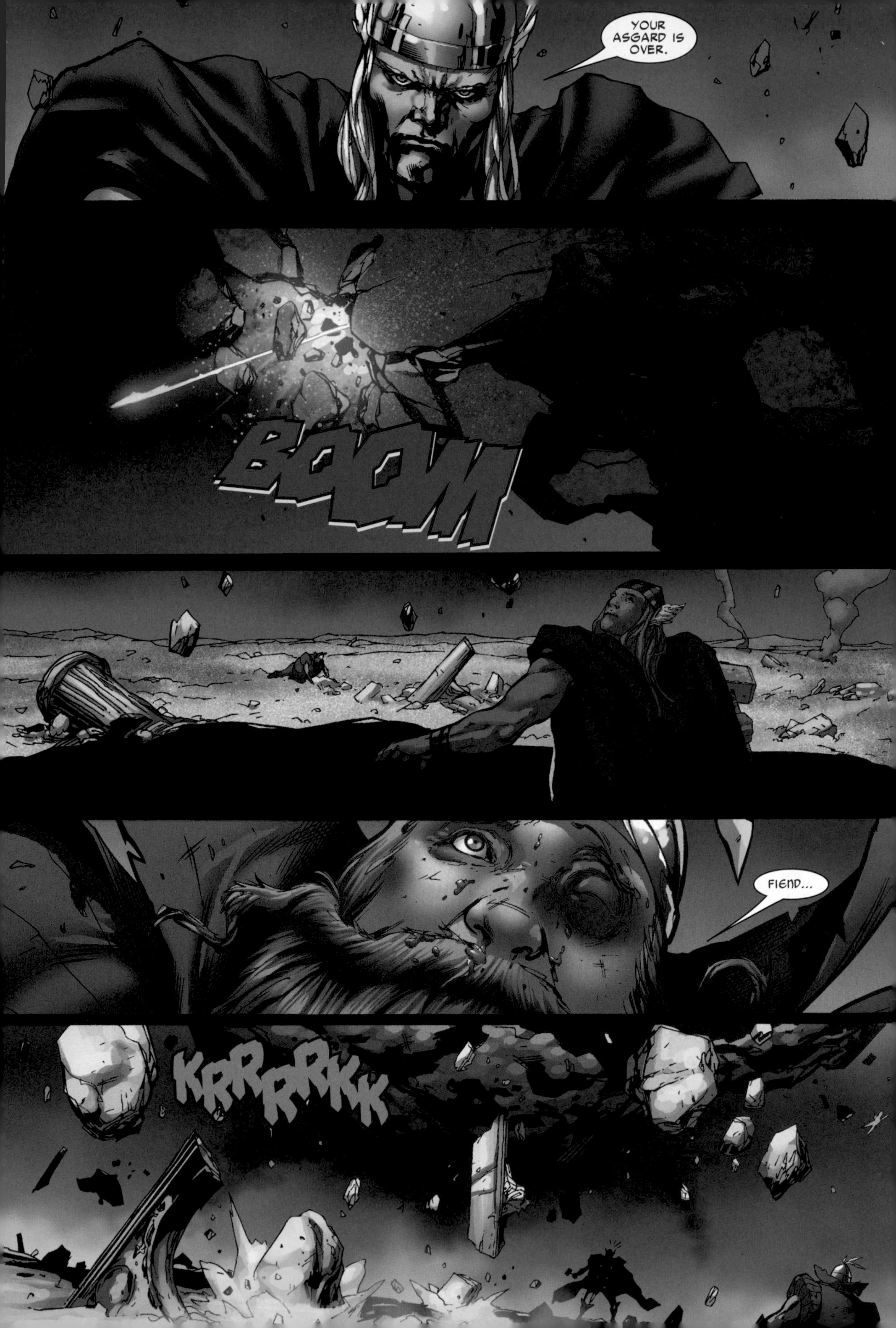
YOUR ASGARD IS OVER.
BOOM
FIEND...
KRRRRKK

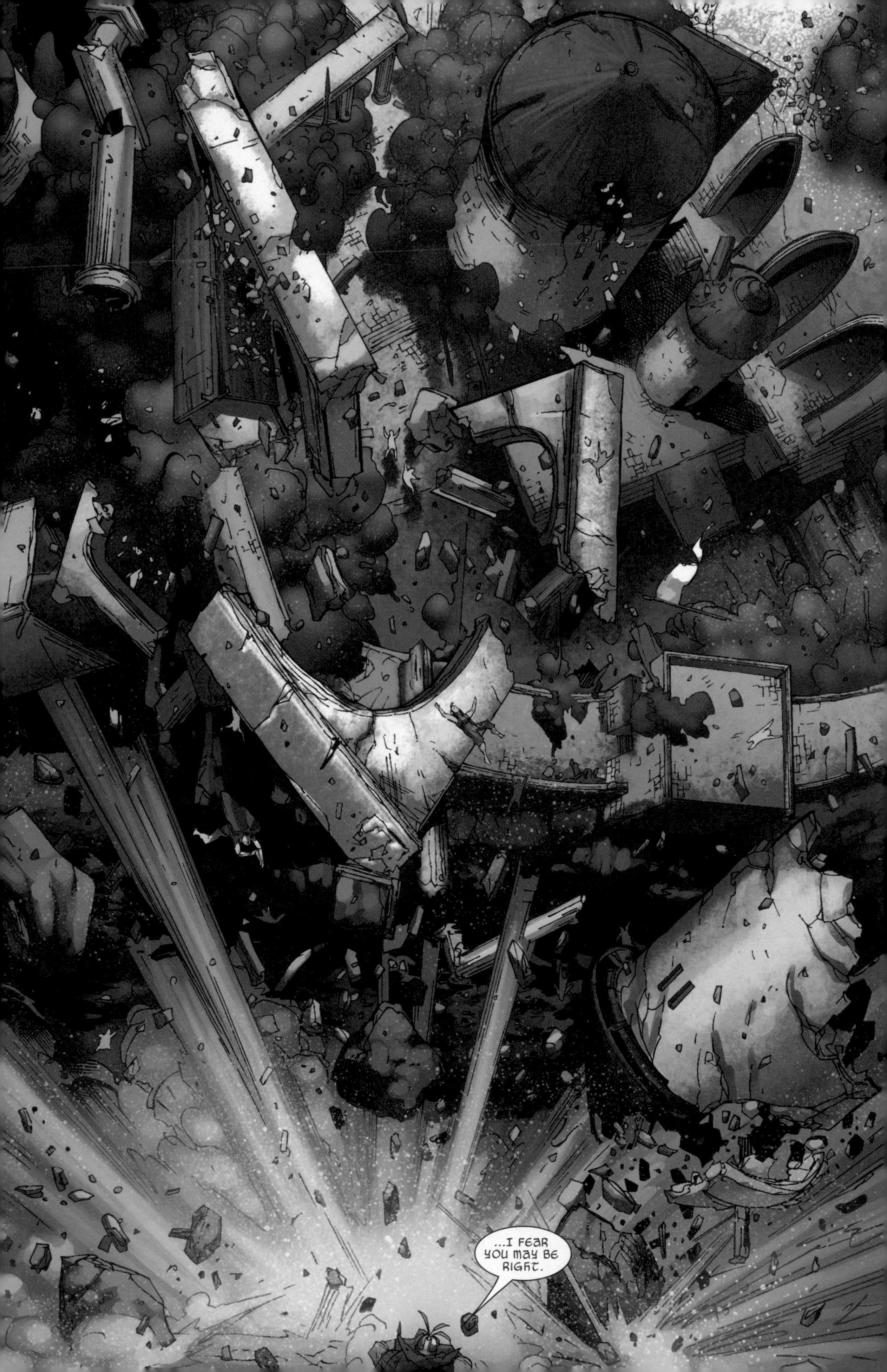
...I FEAR YOU MAY BE RIGHT.

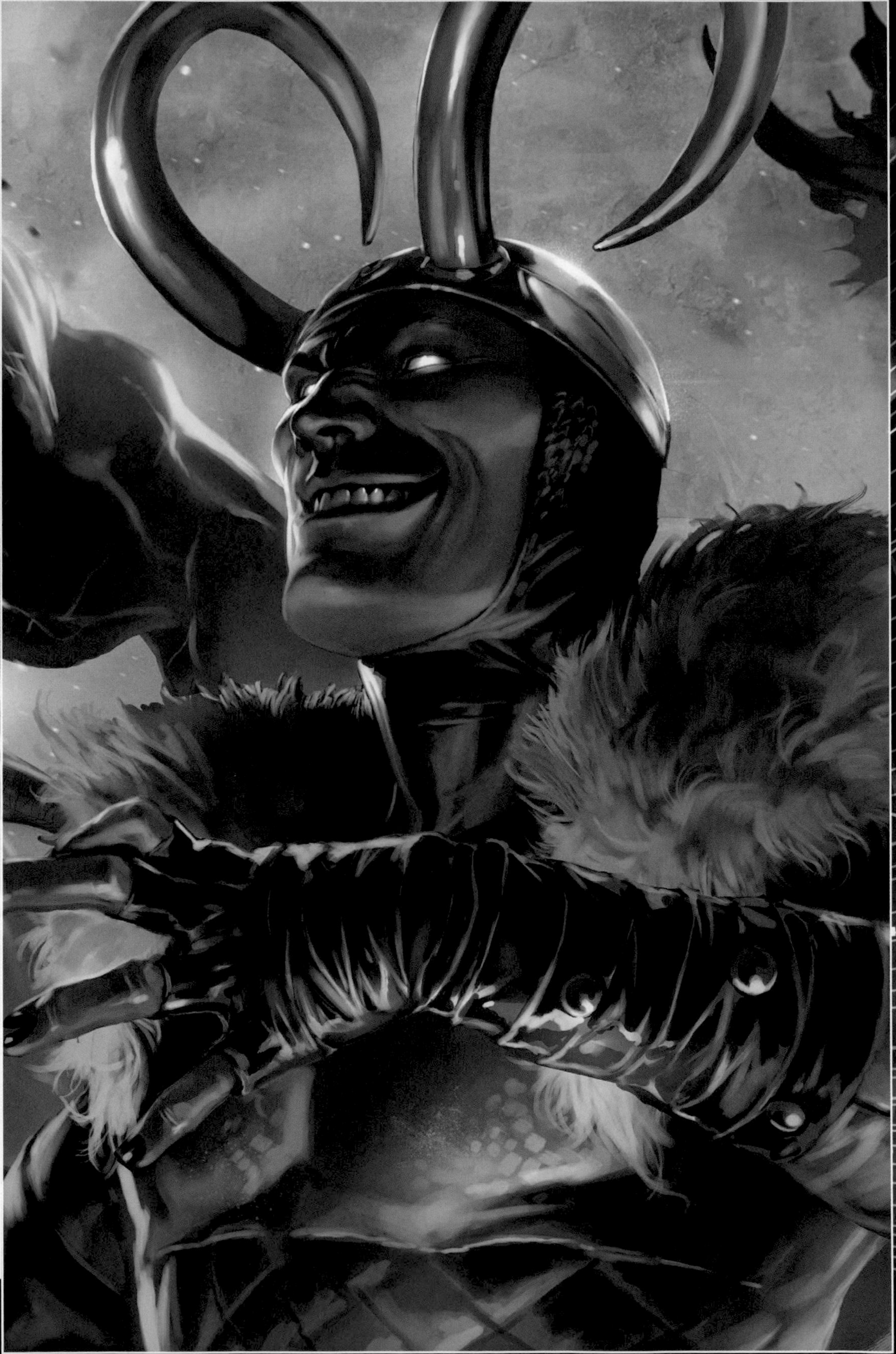

SIEGE: LOKI

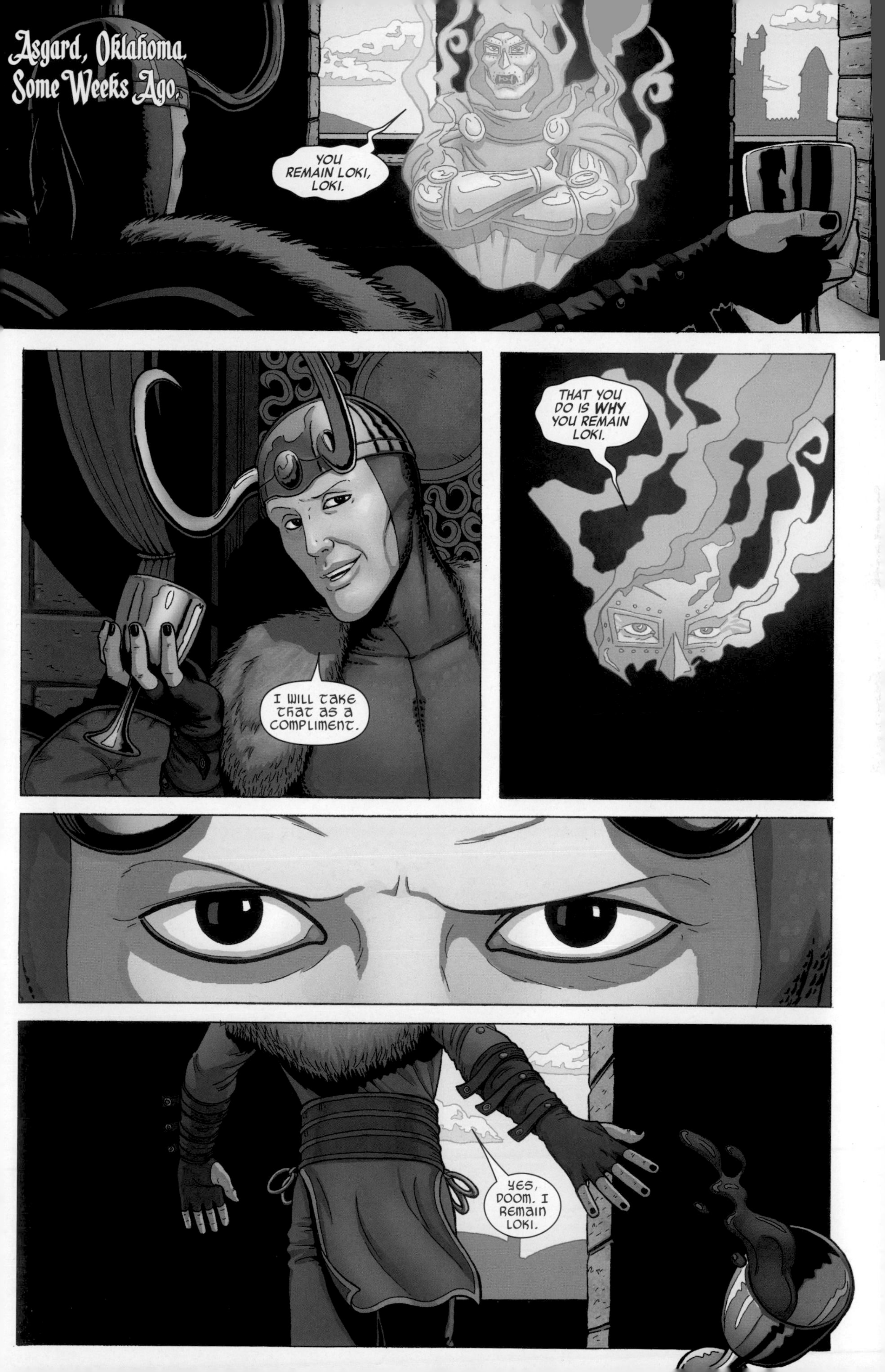
Asgard, Oklahoma. Some Weeks Ago.
YOU REMAIN LOKI, LOKI.
I WILL TAKE THAT AS A COMPLIMENT.
THAT YOU DO IS WHY YOU REMAIN LOKI.
YES, DOOM. I REMAIN LOKI.

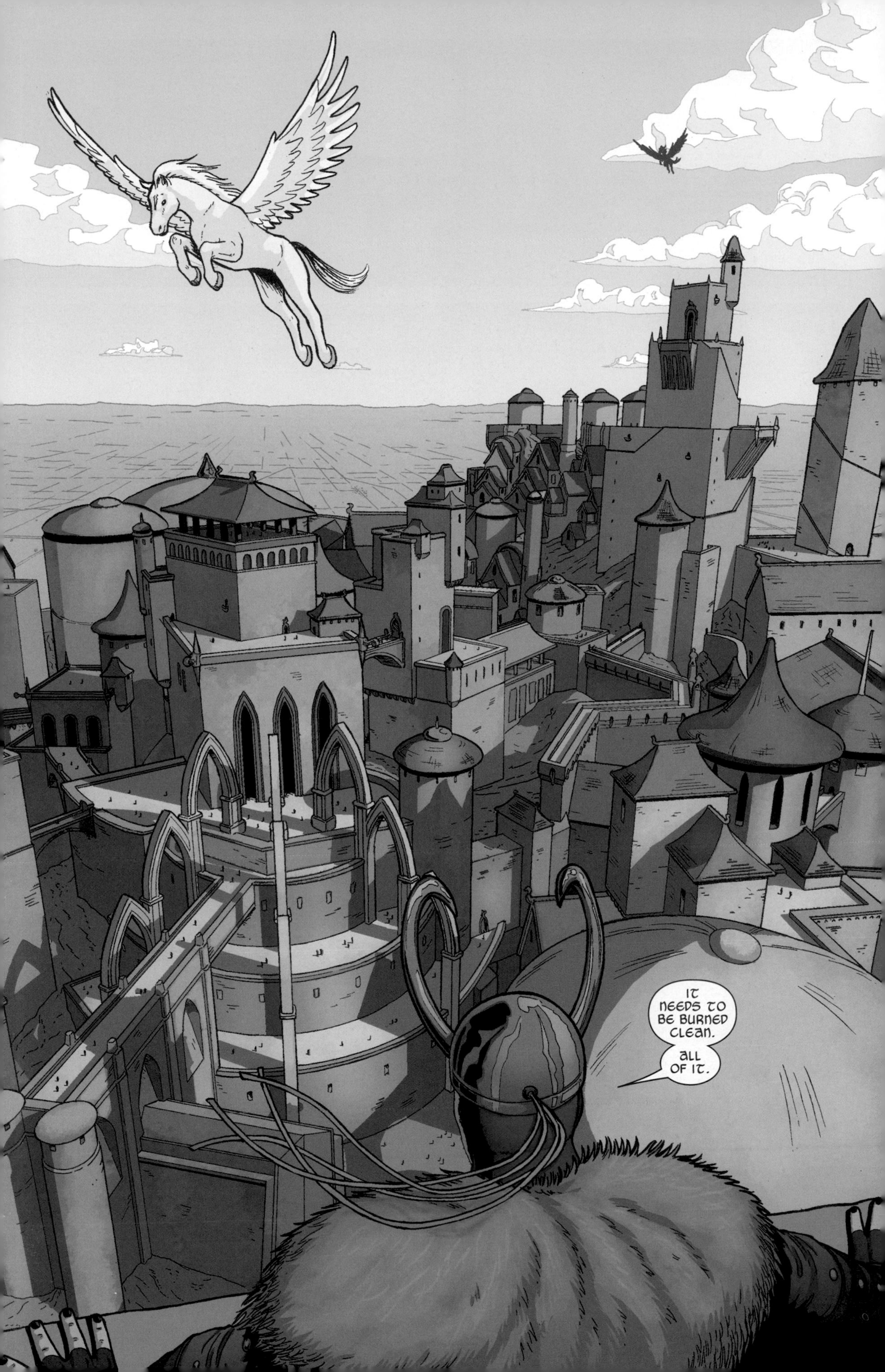
IT NEEDS TO BE BURNED CLEAN.
ALL OF IT.

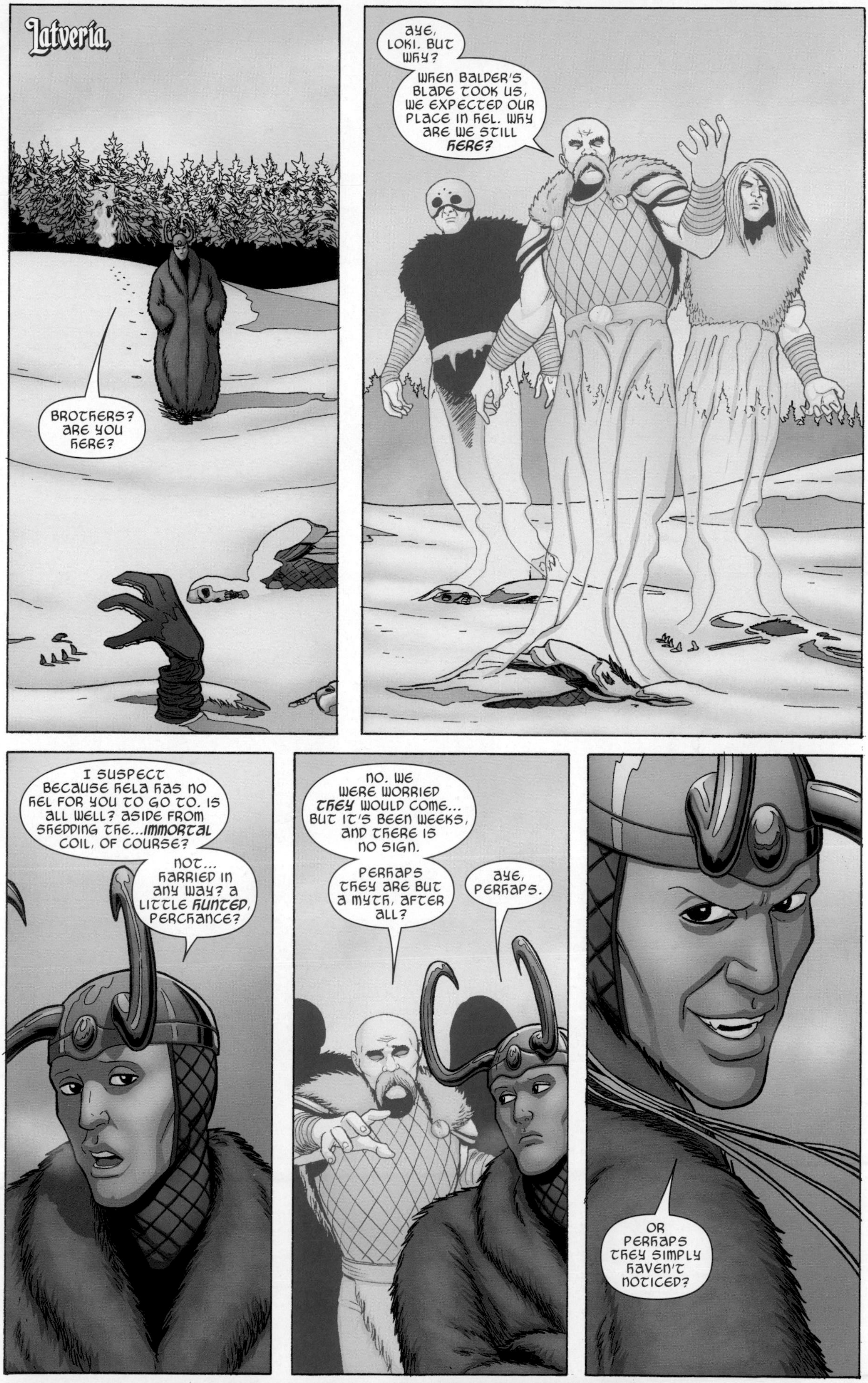
Latveria.
BROTHERS? ARE YOU HERE?
AYE, LOKI. BUT WHY?
WHEN BALDER'S BLADE TOOK US, WE EXPECTED OUR PLACE IN HEL. WHY ARE WE STILL HERE?
I SUSPECT BECAUSE HELA HAS NO HEL FOR YOU TO GO TO. IS ALL WELL? ASIDE FROM SHEDDING THE...IMMORTAL COIL, OF COURSE?
NOT... HARRIED IN ANY WAY? A LITTLE HUNTED, PERCHANCE?
NO. WE WERE WORRIED THEY WOULD COME... BUT IT'S BEEN WEEKS, AND THERE IS NO SIGN.
PERHAPS THEY ARE BUT A MYTH, AFTER ALL?
AYE, PERHAPS.
OR PERHAPS THEY SIMPLY HAVEN'T NOTICED?

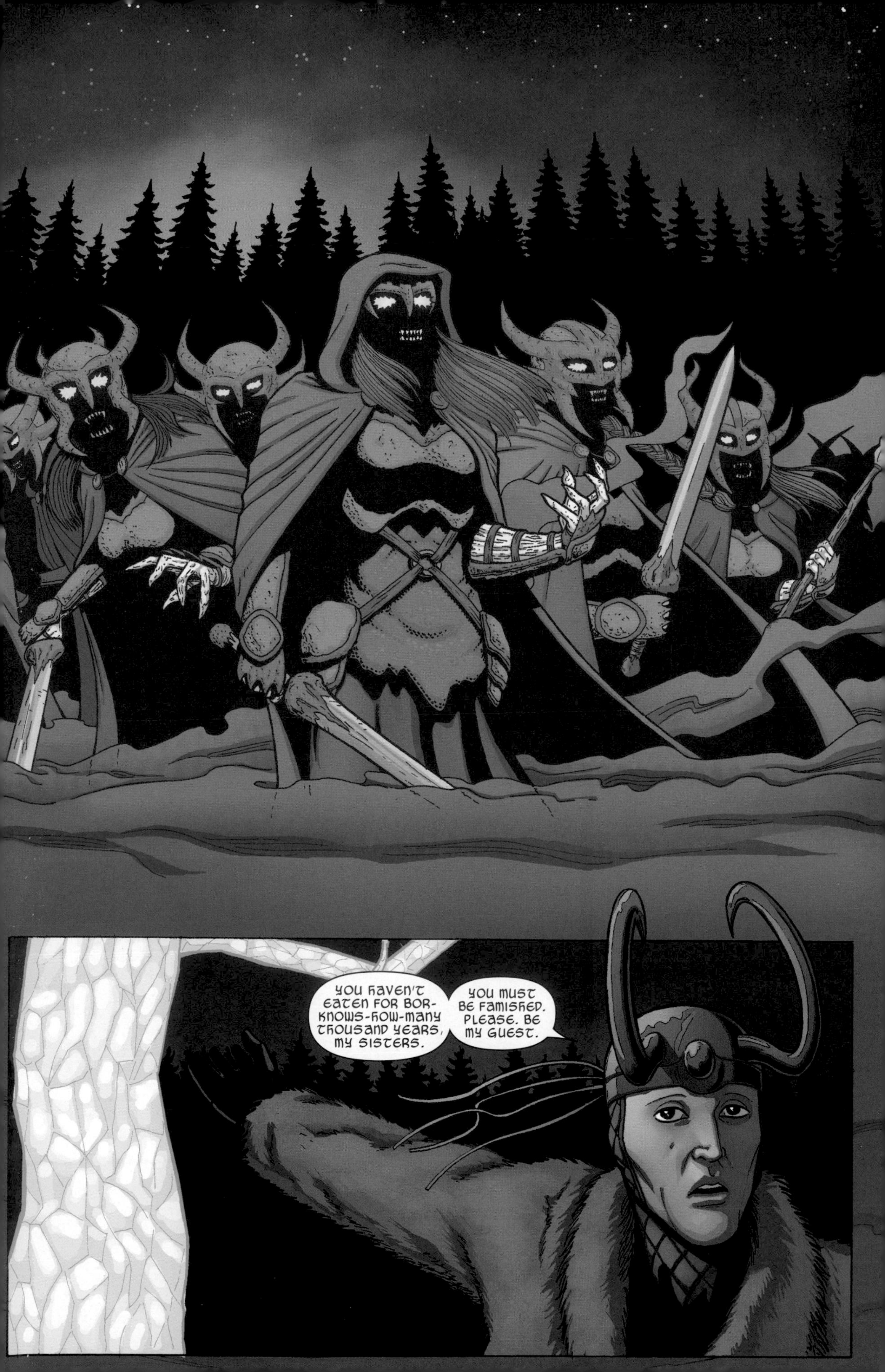
YOU HAVEN'T EATEN FOR BOR-KNOWS-HOW-MANY THOUSAND YEARS, MY SISTERS.
YOU MUST BE FAMISHED. PLEASE. BE MY GUEST.

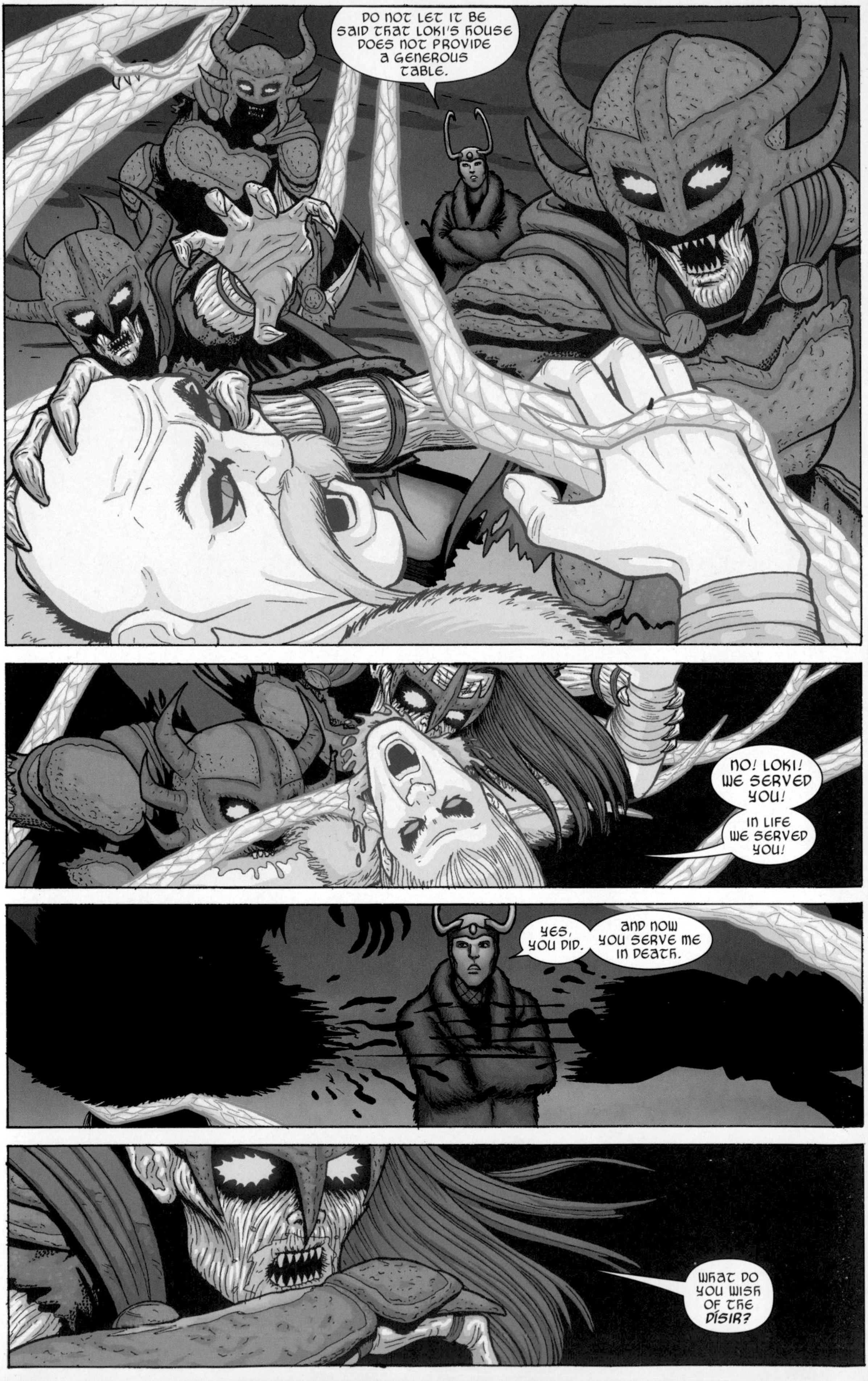
DO NOT LET IT BE SAID THAT LOKI'S HOUSE DOES NOT PROVIDE A GENEROUS TABLE.
NO! LOKI! WE SERVED YOU!
IN LIFE WE SERVED YOU!
YES, YOU DID.
AND NOW YOU SERVE ME IN DEATH.
WHAT DO YOU WISH OF THE DÍSIR?

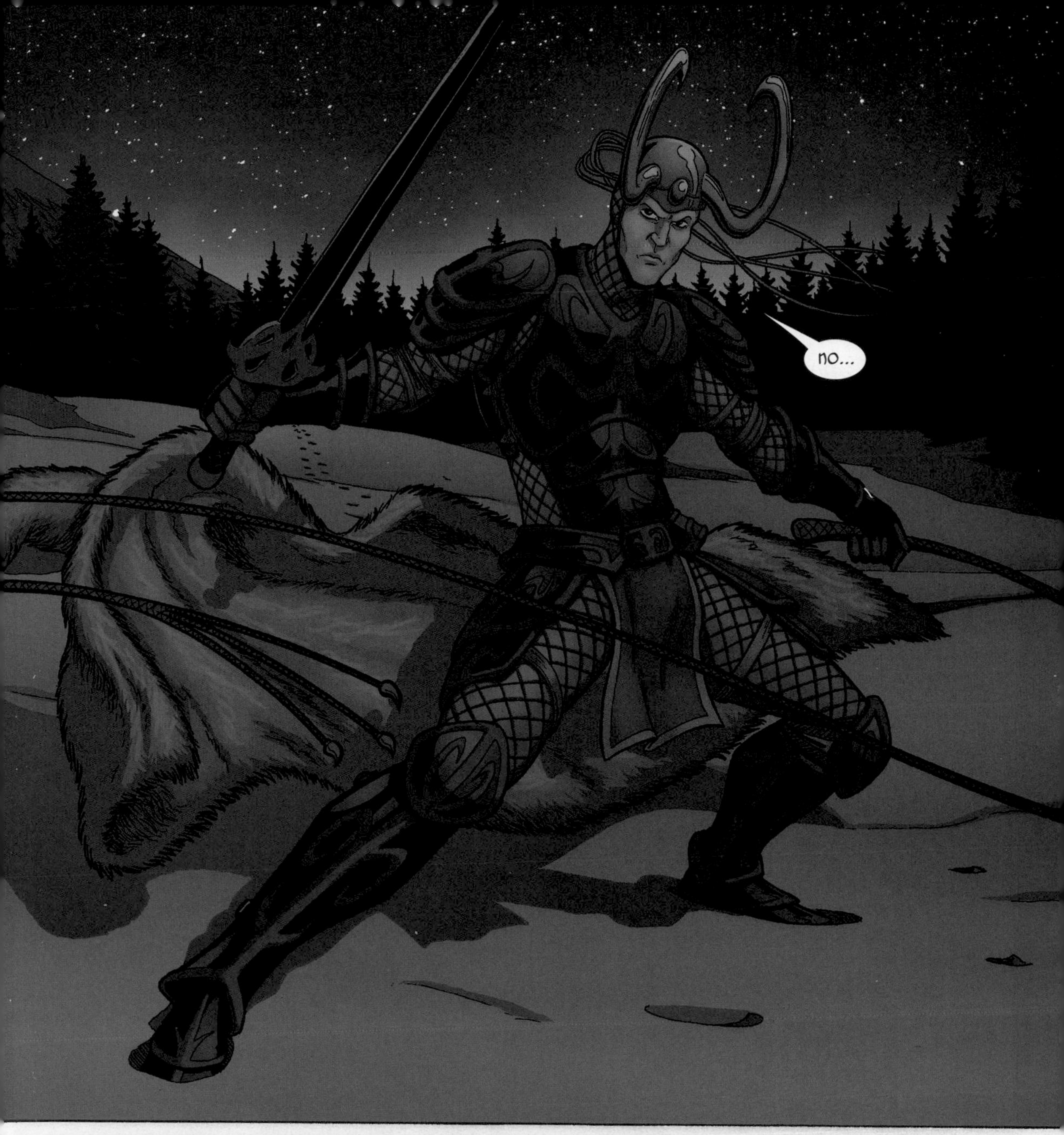
no...

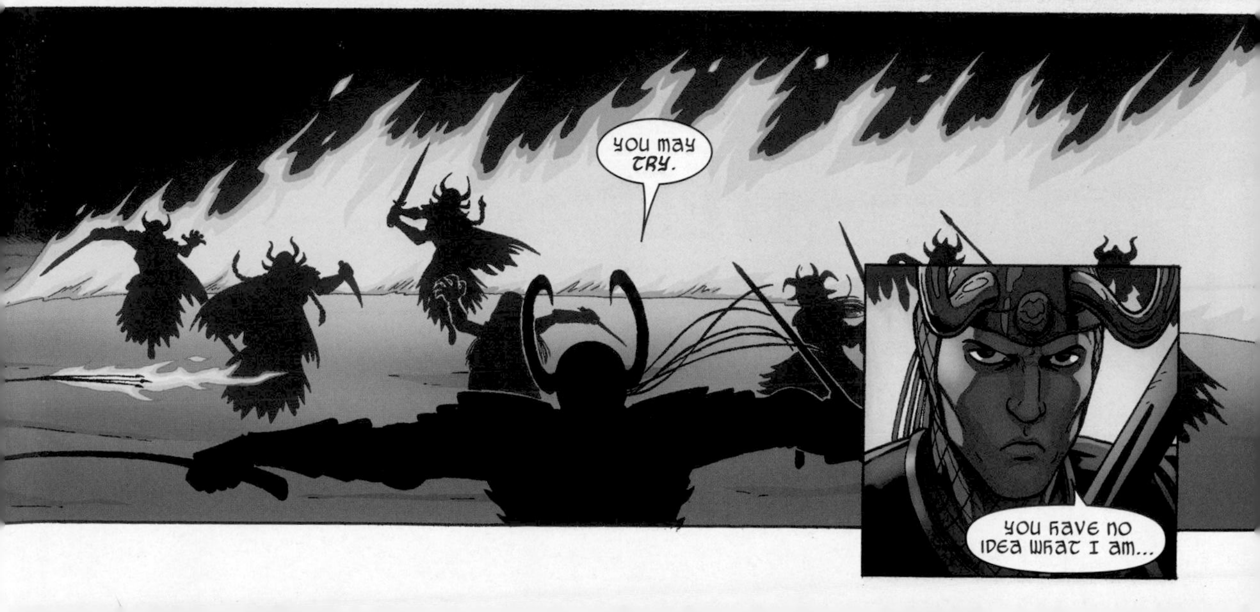
YOU MAY TRY.
YOU HAVE NO IDEA WHAT I AM...

...NO ONE DOES.

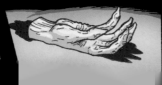
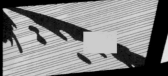

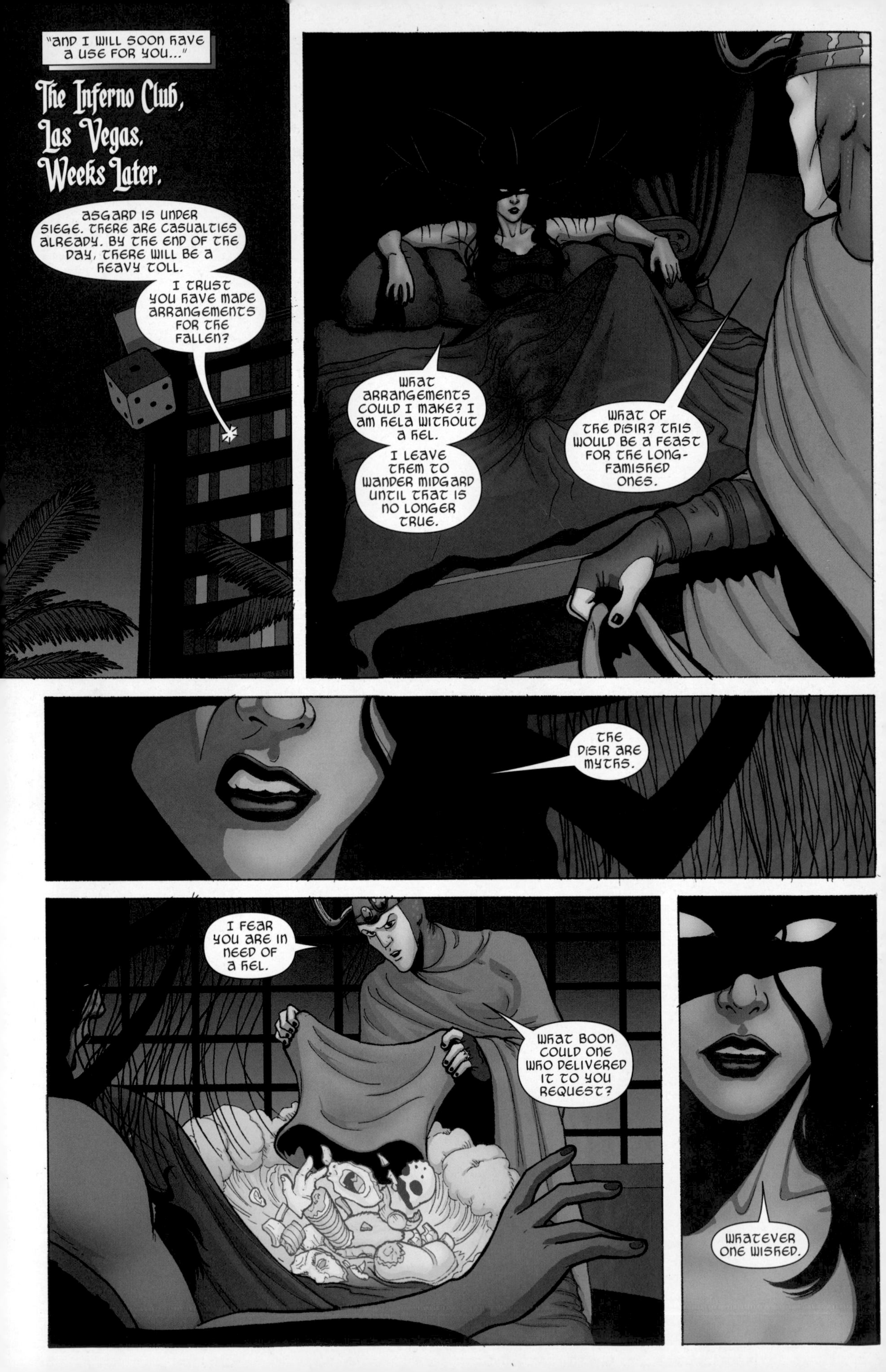
"AND I WILL SOON HAVE A USE FOR YOU..."
The Inferno Club, Las Vegas, Weeks Later.
ASGARD IS UNDER SIEGE. THERE ARE CASUALTIES ALREADY. BY THE END OF THE DAY, THERE WILL BE A HEAVY TOLL.
I TRUST YOU HAVE MADE ARRANGEMENTS FOR THE FALLEN?
WHAT ARRANGEMENTS COULD I MAKE? I AM HELA WITHOUT A HEL.
I LEAVE THEM TO WANDER MIDGARD UNTIL THAT IS NO LONGER TRUE.
WHAT OF THE DISIR? THIS WOULD BE A FEAST FOR THE LONG-FAMISHED ONES.
THE DISIR ARE MYTHS.
I FEAR YOU ARE IN NEED OF A HEL.
WHAT BOON COULD ONE WHO DELIVERED IT TO YOU REQUEST?
WHATEVER ONE WISHED.

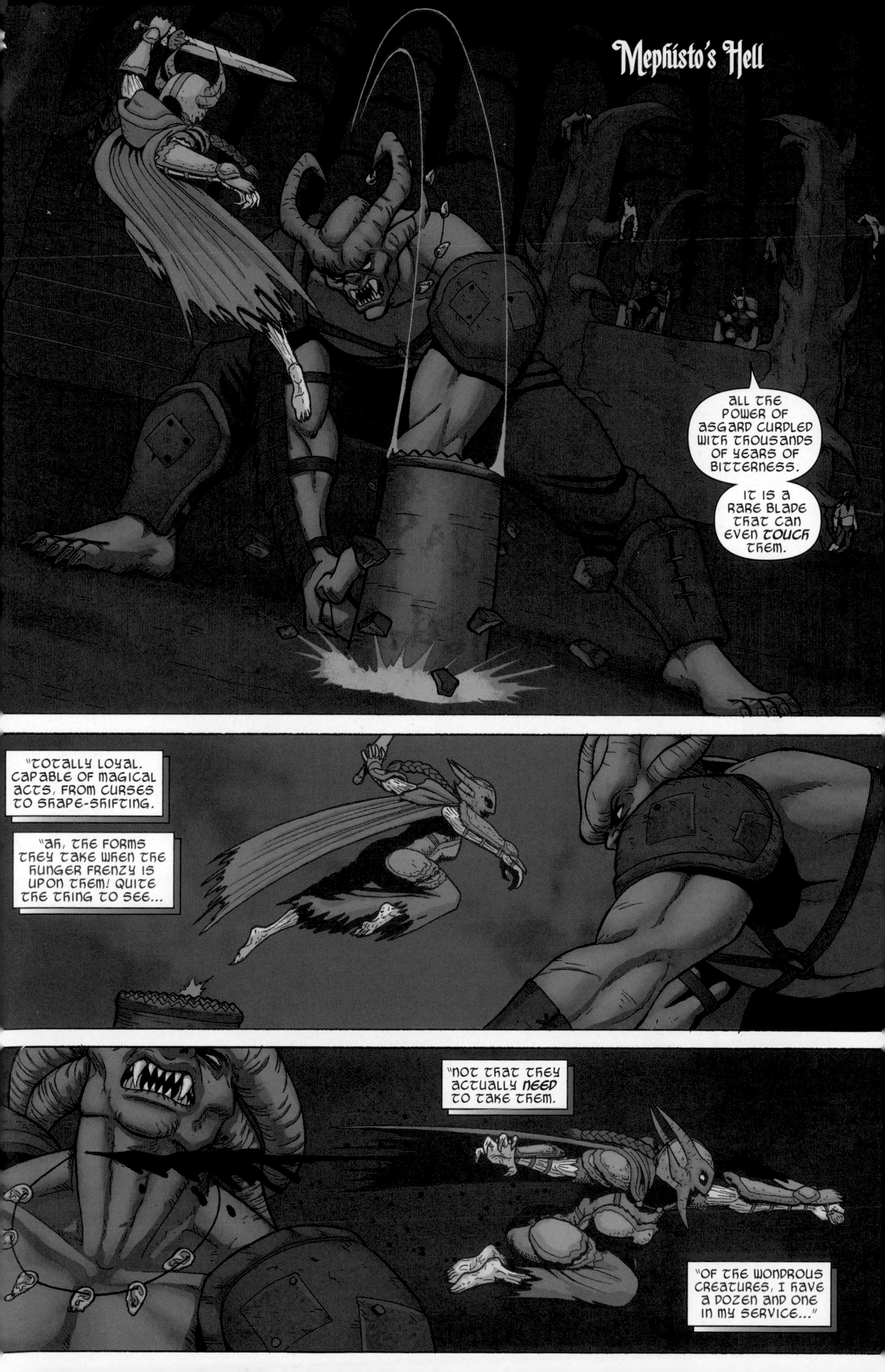
Mephisto's Hell
ALL THE POWER OF ASGARD CURDLED WITH THOUSANDS OF YEARS OF BITTERNESS.
IT IS A RARE BLADE THAT CAN EVEN TOUCH THEM.
"TOTALLY LOYAL. CAPABLE OF MAGICAL ACTS, FROM CURSES TO SHAPE-SHIFTING.
"AH, THE FORMS THEY TAKE WHEN THE HUNGER FRENZY IS UPON THEM! QUITE THE THING TO SEE...
"NOT THAT THEY ACTUALLY NEED TO TAKE THEM.
"OF THE WONDROUS CREATURES, I HAVE A DOZEN AND ONE IN MY SERVICE..."

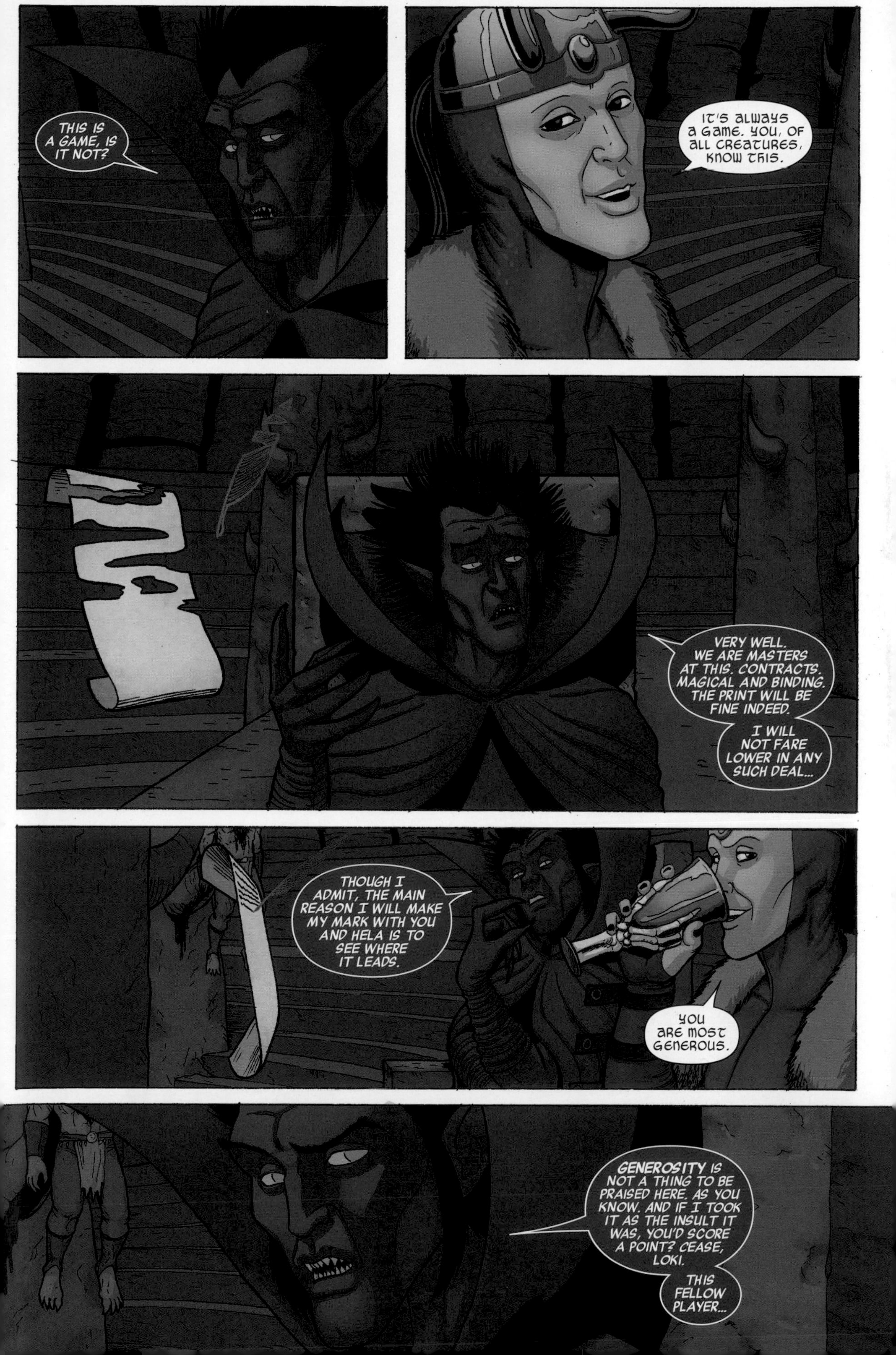

THIS IS A GAME, IS IT NOT?
IT'S ALWAYS A GAME. YOU, OF ALL CREATURES, KNOW THIS.
VERY WELL. WE ARE MASTERS AT THIS. CONTRACTS. MAGICAL AND BINDING. THE PRINT WILL BE FINE INDEED.
I WILL NOT FARE LOWER IN ANY SUCH DEAL...
THOUGH I ADMIT, THE MAIN REASON I WILL MAKE MY MARK WITH YOU AND HELA IS TO SEE WHERE IT LEADS.
YOU ARE MOST GENEROUS.
GENEROSITY IS NOT A THING TO BE PRAISED HERE, AS YOU KNOW. AND IF I TOOK IT AS THE INSULT IT WAS, YOU'D SCORE A POINT? CEASE, LOKI.
THIS FELLOW PLAYER...

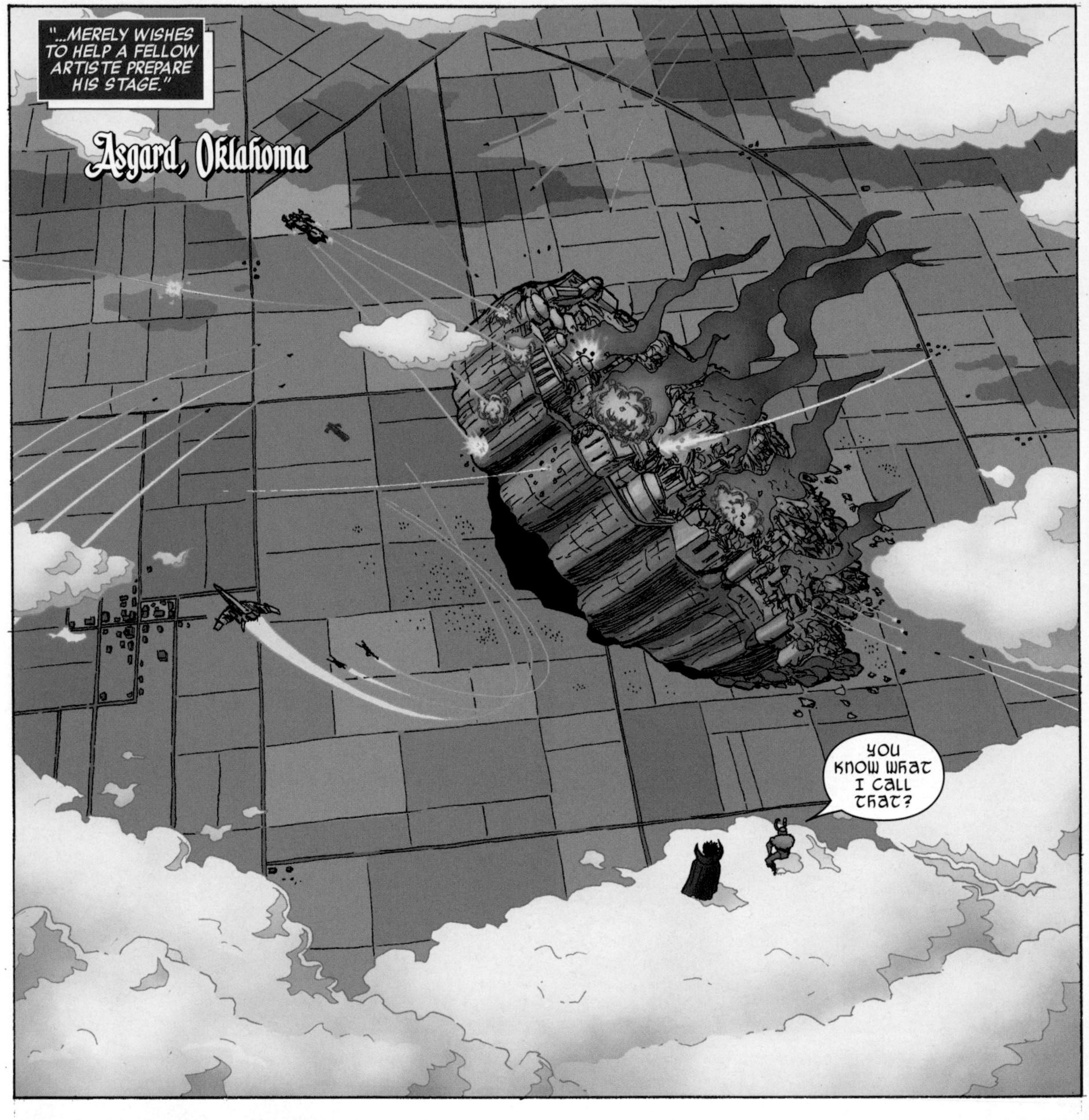
"...MERELY WISHES TO HELP A FELLOW ARTISTE PREPARE HIS STAGE."
Asgard, Oklahoma
YOU KNOW WHAT I CALL THAT?

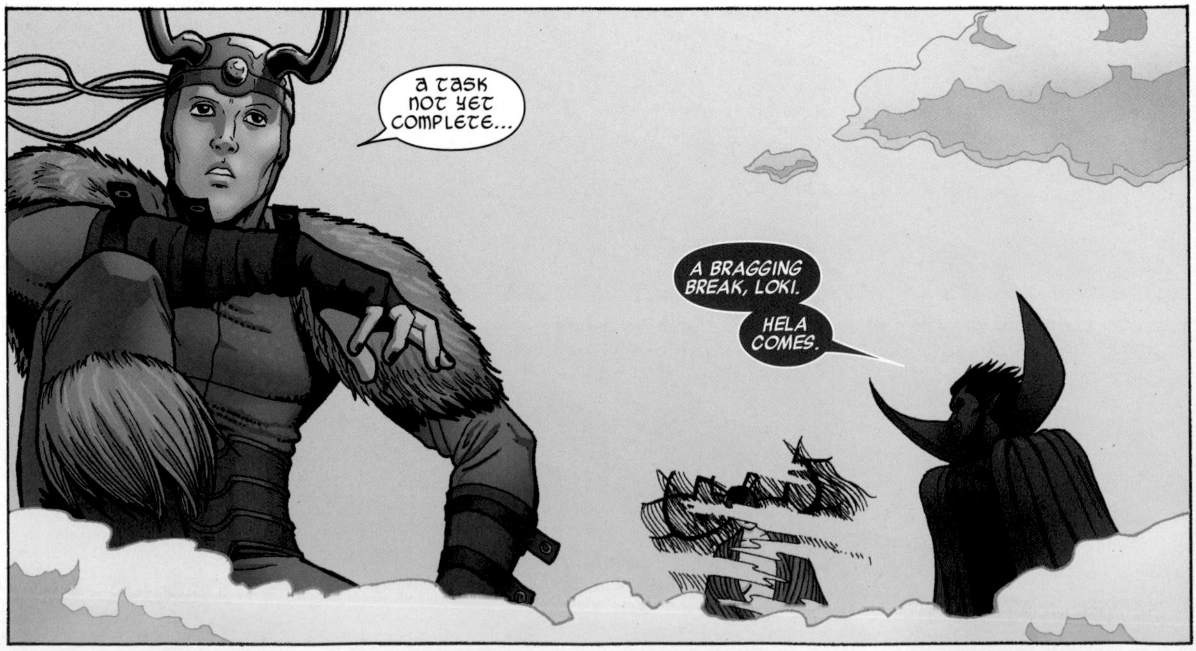
A TASK NOT YET COMPLETE...
A BRAGGING BREAK, LOKI.
HELA COMES.

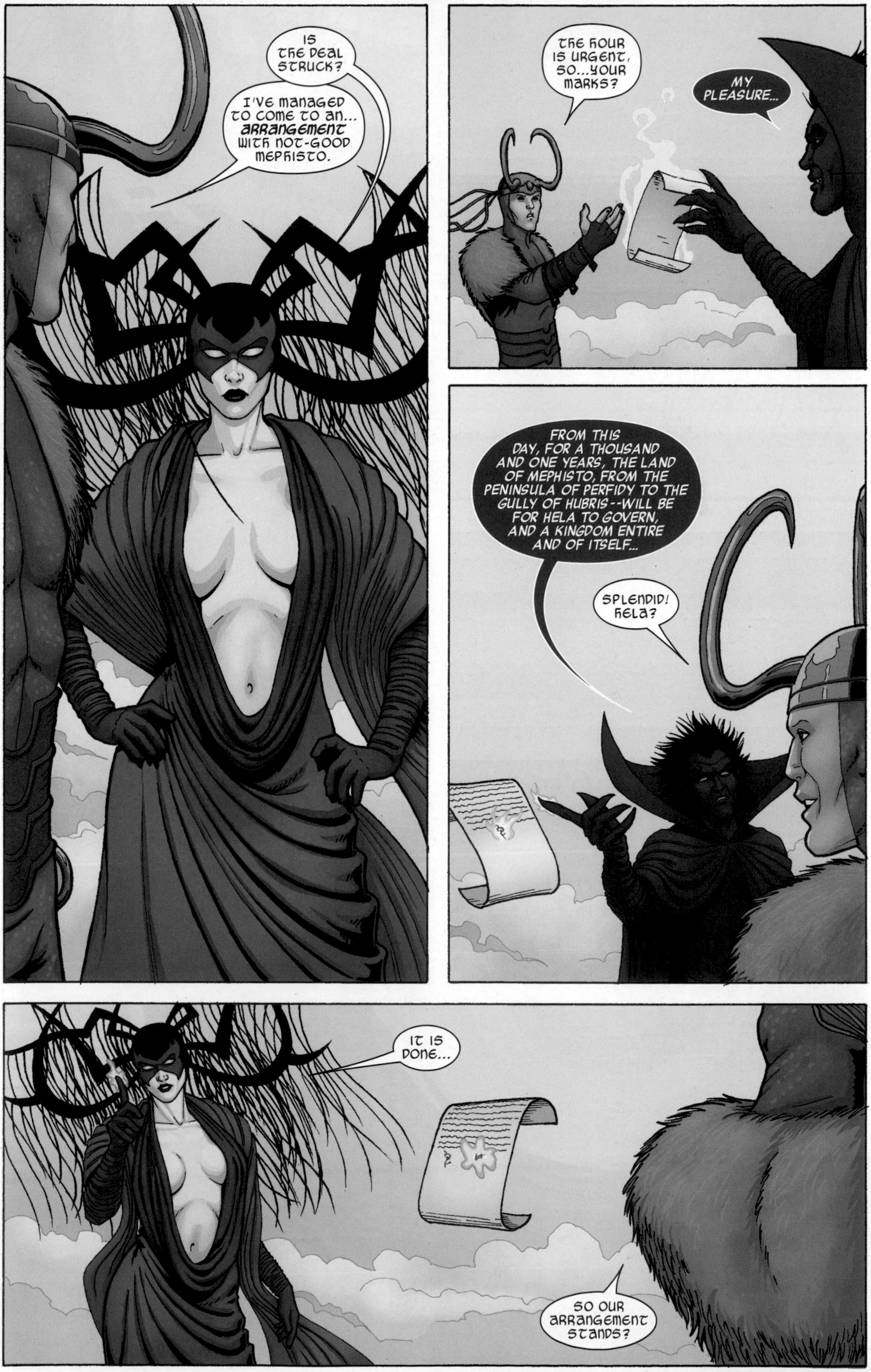
IS THE DEAL STRUCK?
I'VE MANAGED TO COME TO AN... ARRANGEMENT WITH NOT-GOOD MEPHISTO.
THE HOUR IS URGENT, SO...YOUR MARKS?
MY PLEASURE...
FROM THIS DAY, FOR A THOUSAND AND ONE YEARS, THE LAND OF MEPHISTO, FROM THE PENINSULA OF PERFIDY TO THE GULLY OF HUBRIS--WILL BE FOR HELA TO GOVERN, AND A KINGDOM ENTIRE AND OF ITSELF...
SPLENDID! HELA?
IT IS DONE...
SO OUR ARRANGEMENT STANDS?

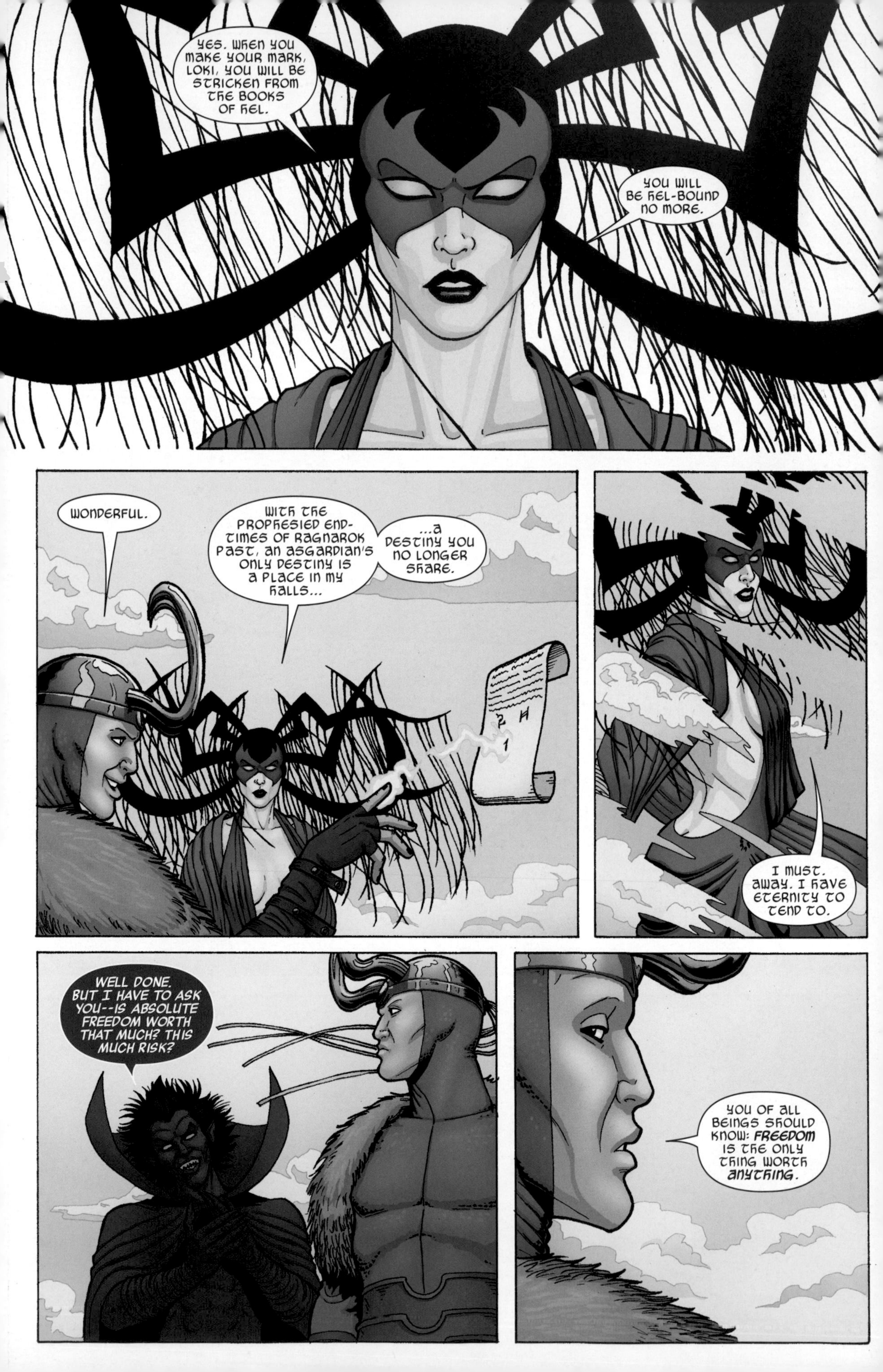
YES. WHEN YOU MAKE YOUR MARK, LOKI, YOU WILL BE STRICKEN FROM THE BOOKS OF HEL.
YOU WILL BE HEL-BOUND NO MORE.
WONDERFUL.
WITH THE PROPHESIED END-TIMES OF RAGNAROK PAST, AN ASGARDIAN'S ONLY DESTINY IS A PLACE IN MY HALLS...
...A DESTINY YOU NO LONGER SHARE.
I MUST. AWAY. I HAVE ETERNITY TO TEND TO.
WELL DONE. BUT I HAVE TO ASK YOU--IS ABSOLUTE FREEDOM WORTH THAT MUCH? THIS MUCH RISK?
YOU OF ALL BEINGS SHOULD KNOW: FREEDOM IS THE ONLY THING WORTH ANYTHING.

QUITE. AND WELL PLAYED-- YOU CREATED A PERIL AND SOLD HER A SOLUTION.

WHICH ALSO BEGS A QUESTION...

WHY NOT SELL HER THE SOLUTION DIRECT? THE DISIR ARE YOURS. YOU COULD HAVE PREVENTED WHAT SHE FEARED YOURSELF.

AND STOPPED THEM FROM RAVAGING THE DEAD? PREVENTED THE LAMENTING WHEN ALL DISCOVER THE FALLEN'S SOULS HAVE NOT GONE TO HELA'S HALLS, BUT THE BELLIES OF LONG-PAST MONSTERS?

MISSED THE SIGHT OF MISTRESS HELA SCURRYING LIKE A SCHOOLGIRL?

WHERE WOULD BE THE AMUSEMENT IN THAT?

ALL THIS EFFORT TO ESCAPE ALL PREDESTINATION... AND STILL YOU TURN TO MISCHIEF.

NO, MISCHIEF IS A SMALL THING, A TOY I'VE WELL USED AND DISCARDED.

THIS ISN'T MISCHIEF. THIS IS MAYHEM.

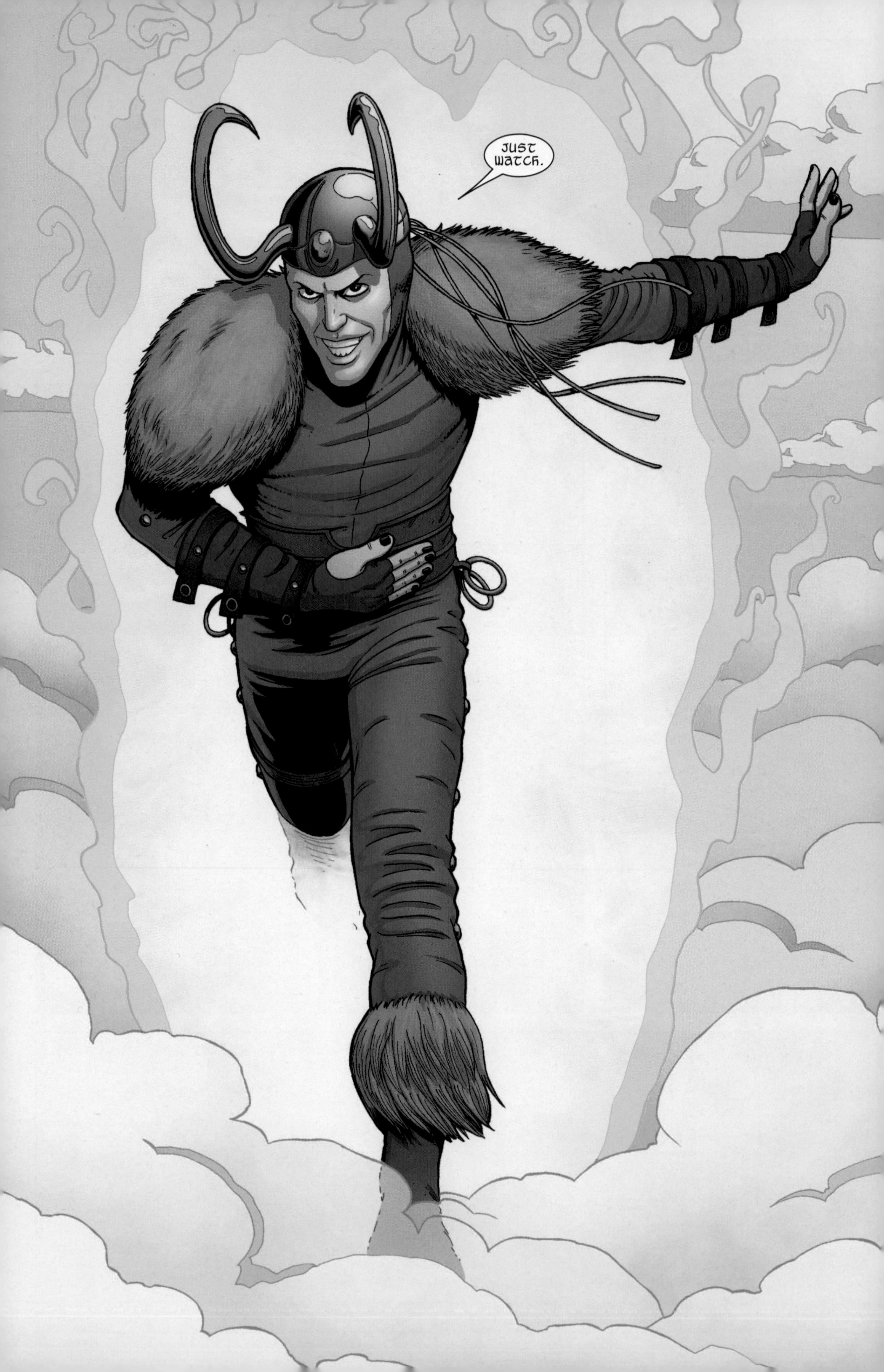
JUST WATCH.

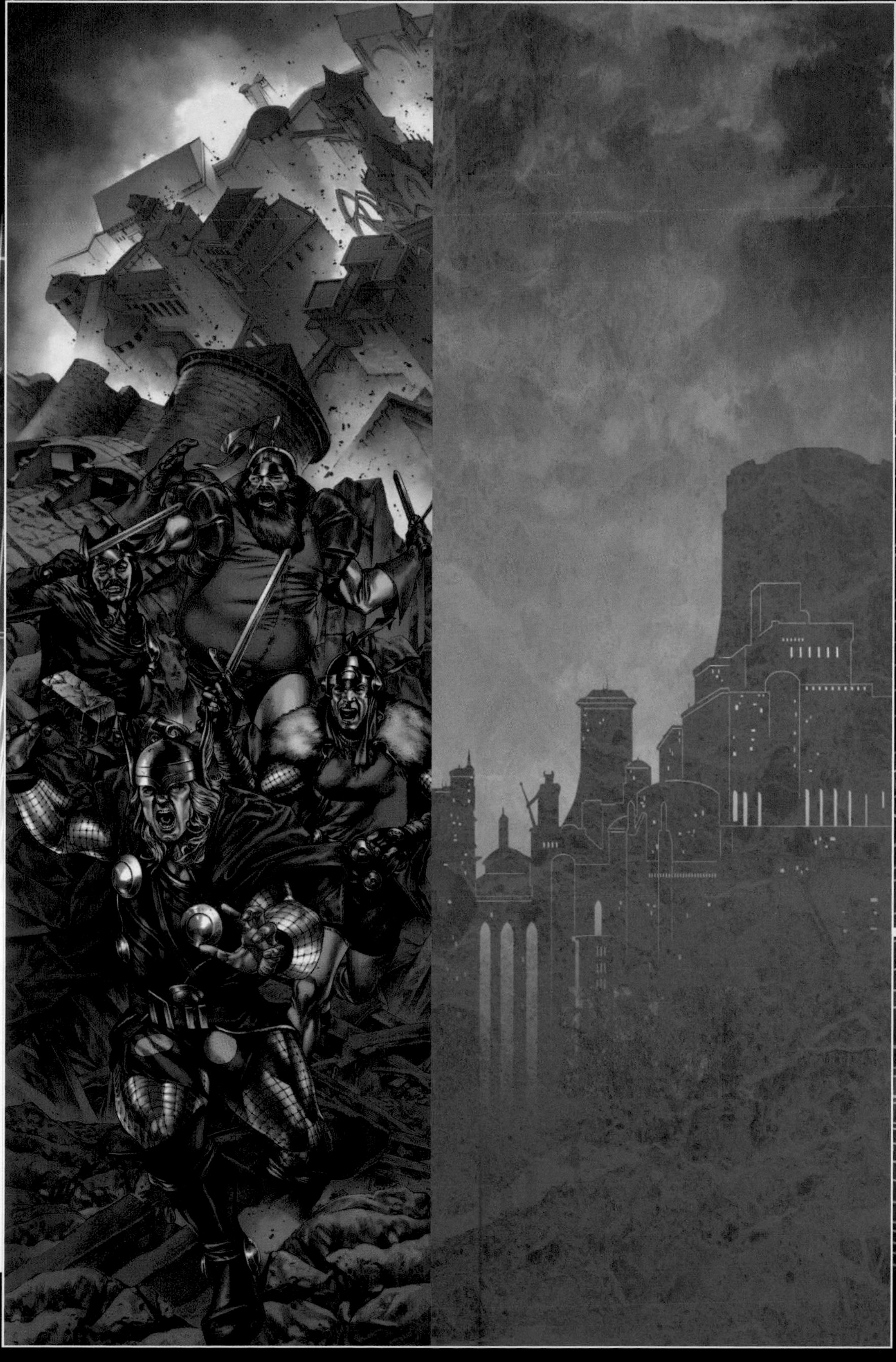

THOR #609

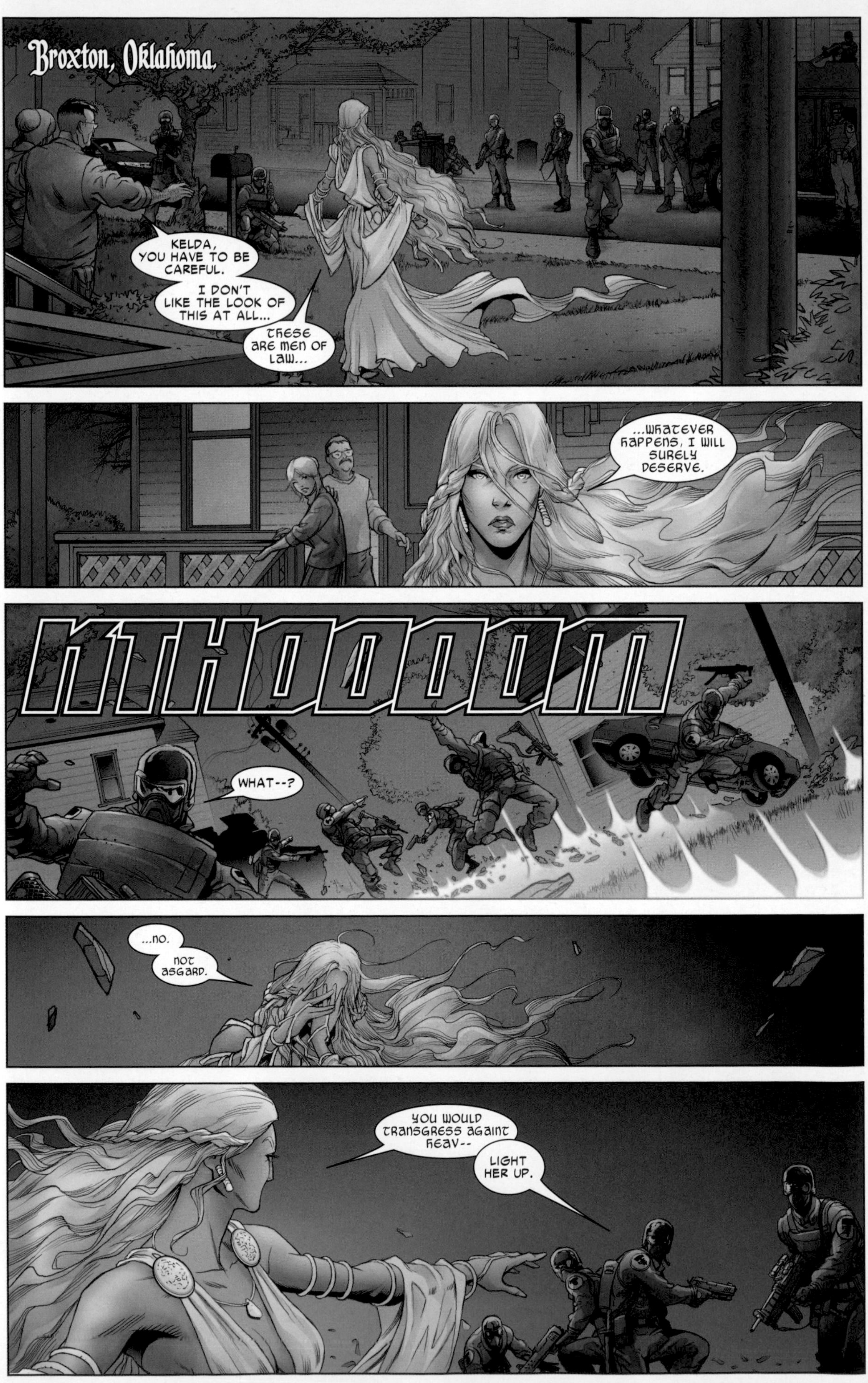
Broxton, Oklahoma.
KELDA, YOU HAVE TO BE CAREFUL.
I DON'T LIKE THE LOOK OF THIS AT ALL...
THESE ARE MEN OF LAW...
...WHATEVER HAPPENS, I WILL SURELY DESERVE.
KTHOOOOM
WHAT--?
...NO. NOT ASGARD.
YOU WOULD TRANSGRESS AGAINT HEAV--
LIGHT HER UP.

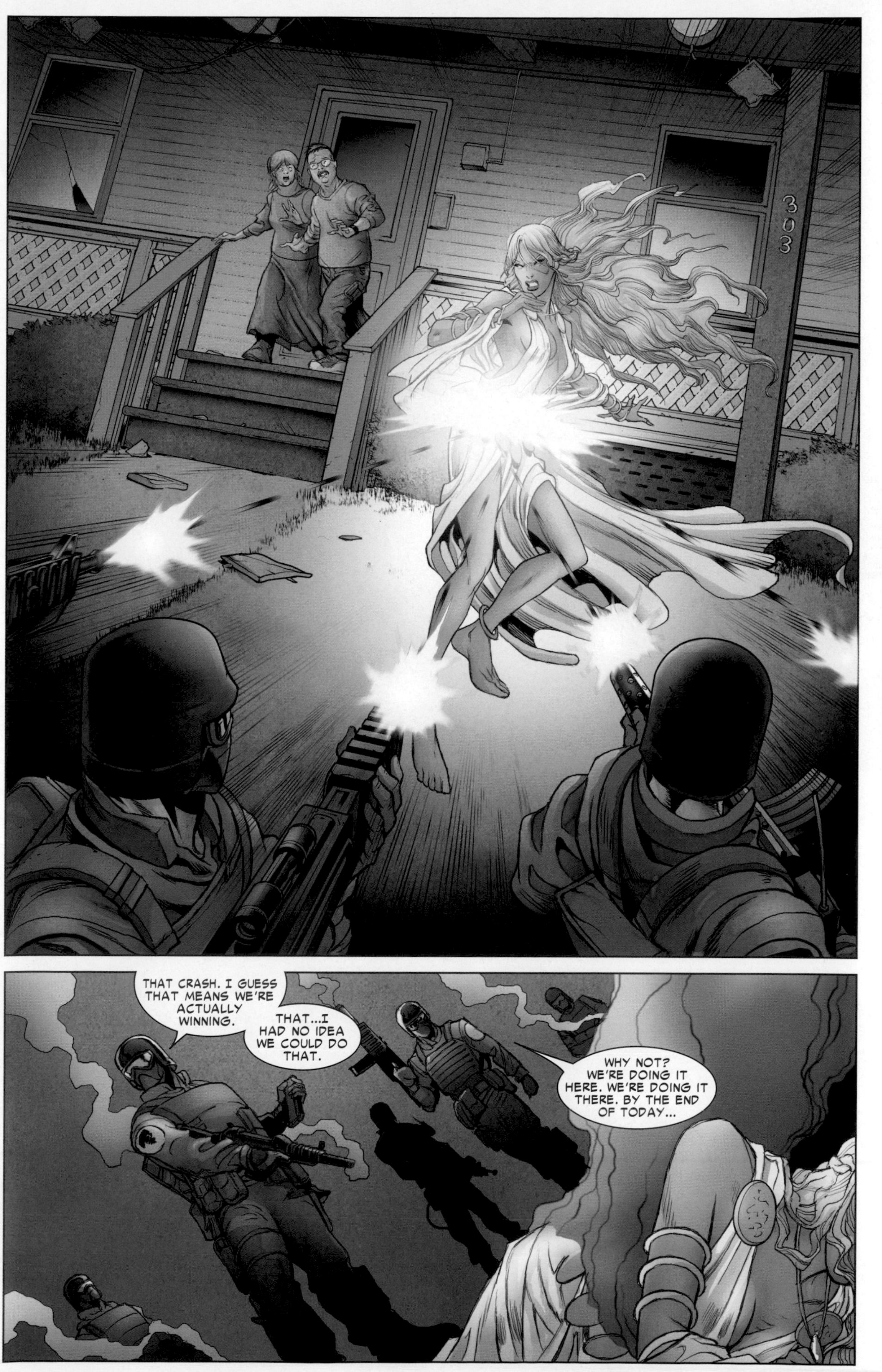
THAT CRASH. I GUESS THAT MEANS WE'RE ACTUALLY WINNING.
THAT...I HAD NO IDEA WE COULD DO THAT.
WHY NOT? WE'RE DOING IT HERE. WE'RE DOING IT THERE. BY THE END OF TODAY...

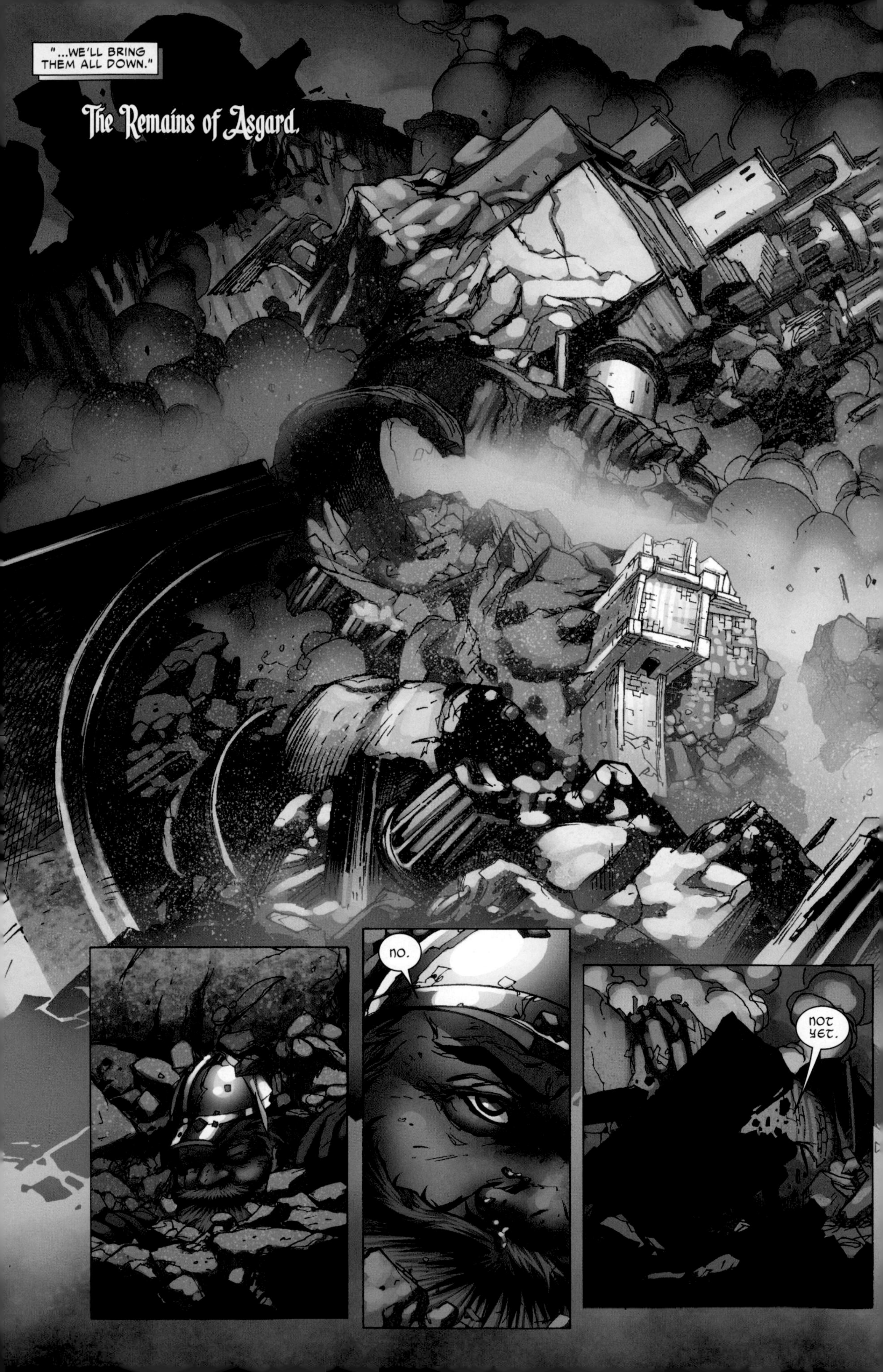
"...WE'LL BRING THEM ALL DOWN."
The Remains of Asgard.
no.
not yet.

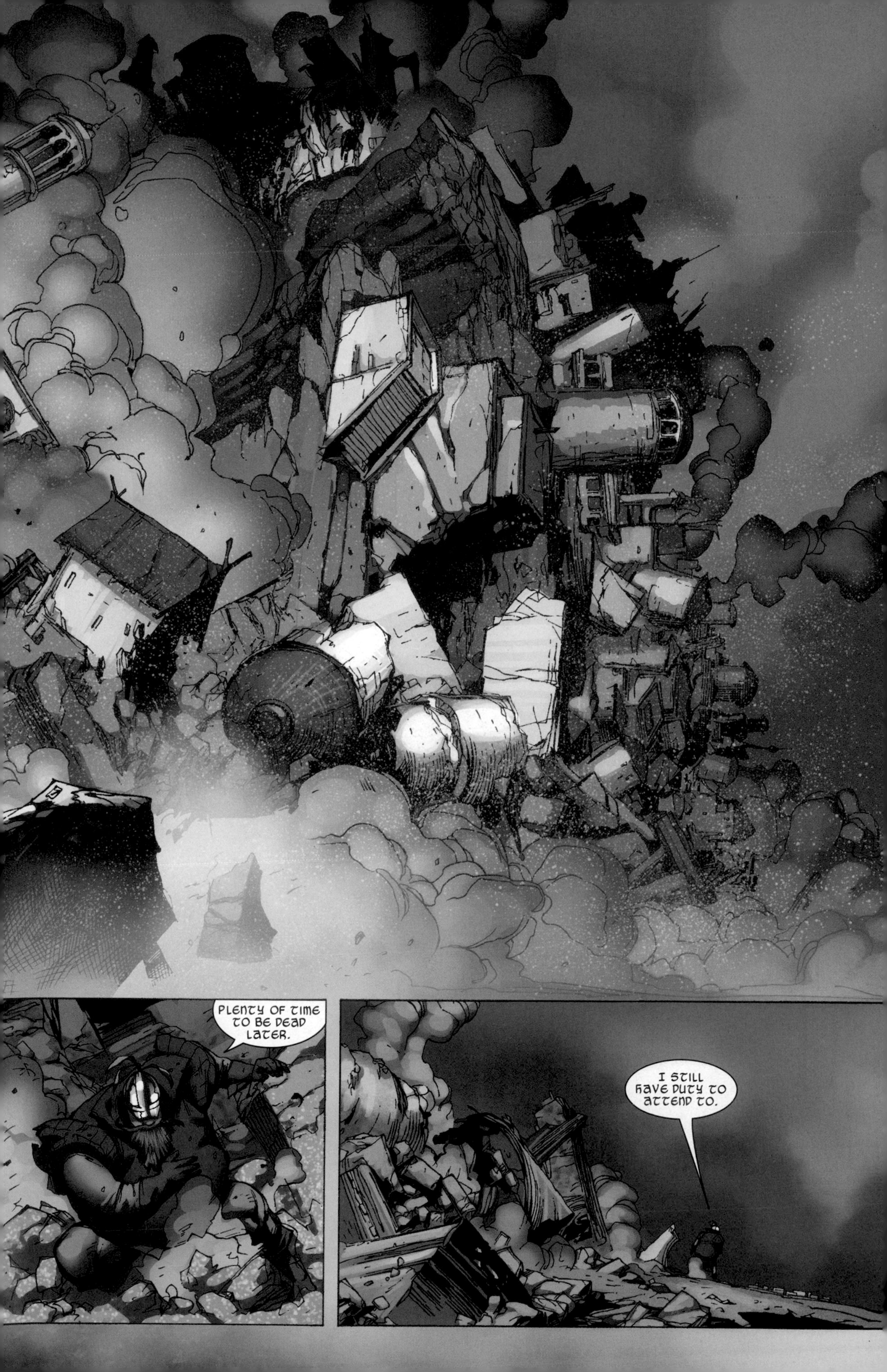
PLENTY OF TIME TO BE DEAD LATER.
I STILL HAVE DUTY TO ATTEND TO.

OF COURSE...

...THAT I'M BUZZING ON STOLEN NORSE-POWER JUST MAKES THIS ALL THE MORE IRONIC.

HUH?

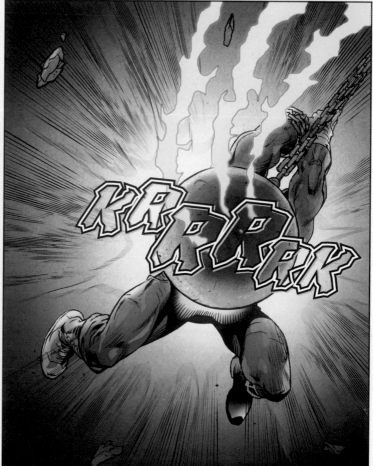

KRRRAK

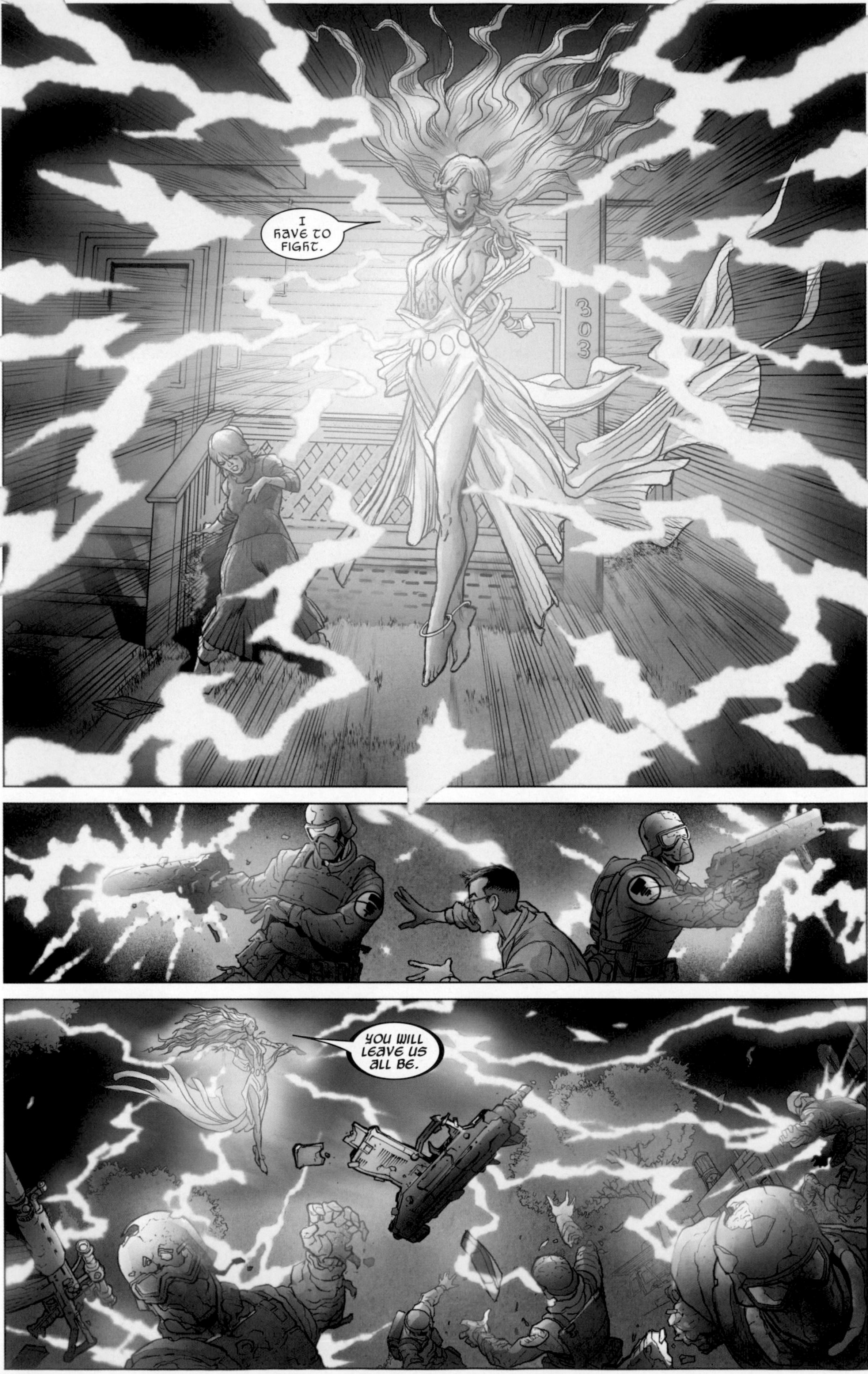
I HAVE TO FIGHT.
303
YOU WILL LEAVE US ALL BE.

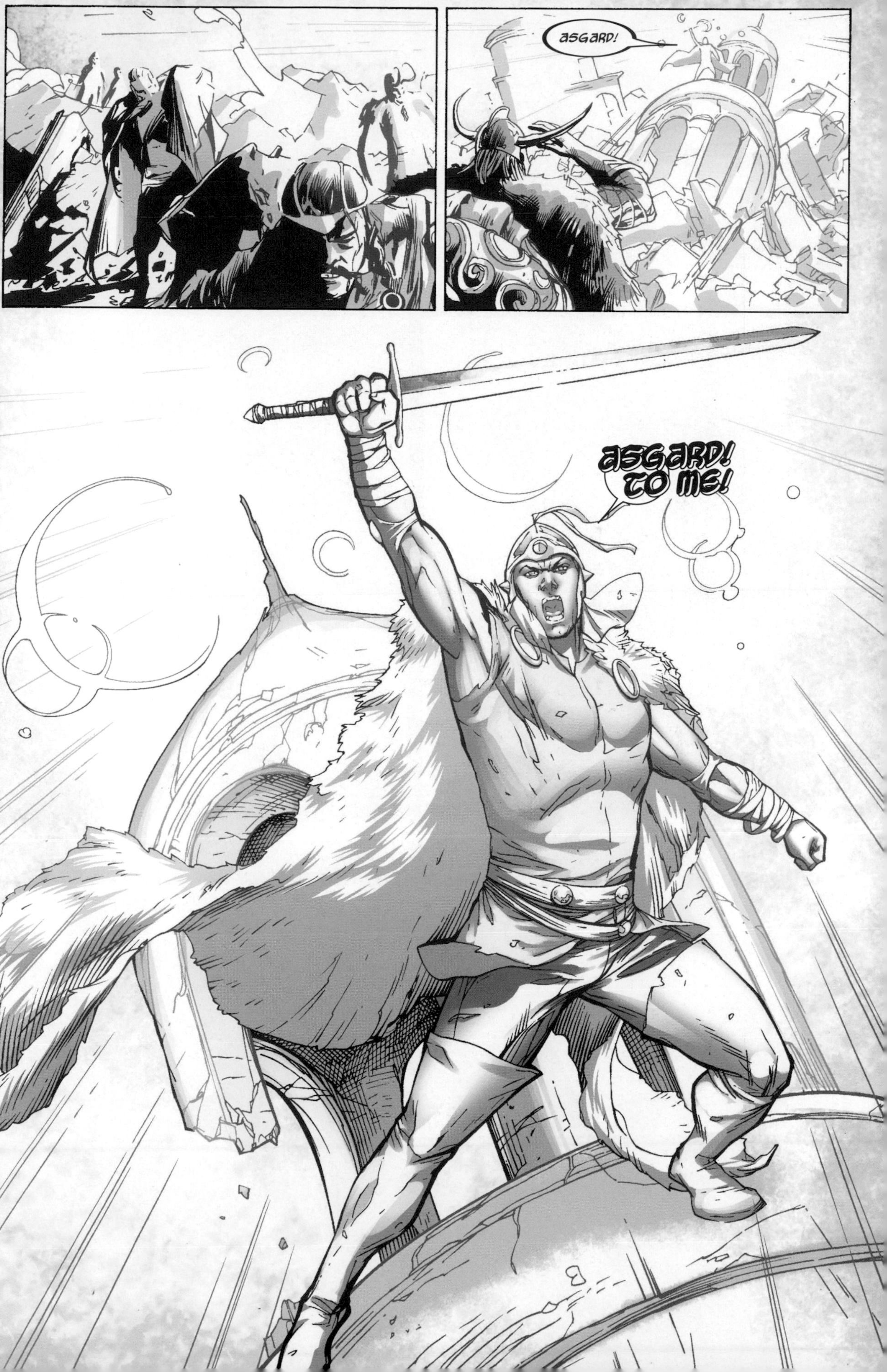
ASGARD!
ASGARD! TO ME!

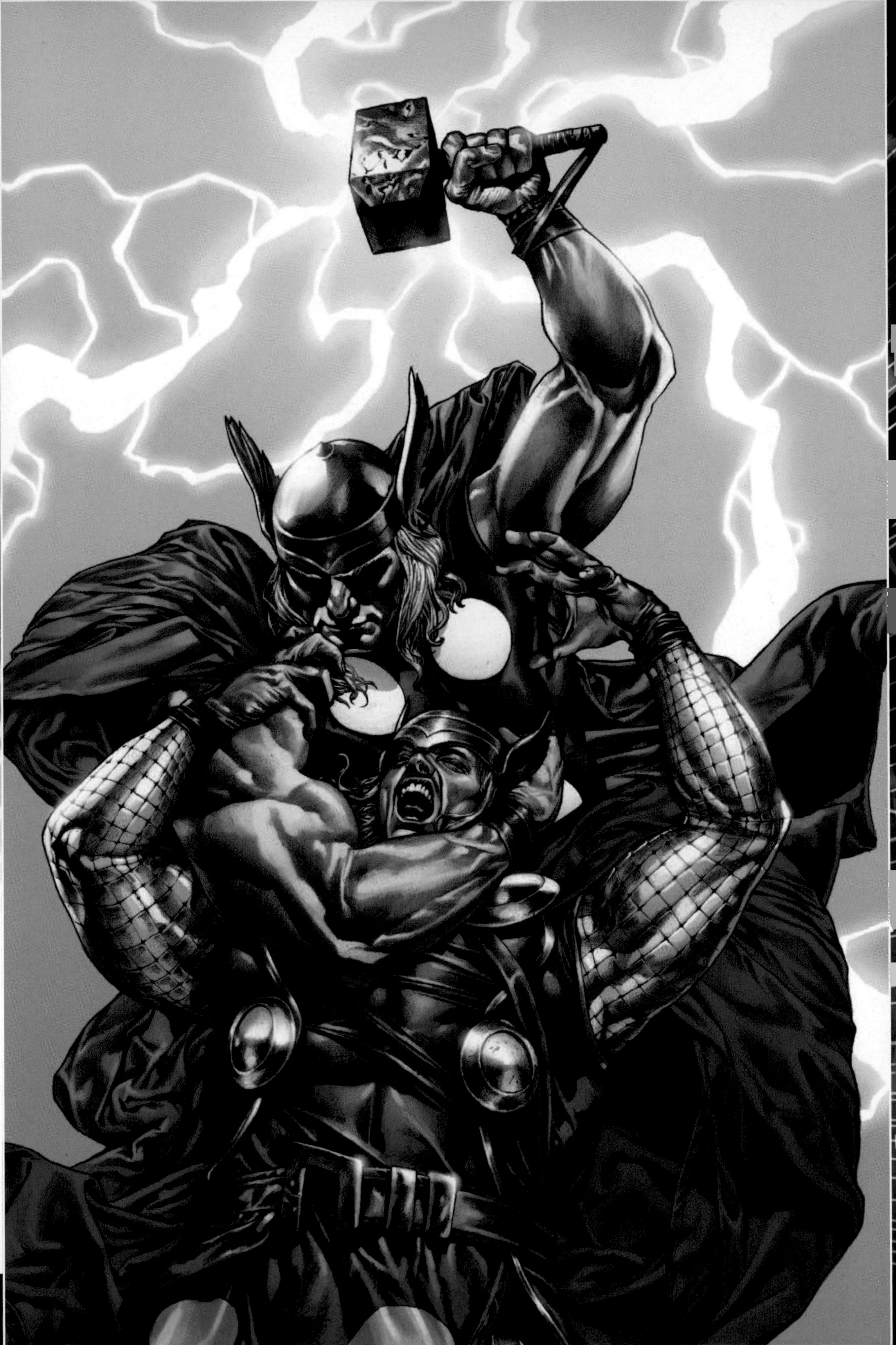

THOR #610

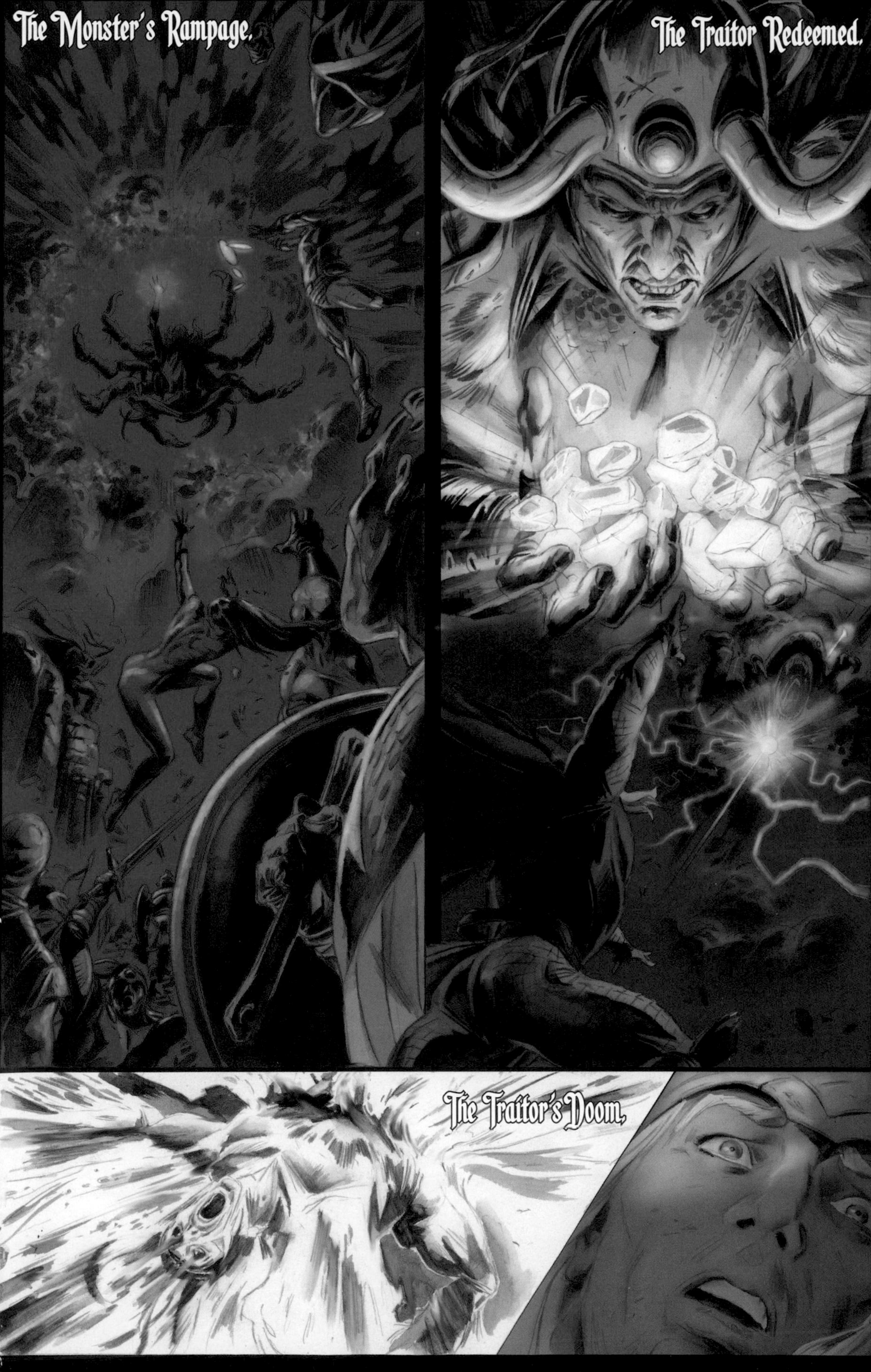

The Monster's Rampage,
The Traitor Redeemed,
The Traitor's Doom,

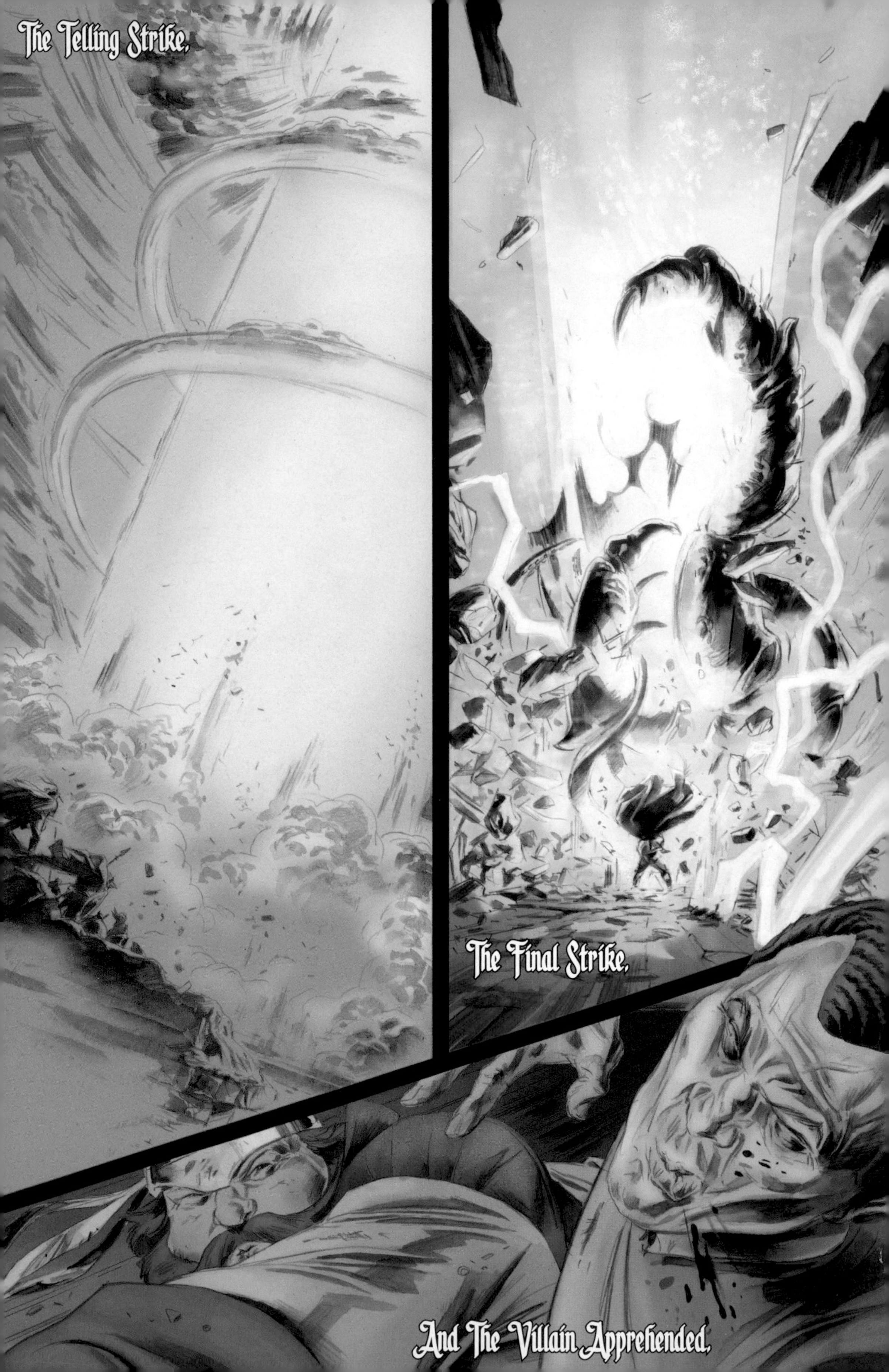
The Telling Strike,
The Final Strike,
And The Villain Apprehended.

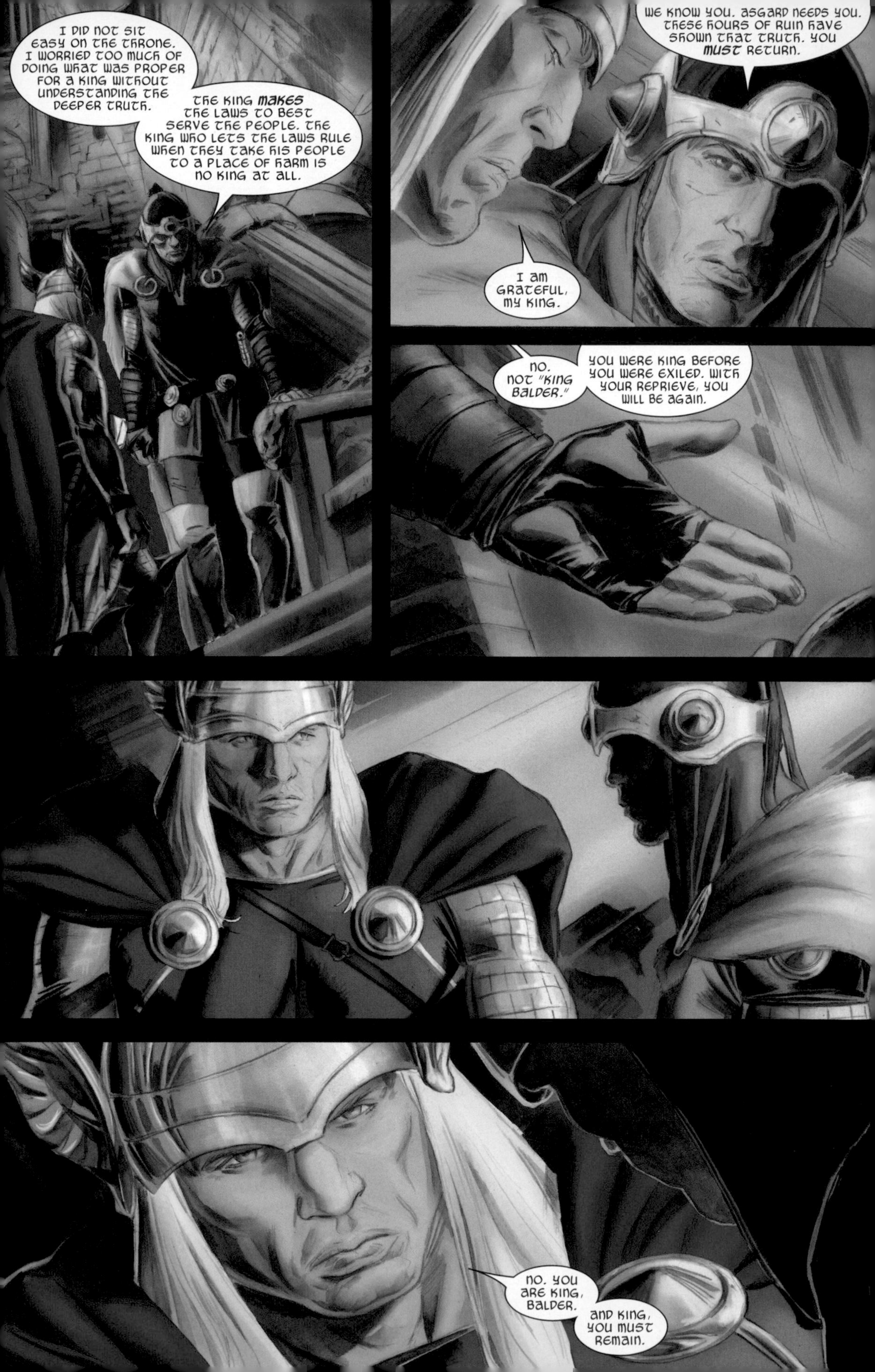
I DID NOT SIT EASY ON THE THRONE. I WORRIED TOO MUCH OF DOING WHAT WAS PROPER FOR A KING WITHOUT UNDERSTANDING THE DEEPER TRUTH.
THE KING MAKES THE LAWS TO BEST SERVE THE PEOPLE. THE KING WHO LETS THE LAWS RULE WHEN THEY TAKE HIS PEOPLE TO A PLACE OF HARM IS NO KING AT ALL.
WE KNOW YOU. ASGARD NEEDS YOU. THESE HOURS OF RUIN HAVE SHOWN THAT TRUTH. YOU MUST RETURN.
I AM GRATEFUL, MY KING.
NO. NOT "KING BALDER."
YOU WERE KING BEFORE YOU WERE EXILED. WITH YOUR REPRIEVE, YOU WILL BE AGAIN.
NO. YOU ARE KING, BALDER.
AND KING, YOU MUST REMAIN.

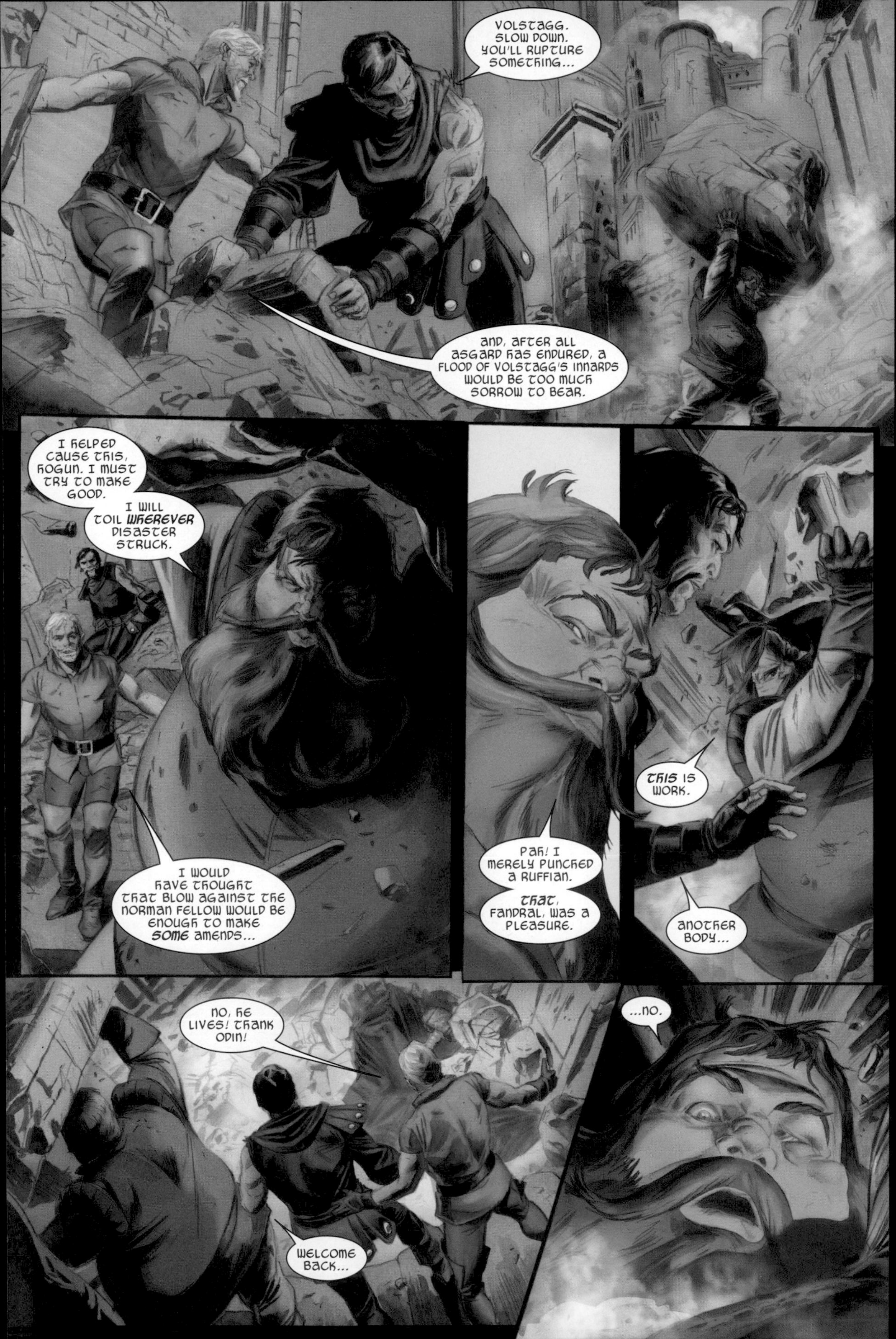
VOLSTAGG. SLOW DOWN. YOU'LL RUPTURE SOMETHING...
AND, AFTER ALL ASGARD HAS ENDURED, A FLOOD OF VOLSTAGG'S INNARDS WOULD BE TOO MUCH SORROW TO BEAR.
I HELPED CAUSE THIS, HOGUN. I MUST TRY TO MAKE GOOD.
I WILL TOIL WHEREVER DISASTER STRUCK.
I WOULD HAVE THOUGHT THAT BLOW AGAINST THE NORMAN FELLOW WOULD BE ENOUGH TO MAKE SOME AMENDS...
PAH! I MERELY PUNCHED A RUFFIAN.
THAT, FANDRAL, WAS A PLEASURE.
THIS IS WORK.
ANOTHER BODY...
NO, HE LIVES! THANK ODIN!
WELCOME BACK...
...NO.

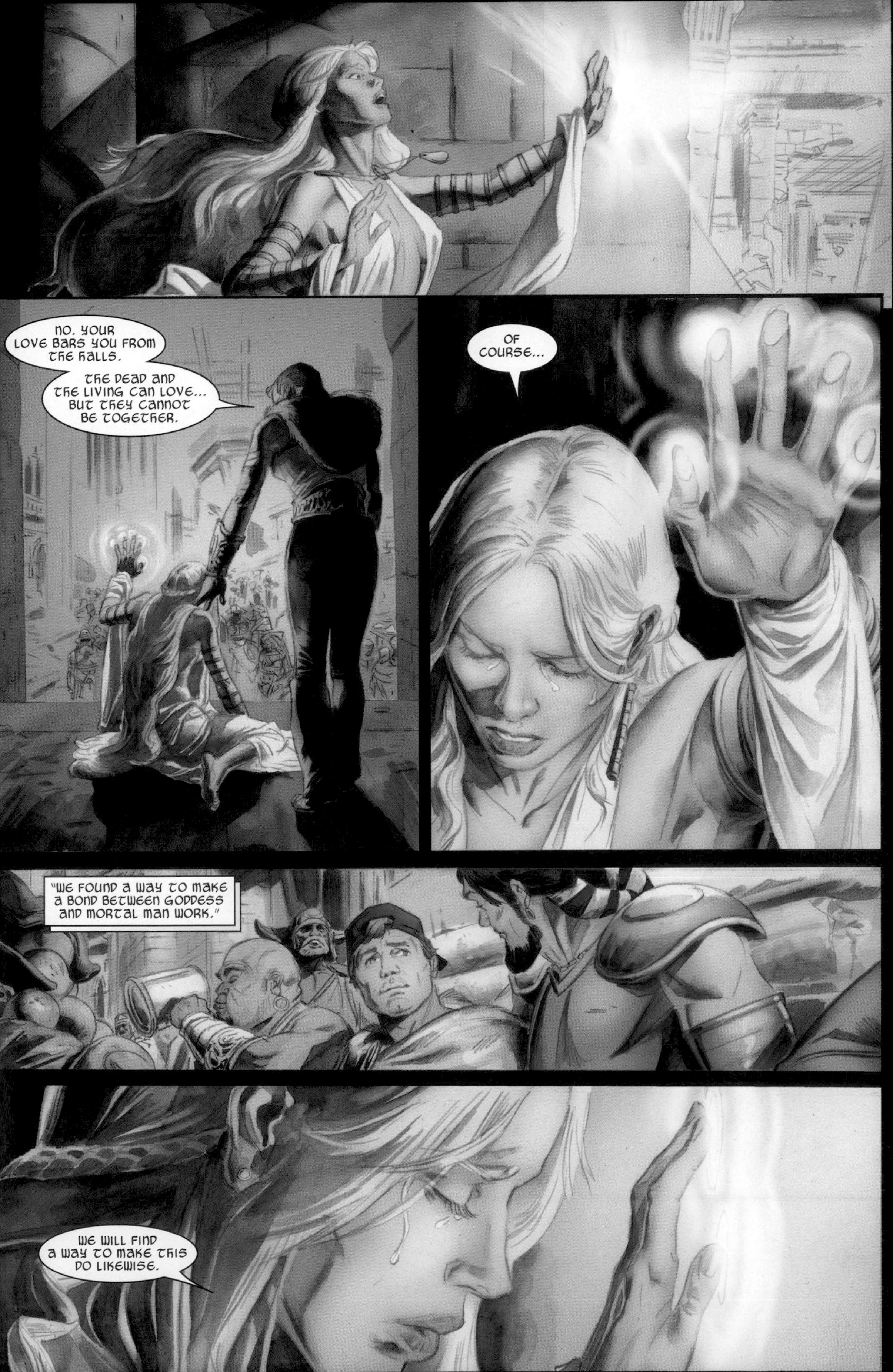
NO. YOUR LOVE BARS YOU FROM THE HALLS.
THE DEAD AND THE LIVING CAN LOVE... BUT THEY CANNOT BE TOGETHER.
OF COURSE...
"WE FOUND A WAY TO MAKE A BOND BETWEEN GODDESS AND MORTAL MAN WORK."
WE WILL FIND A WAY TO MAKE THIS DO LIKEWISE.

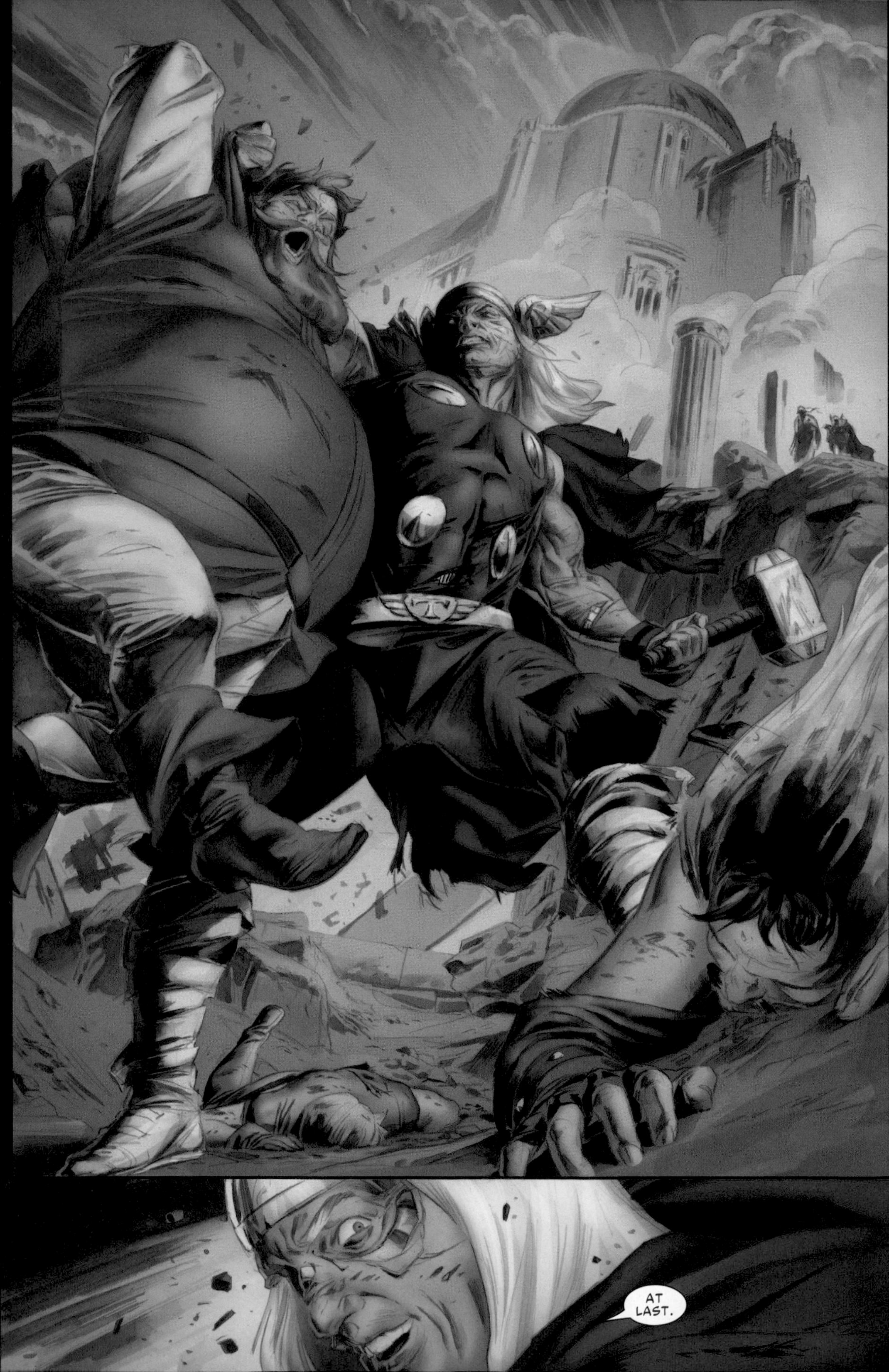
AT LAST.

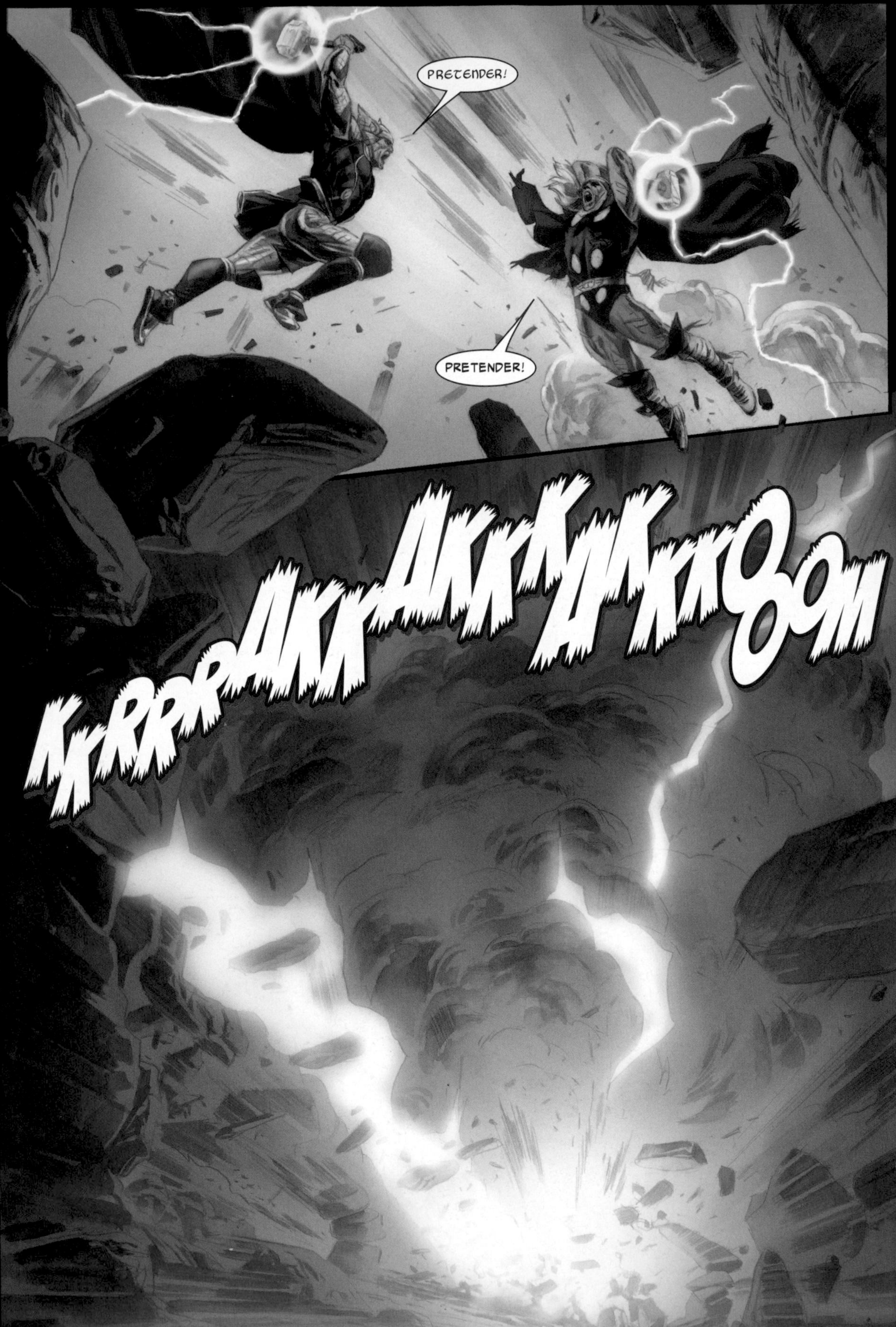
PRETENDER!
PRETENDER!

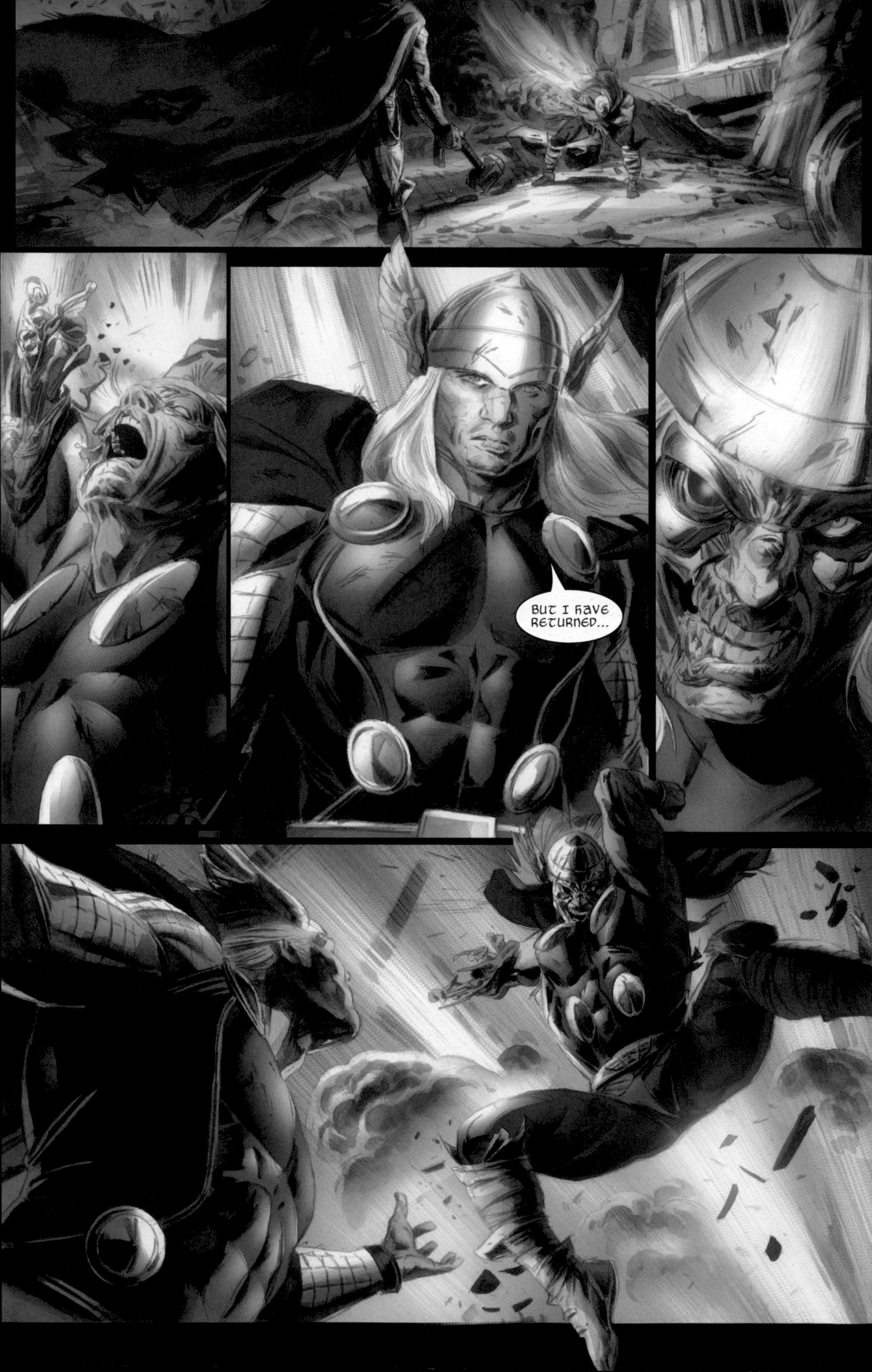
BUT I HAVE RETURNED...

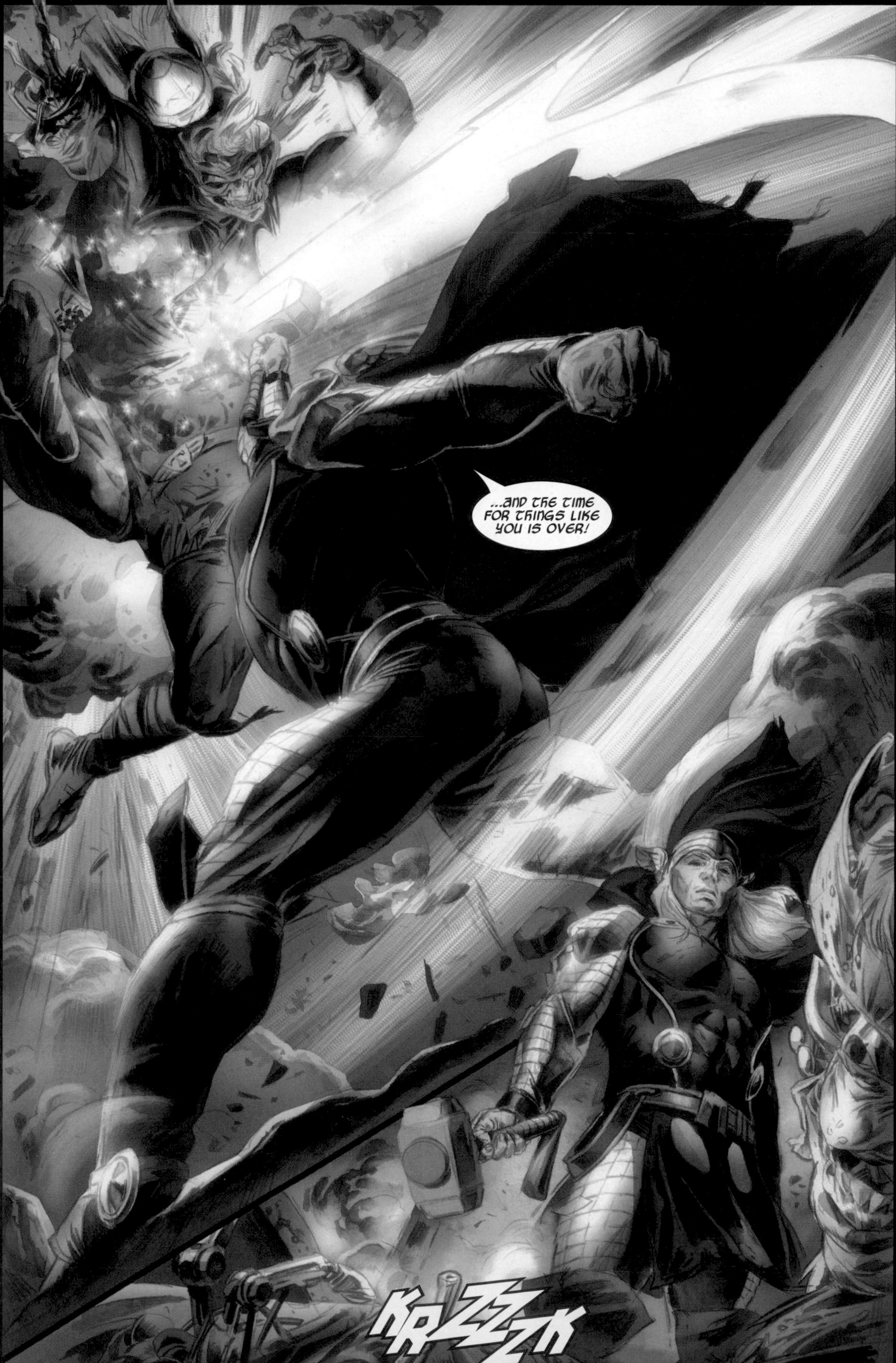
...AND THE TIME FOR THINGS LIKE YOU IS OVER!
KRZZZK

THOR #610 HEROIC AGE VARIANT

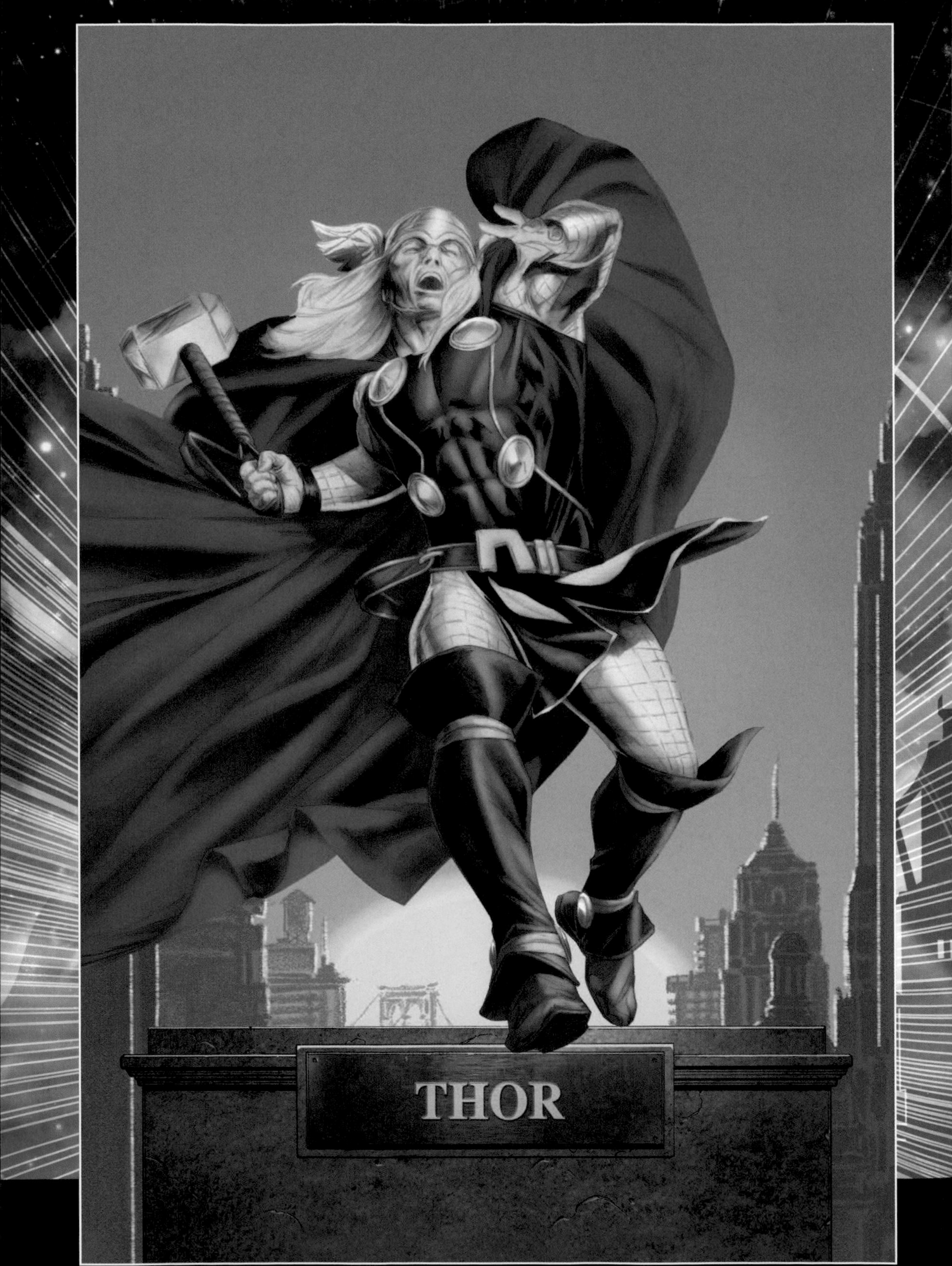
THOR

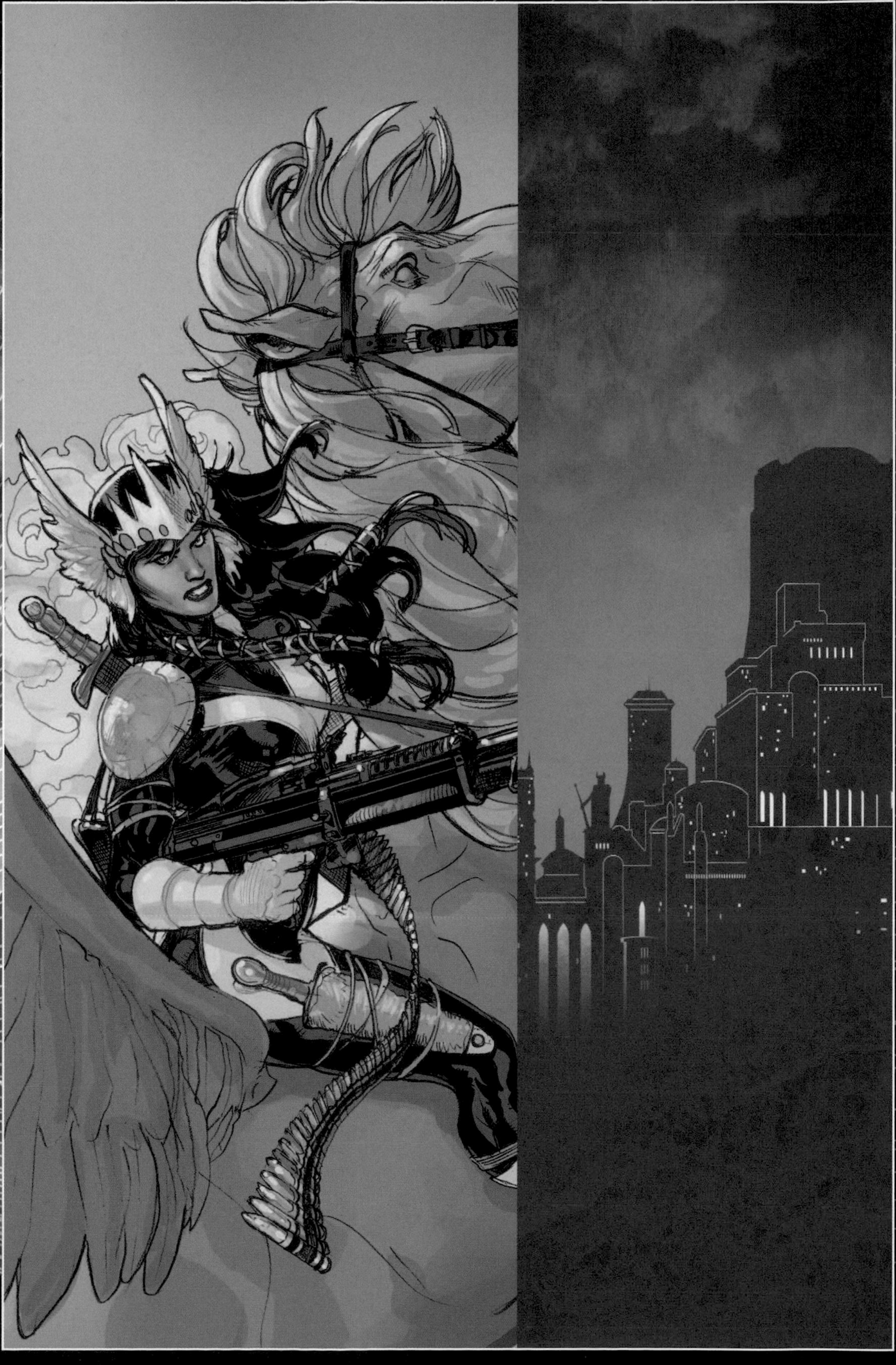

NEW MUTANTS #11

NEW MUTANTS

When Norman Obsorn, leader of the Dark Avengers, waged war on the X-Men, team leader Cyclops created a plan for fighting back. A key component of his strategy involved Dani Moonstar—depowered mutant and former Asgardian Valkyrie. Moonstar went to Hela, Asgardian goddess of death, and made a bargain with her: Hela would imbue Moonstar with the power of a Valkyrie once more so that she could repel the Dark Avengers' attack on the X-Men, but in turn, Moonstar would be indebted to the goddess.

"HEL'S VALKYRIE"

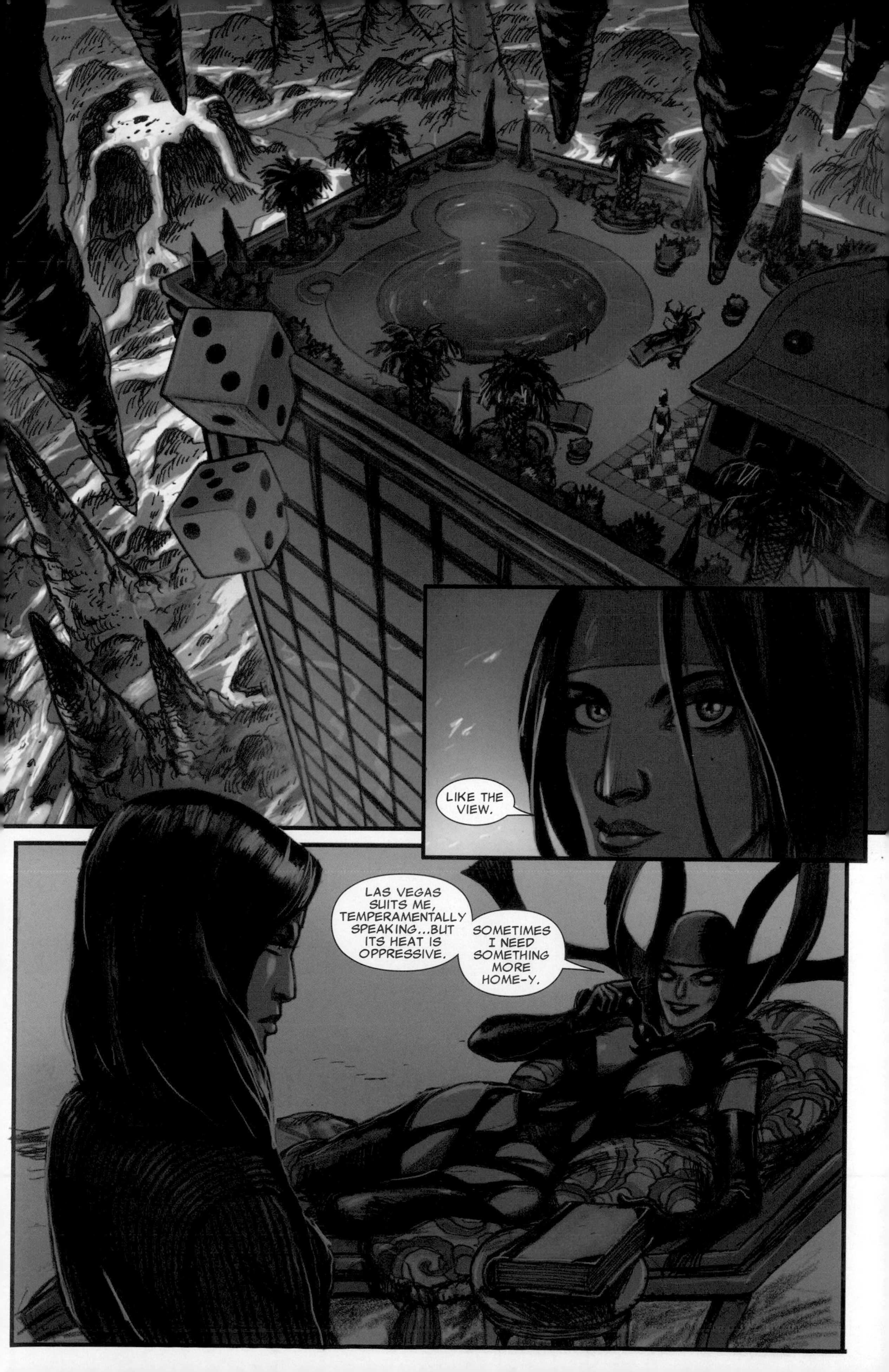
LIKE THE VIEW.
LAS VEGAS SUITS ME, TEMPERAMENTALLY SPEAKING...BUT ITS HEAT IS OPPRESSIVE.
SOMETIMES I NEED SOMETHING MORE HOME-Y.

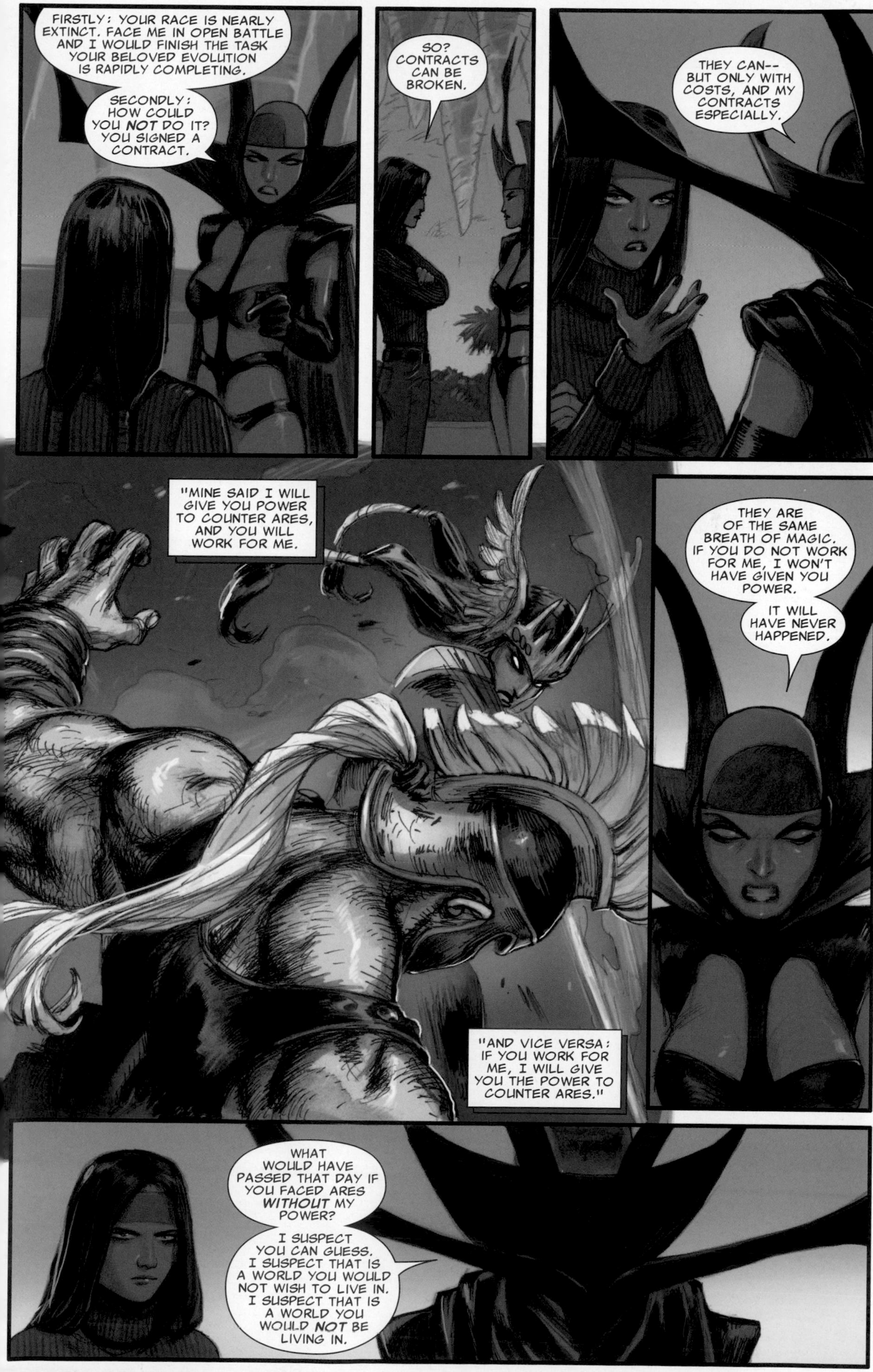
FIRSTLY: YOUR RACE IS NEARLY EXTINCT. FACE ME IN OPEN BATTLE AND I WOULD FINISH THE TASK YOUR BELOVED EVOLUTION IS RAPIDLY COMPLETING.
SECONDLY: HOW COULD YOU *NOT* DO IT? YOU SIGNED A CONTRACT.
SO? CONTRACTS CAN BE BROKEN.
THEY CAN-- BUT ONLY WITH COSTS, AND MY CONTRACTS ESPECIALLY.
"MINE SAID I WILL GIVE YOU POWER TO COUNTER ARES, AND YOU WILL WORK FOR ME.
"AND VICE VERSA: IF YOU WORK FOR ME, I WILL GIVE YOU THE POWER TO COUNTER ARES."
THEY ARE OF THE SAME BREATH OF MAGIC. IF YOU DO NOT WORK FOR ME, I WON'T HAVE GIVEN YOU POWER.
IT WILL HAVE NEVER HAPPENED.
WHAT WOULD HAVE PASSED THAT DAY IF YOU FACED ARES *WITHOUT* MY POWER?
I SUSPECT YOU CAN GUESS. I SUSPECT THAT IS A WORLD YOU WOULD NOT WISH TO LIVE IN. I SUSPECT THAT IS A WORLD YOU WOULD *NOT* BE LIVING IN.

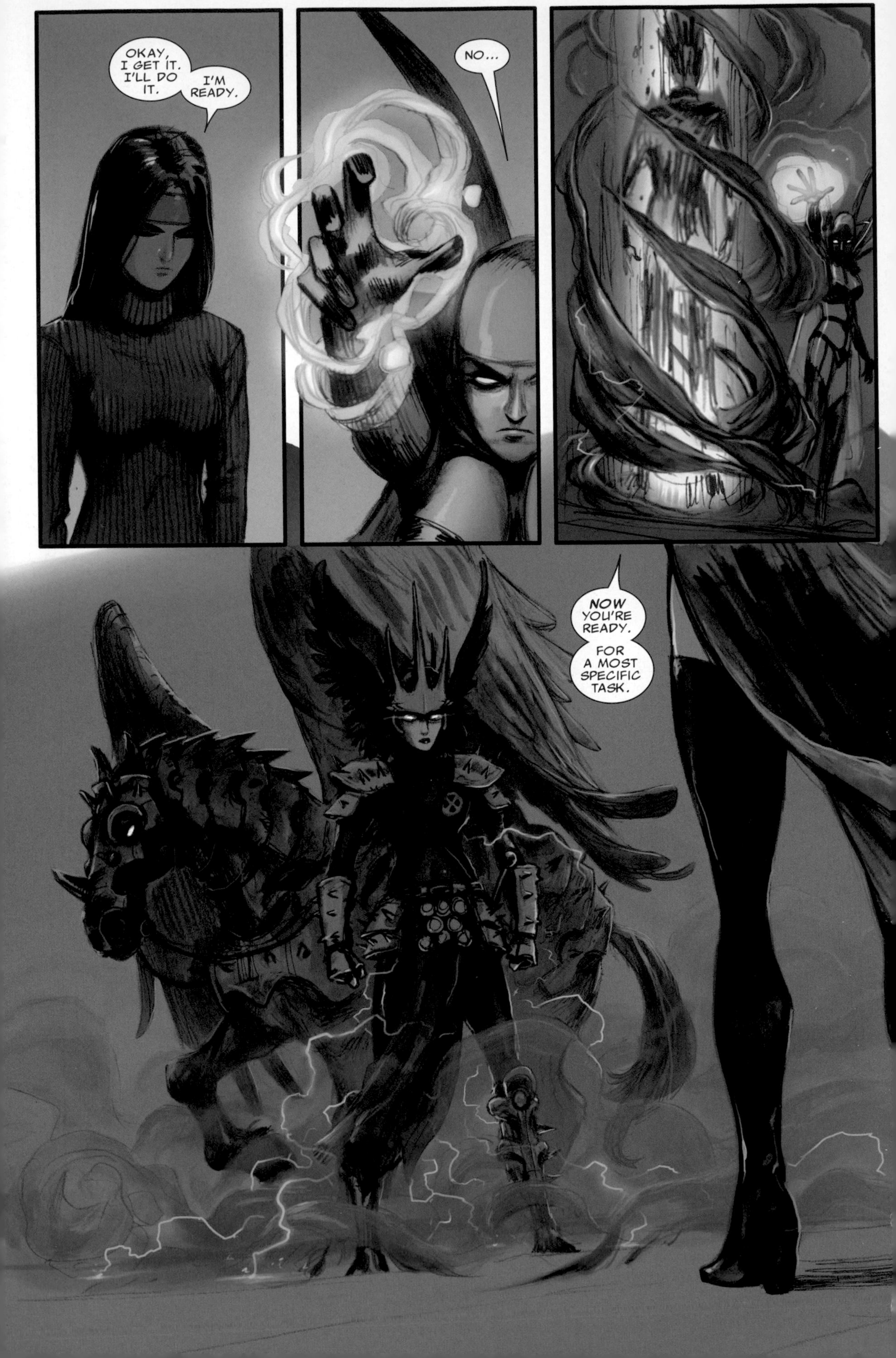
OKAY, I GET IT. I'LL DO IT.
I'M READY.
NO...
NOW YOU'RE READY.
FOR A MOST SPECIFIC TASK.

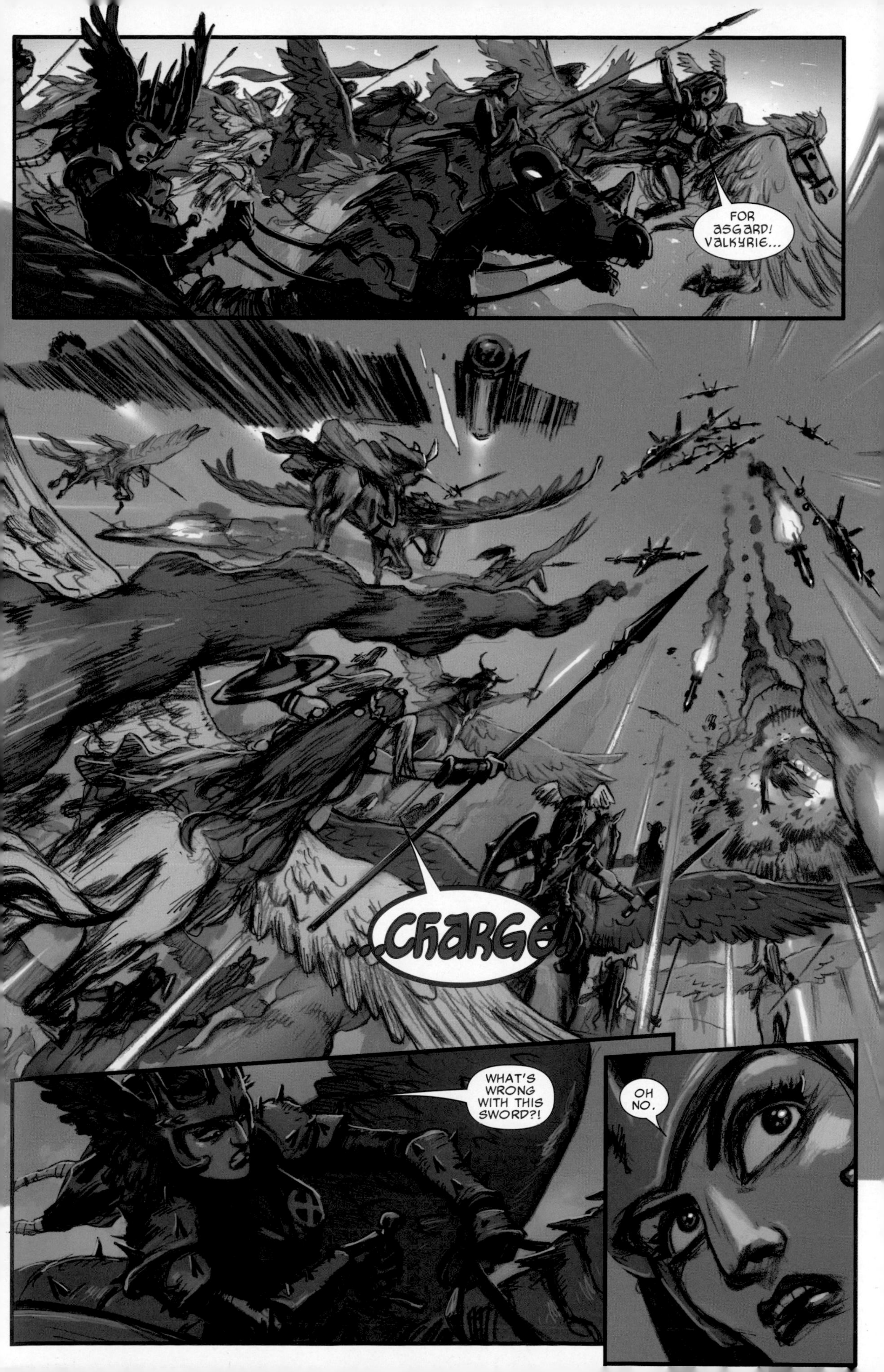
FOR ASGARD! VALKYRIE...
...CHARGE!
WHAT'S WRONG WITH THIS SWORD?!
OH NO.

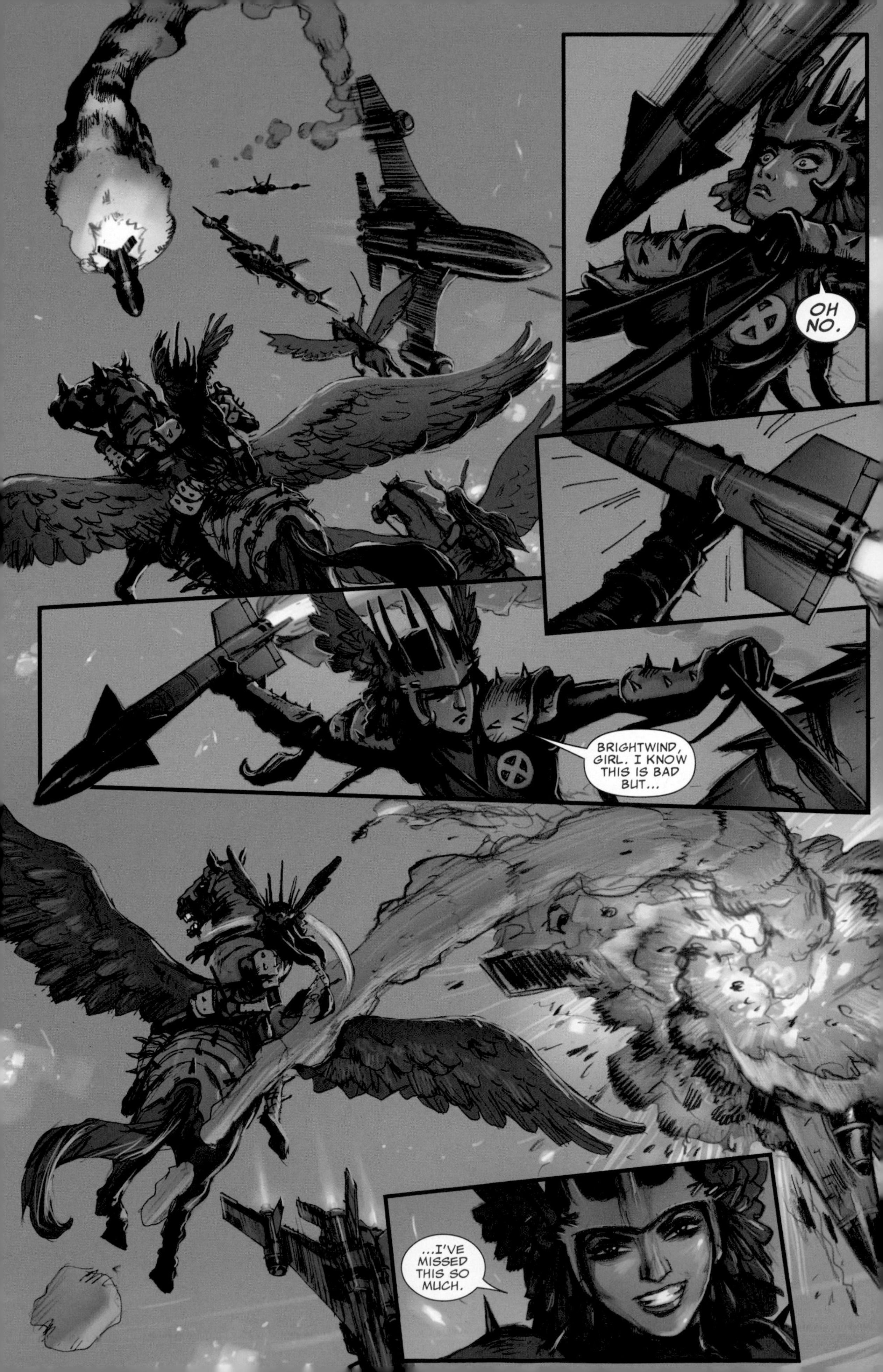
OH NO.
BRIGHTWIND, GIRL. I KNOW THIS IS BAD BUT...
...I'VE MISSED THIS SO MUCH.

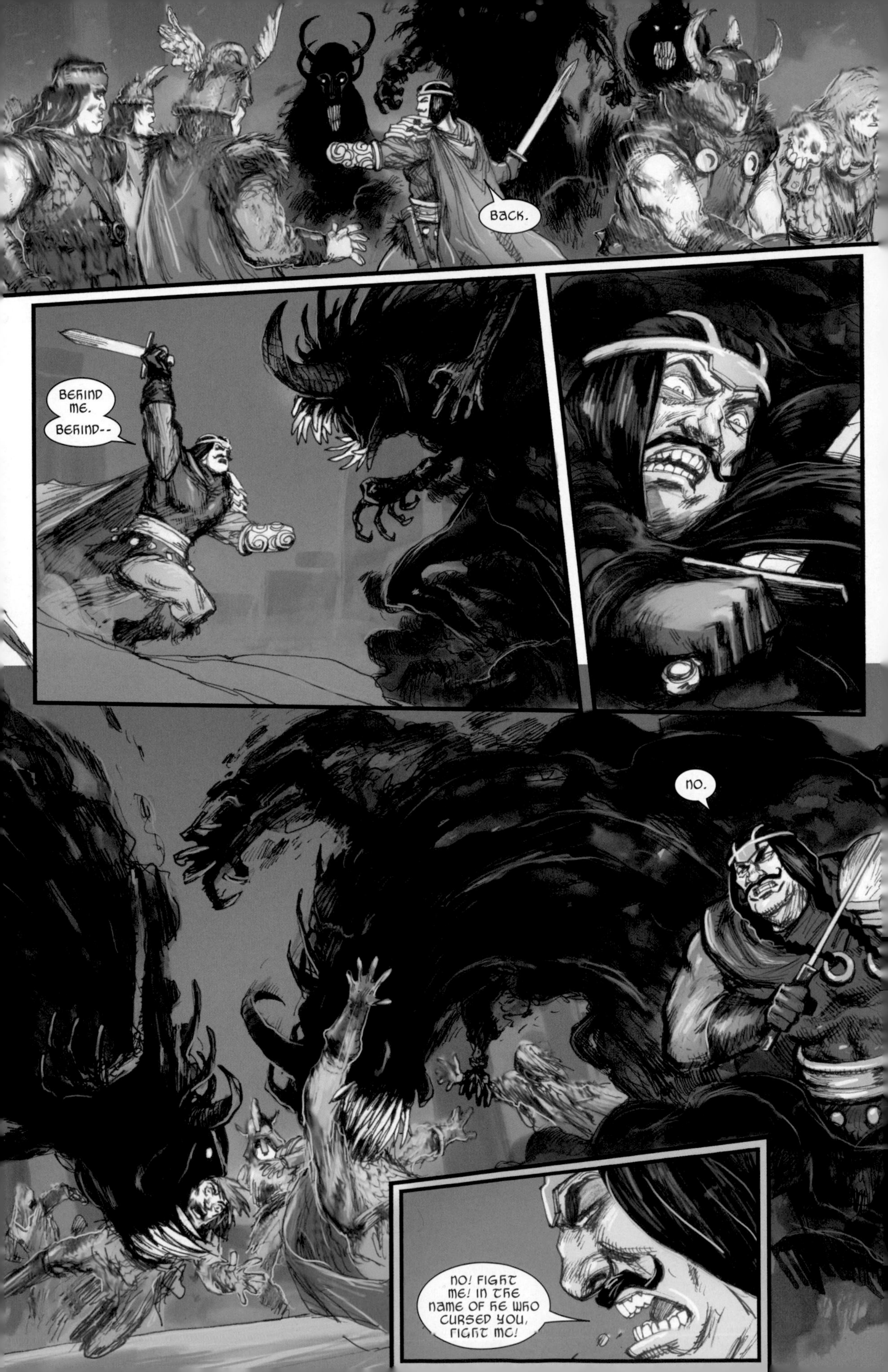
BACK.
BEHIND ME.
BEHIND--
NO.
NO! FIGHT ME! IN THE NAME OF HE WHO CURSED YOU, FIGHT ME!

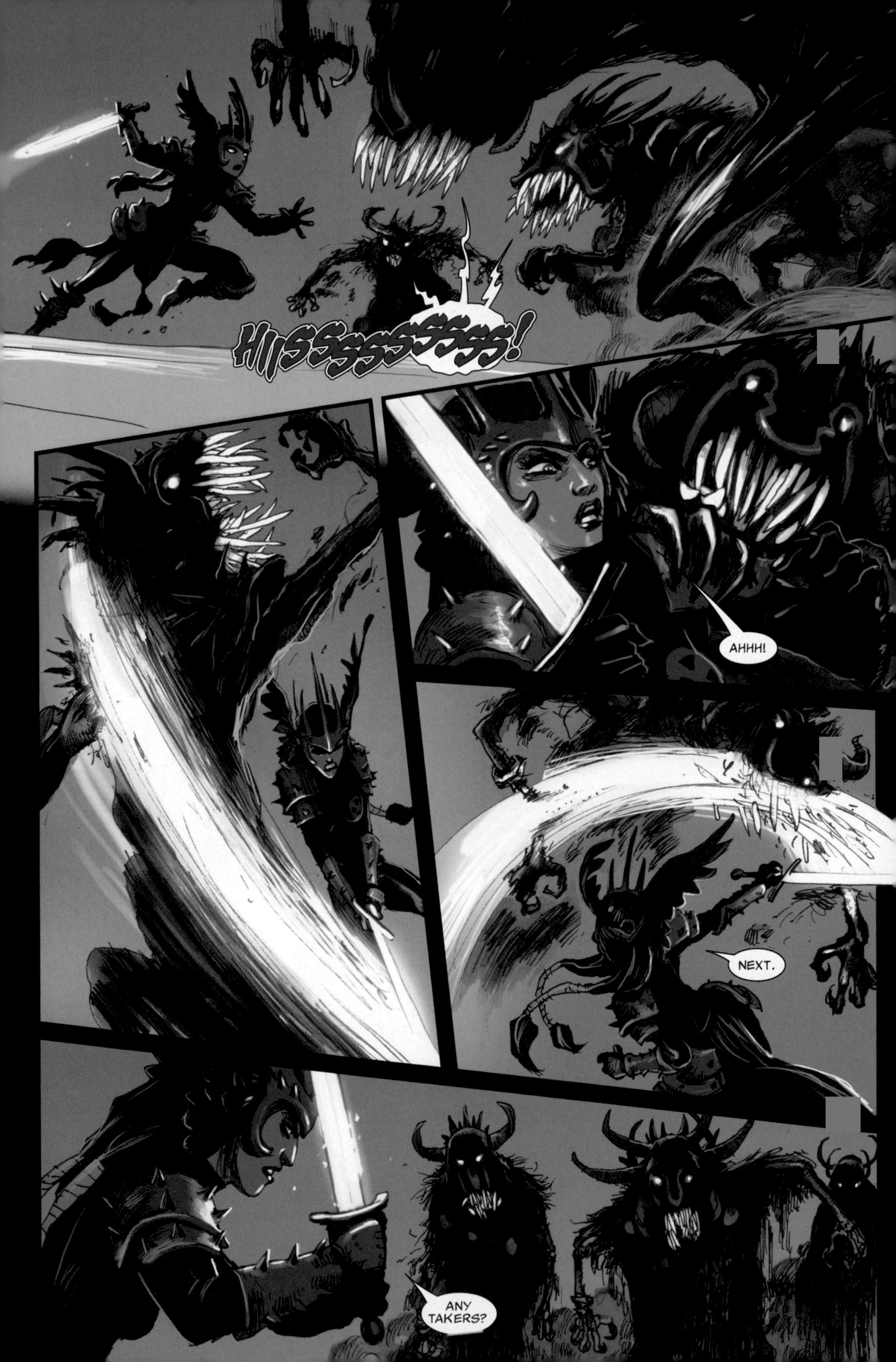
HIISSSSSSSSS!
AHHH!
NEXT.
ANY TAKERS?

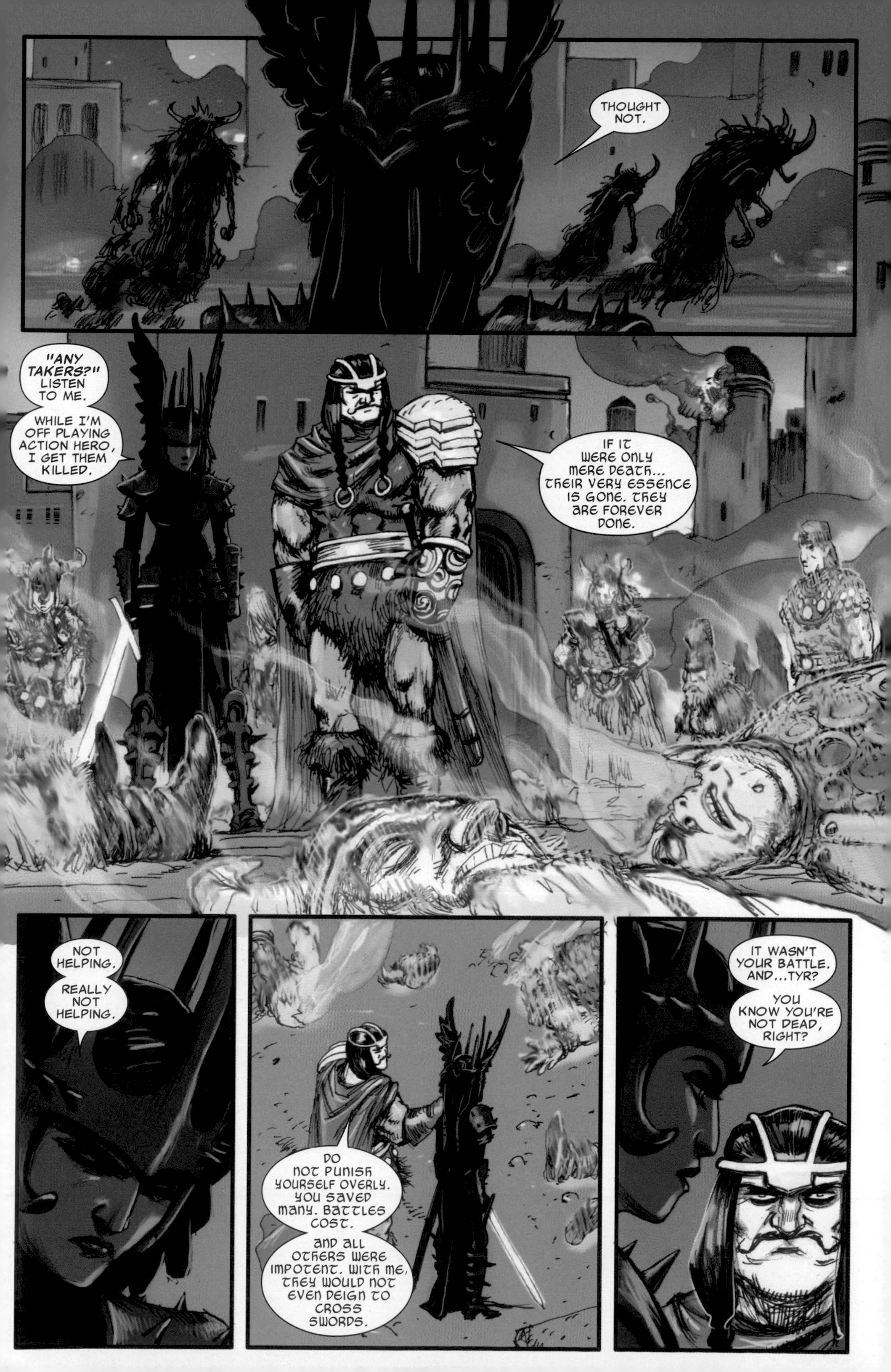
THOUGHT NOT.
"ANY TAKERS?" LISTEN TO ME.
WHILE I'M OFF PLAYING ACTION HERO, I GET THEM KILLED.
IF IT WERE ONLY MERE DEATH... THEIR VERY ESSENCE IS GONE. THEY ARE FOREVER DONE.
NOT HELPING.
REALLY NOT HELPING.
DO NOT PUNISH YOURSELF OVERLY. YOU SAVED MANY. BATTLES COST.
AND ALL OTHERS WERE IMPOTENT. WITH ME, THEY WOULD NOT EVEN DEIGN TO CROSS SWORDS.
IT WASN'T YOUR BATTLE. AND...TYR?
YOU KNOW YOU'RE NOT DEAD, RIGHT?